The Spirited Horse

The Spirited Horse

Equid – Human Relations in The Bronze Age Near East

Lærke Recht

BLOOMSBURY ACADEMIC
LONDON • NEW YORK • OXFORD • NEW DELHI • SYDNEY

BLOOMSBURY ACADEMIC
Bloomsbury Publishing Plc
50 Bedford Square, London, WC1B 3DP, UK
1385 Broadway, New York, NY 10018, USA
29 Earlsfort Terrace, Dublin 2, Ireland

BLOOMSBURY, BLOOMSBURY ACADEMIC and the Diana logo
are trademarks of Bloomsbury Publishing Plc

First published in Great Britain 2022
Paperback edition published 2024

For legal purposes the Acknowledgements on p. xviii constitute an extension
of this copyright page.

Cover image: Seal of Isharbeli © The International Institute for Mesopotamian Area Studies
Cover design: Inger Recht

A catalogue record for this book is available from the British Library.

Library of Congress Cataloging-in-Publication Data
Names: Recht, Laerke, author.
Title: The spirited horse : equid-human relations in the Bronze Age Near East /
Laerke Recht.
Description: New York : Bloomsbury Academic, 2022. | Series: Ancient environments |
Includes bibliographical references.
Identifiers: LCCN 2021056128 | ISBN 9781350158917 (hardback) |
ISBN 9781350274310 (paperback) | ISBN 9781350158924 (ebook) |
ISBN 9781350158931 (epub) | ISBN 9781350158948
Subjects: LCSH: Equidae–Middle East–History–To 1500. | Horses–Middle East–History–To
1500. | Human-animal relationships–History–To 1500. | Domestication–History–To 1500.
Classification: LCC SF285.3 .R43 2022 | DDC 636.10956—dc23/eng/20211216
LC record available at https://lccn.loc.gov/2021056128

ISBN: HB: 978-1-3501-5891-7
         PB: 978-1-3502-7431-0
         ePDF: 978-1-3501-5892-4
         eBook: 978-1-3501-5893-1

Series: Ancient Environments

Typeset by RefineCatch Limited, Bungay, Suffolk

To find out more about our authors and books visit www.bloomsbury.com
and sign up for our newsletters.

To Charlie

Contents

Illustrations

Drawings by the author and Stefani Recht unless otherwise noted.

Tables

Acknowledgements

This book has been many years in the making, and a great number of people have helped and supported me in the process. A large bulk of the research was carried out during my time at University of Cambridge as Marie Skłodowska-Curie Fellow and Teaching Associate in Mesopotamian Archaeology. My first thanks therefore go to the Horizon2020 programme (project *The Spirited Horse* – TSH 742303), and to the many people at the McDonald Institute of Archaeological Research who have endured my many equid-related discussions and helped with various aspects of the work: Jess Beck, Katherine Boyle, Marjolein Bosch, Matthew Collins, Nancy Highcock, Alexandra Ion, John MacGinnis, Augusta McMahon, Preston Miracle, Ioanna Moutafi, Jess Rippengal, Akshyeta Suryanarayan, Marie Louise Sørensen, Toby Wilkinson, and especially Christina Tsouparopoulou and Nicholas Postgate for their patience in helping me with the ancient languages.

The same goes for others in Cambridge, Newmarket, Sidmouth, Moulton and other parts of the world, many of whom kindly shared their expertise and resources: Troels Arbøll, Guy Bar-Oz, Ilona Bede, Laure Bonner, Giorgio Buccellati, Paul Croft, Lonneke Delpeut, Hekmat Dirbas, Yannis Galanakis, Jill Goulder, Rick Hauser, Irene Holm, Flemming Højlund, Sara Heil Jensen, Marilyn Kelly-Buccellati, Jacob Kveiborg, Steffen Terp Laursen, Joanna Lawrence, Christine Morris, David Mountford, Lubna Omar, David Owen, Chris Pearce, Melina Seabrook, David Reese, Colin Roberts, Emma Saunders, William Taylor, Janice Stargardt, James Walker, Selena Wisnom, James Wood, Lesley Young (and Roscoe and Grumpy for their tolerance and showmanship) and Chikako Watanabe.

Museums and other institutions have facilitated me at different stages of the journey and provided access to material, resources and the equids at the very heart of this book, including the Ashmolean Museum in Oxford (Paul Collins and Anja Ulbrich), the British Museum, the Fitzwilliam Museum (Anastasia Christophilopoulou), the Cambridge Museum of Archaeology and Anthropology, the Cambridge Museum of Zoology (Matthew Lowe), the Department of Archaeology and Heritage Studies, Aarhus University (Helle Vandkilde), and the Donkey Sanctuary Sidmouth, where my gratitude goes to Faith Burden and her colleagues for all their help and extremely fruitful discussions. The final stages of writing have taken place while at the University of Graz, with wonderful support from my colleagues here, and the invaluable help of Eirini Paizi and Marina Schutti in chasing down references and final formatting.

I have greatly benefitted from comments and suggestions made by readers who have kindly gone through parts or all of the manuscript: Marjolein Bosch, Haskel Greenfield, Nancy Highcock, Alexandra Ion, Nicholas Postgate, Glenn Schwartz, Christina Tsouparopoulou and Jill Weber. Their suggestions have helped improve the text, although any errors are entirely my own. A massive thank you also goes to the many people who have drawn (Stefani Recht, Inger Recht), generously given permission to reproduce illustrations (listed for each figure), and helped chase down images (especially Hans Curvers, Geralda Jurriaans-Helle and staff at the Oriental Institute Museum and Penn Museum). I would also like to thank the editors of the 'Ancient Environments' series and staff at Bloomsbury (especially Lily Mac Mahon) for their help, flexibility and for putting up with multiple delays and odd requests, and Brigid Clark for proofreading the final manuscript.

Finally, and most importantly, my gratitude goes to my family, who have provided the emotional and practical support that made this endeavour possible, along with the platform for many years of interaction with animals. I write this from the perspective of an archaeologist who has grown up with and shared the vast majority of her life with horses. Through this, I have had the privilege of meeting many equids, each with their individual way of being, and each having influenced me in their own way. More than anything, they, and their ancient counterparts, are the inspiration for this work. I hope you will find their presence as enriching as I have.

Abbreviations

ARM	Archives Royales de Mari
ARMT	Archives Royales de Mari, traduction
BDTNS	Database of Neo-Sumerian Texts (http://bdtns.filol.csic.es/)
BM	British Museum – collection number
CAD	The Assyrian Dictionary of the University of Chicago
CCT	Cuneiform Texts from Cappadocian Tablets in the British Museum
CDLI	Cuneiform Digital Library Initiative (https://cdli.ucla.edu/)
CT	Cuneiform Texts from Babylonian Tablets in the British Museum
EA	Amarna Letter number
ePDS2	electronic Pennsylvania Sumerian Dictionary Project, 2nd edn (http://oracc.museum.upenn.edu/epsd2/sux)
ETCSL	*Electronic Text Corpus of Sumerian Literature,* Oxford 1998–2006 (www.orinst.ac.uk/)
IM	National Museum of Iraq, Baghdad – collection number
P000000	CDLI identification number
RIME	The Royal Inscriptions of Mesopotamia, Early Periods
RLA	Reallexikon Assyriologie
RS	Ugarit (Ras Shamra) identification number
TM	Ebla (Tell Mardikh) identification number

Online Appendices

Available at: bloomsbury.pub/spirited-horse

For Appendix A, please see pages 185–6 of this book.

B Ancient terminology related to equids
C Equine physical attributes according to species
D Zooarchaeological identification of *Equidae* from the ancient Near East
E Estimation of withers heights based on faunal remains
F Catalogue of sites with equid remains
G Catalogue of sites with terracotta equid figurines
H Catalogue of iconography of equids with wheeled vehicles
J Catalogue of other iconography depicting equids
K Additional distribution maps

Series Preface

While our intention in writing this preface was to provide a neutral introduction that could stand for the whole series, recent events are too dramatic and relevant to ignore. The Covid-19 pandemic and the climate emergency have increased awareness of human reliance and impact on the environments we occupy, dramatically emphasised human inability to control nature, and reinforced perceptions that the environment is the most pressing political and social issue of our time. It confirms our belief that the time is right to situate our current (abnormal?) relationship with nature within an examination of human interactions with the environment over the *longue durée* – a belief that has given rise to this series.

Ancient Environments sets out to explore (from a variety of perspectives) different constructions of the 'environment' and understandings of humankind's place within it, across and around the Mediterranean from 3500 BCE–750 CE. By 'environment' we mean the worlds of living and non-living things in which human societies and cultures exist and with which they interact. The series focuses on the *co-construction* of humans and the natural world. It examines not only human-led interactions with the environment (e.g. the implications of trade or diet), but also those that foreground earth systems and specific environmental phenomena; it investigates both physical entities and events and ancient, imagined environments and alternate realities. The initial and primary focus of this series is the ancient world, but by explicitly exploring, evaluating and contextualising past human societies and cultures in dialogue with their environments, it also aims to illuminate the development and reception of environmental ideas and concepts, and to provoke a deeper understanding of more long-term and widespread environmental dynamics.

The geographical remit of this series includes not only the cultures of the Mediterranean and Near East, but also those of southern Europe, North Africa including Egypt, northern Europe, the Balkans and the shores of the Black Sea. We believe that encompassing this broader geographical extent supports a more dynamic, cross-disciplinary and comparative approach – enabling the series to transcend traditional boundaries in scholarship. Its temporal range is also far-reaching: it begins with the Neolithic (a dynamic date range, depending on location in the Near East/Europe) because it marks a distinct change in the ways in which human beings interacted with their environment. We have chosen c. 750 CE as our end date because it captures the broadest understanding of the end of Late Antiquity in the Central Mediterranean area, marking the rise of the Carolingians in the West, and the fall of the Umayyad Caliphate in the East.

Our series coincides with, and is inspired by, a particular focus on 'the environmental turn' in studies of the ancient world, as well as across humanities more generally. This focus is currently provoking a reassessment of approaches that have tended to focus solely on people and their actions, prompting scholars to reflect instead (or alongside) on the key role of the environments in which their historical subjects lived, and which shaped and were shaped by them. By extending beyond the chronological and geographical boundaries that often define — and limit — understanding of the meaning of 'antiquity', we intend that this series should encourage and enable broader participation from within and beyond relevant academic disciplines. This series will, we hope, not only advance the investigation of ancient ecological experiences, but also stimulate reflection on responses to contemporary ecological challenges.

The editors would like to express heartfelt thanks to everyone at Bloomsbury Press, especially Alice Wright who first conceived of the idea and suggested it to Esther, and who has done so much to develop it, and to Georgina Leighton, for her work in launching the series and her continued support. We are extremely grateful to the members of the Series Board, who have provided such wonderful encouragement and support, and to our authors (current and future) who have entrusted their work to this 'home'. Thanks also to the Leverhulme Trust for crucial funds that made it possible to initiate the series. We have chosen the 'Mistress of Animals' or *Potnia Theron*, a figure found in Near Eastern, Minoan, Mycenean, Greek and Etruscan art over thousands of years, as the motif for the series.

Anna Collar
Esther Eidinow
Katharina Lorenz

Introduction

I am a mule, most suitable for the road.
I am a horse, whose tail waves on the highway.
I am a stallion of Šakkan, eager to run.

Šulgi A[1]

1.1 Equid–human relations

On 6 November 2011, the Dutch stallion Hickstead died, collapsing after a round of World Cup show-jumping at the Verona tournament (Nir 2011). He was fifteen years old and had a lifetime of achievements behind him, winning gold at the 2008 Beijing Olympics, showing better than his riders at the Rolex Top Four Final, where he was the only horse that cleared the round with four different riders (subsequently earning the *Fédération Équstre Internationale* 'Best Horse in the World' Award), and in high demand as a stallion across the world. The tournament in Verona was discontinued at the request of the riders, who held one minute of silence in memory of Hickstead. This act shows that he was honoured and respected as a champion in his own right, and as a great *athlete*, an attribute more often bestowed on humans. It illustrates a human recognition of animal personhood, skill and intention.

In a broad sense, it is this acknowledgement of an equid's agency and personhood – its ability to act and influence its own lifeworld, and its individuality – that I call 'spirited'. But the 'spirited horse' of this book goes much further than this. 'Spirited' is also a recognition of equid moods and intentions, and of ranges of behaviour and needs specific to different equid species. The ancient writer of Šulgi Hymn A illustrates this nicely with three different attributes associated with three types of equids – one an expert in endurance, one in swishing its tail (however that is interpreted) and one in speed. Here we have the equids of the ancient Near East in a microcosm, with a clear knowledge of what each animal was best at. These few short lines demonstrate acute ancient observation of equids and even hint at their agency. 'The Spirited Horse' is shorthand for not only horses but all the equids of the ancient Near East, and is intended as a tribute to their individuality, moods, intentions and lived experiences, and their deep engagement with humans through mutual becomings, and sharing space, food, learning, travels, work, hunting, war and death.

It is difficult to overstate the impact of nonhuman animals on human lives, both today and in the past – for a sense of how the interaction between humans and other animals featured in all aspects of human existence in the ancient Near East, see e.g. Collins (2002), Arbuckle & McCarty (2014), Greenfield (2014), Mattila et al. (2019), Recht & Tsouparopoulou (2021), and the many papers in the various volumes of *Archaeozoology of the Near East*. The focus in this book is on equid–human *relations*. This approach is firmly situated within the interdisciplinary and multidisciplinary field of Human–Animal Studies (e.g. Ritvo 2004; Flynn 2008; Haraway 2003; 2008; Engel & Jenni 2010; DeMello 2012), closely related to multispecies ethnography, multispecies archaeology and social zooarchaeology (Kirksey & Helmreich 2010; Russell 2011; Hamilakis & Overton 2013; Ogden et al. 2013; Overton & Hamilakis 2013; Kopnina 2017; Pilaar Birch 2018; Stépanoff & Vigne 2019) and part of what is sometimes called 'the animal turn' (Weil 2010). Human–Animal Studies is an extremely diverse field with scholars examining human–nonhuman animal relations from many different perspectives, including those of history, psychology, political science, gender studies, literary studies, animal rights groups, medicine, anthropology and sociology, to name but a few. These kinds of approaches have also made an appearance in archaeology, where nonhuman animals have found voice through studies that explore concepts such as trust, co-becoming, hybridity and entanglement, and moving beyond dichotomies and the 'othering' of nonhuman animals (e.g. Ingold 1994; Manning & Serpell 1994; Armstrong Oma 2010; 2017; Lindstrøm 2012; Boyd 2017). For example, Armstrong Oma has discussed sheep-human relations in Bronze Age Norway, including the mutual becomings through shared habitation and lived experience (2017), and in a paper on canines, Lescureux outlines some of the complexities of human encounters with dogs, wolves and dog-wolf hybrids, and challenges the traditional wild-domestic division (2019). Moving to the equids that are at the centre here, Argent has eloquently explored the role of horses in some of the Pazyryk burials of Inner Asia (e.g. 2010; 2013; 2016). The range in social status associated with these horses are akin to those of humans; their identity and personhood, like that of their human counterparts, were expressed through their burial equipment and individual embodied features such as haircuts and braiding, and some horses were recognized as honoured 'elders'.

The variety in Human–Animal Studies research is naturally based on different methods and data sets, but what they have in common is a desire to decentre humans, moving away from anthropocentrism (or, more accurately, speciesism) to a more equal consideration of all species involved. This is not a call to abolish humans from the equation, but rather to consider all elements equally (in this case humans and nonhuman animals, more specifically equids). The equal *consideration* does not automatically translate to equality in the relationship. On the contrary, we will see that in the vast majority of encounters between equids and humans, humans are the more powerful, dominant agent. We will also see that the relations between equids and humans were extremely complex and varied, as much as those between humans themselves, and that constant negotiations instigated by both sides occurred. When the focus is on the relationship or nature of the interaction between equids and humans, the dynamics and two-way action are emphasized. That is, equids are not passive, mindless objects which humans (actively, deliberately) do things to. Both equids and humans are here recognized and treated as *social actors* (Dornan 2002; Robb 2010; Recht 2019) with *personhood* (Willerslev 2007; Losey et al. 2011; Shir-Vertesh 2012; Recht & Morris 2021). That is, they are individual subjects with intentions and the ability to act upon them (more or less consciously): they profoundly impact each others' lives physically, emotionally, socially and economically.

The challenge in this approach is far from insignificant, since we cannot entirely escape our own human bias. In a sense, I see this as an extension of the problem of intersubjectivity, but merely the fact that I cannot ever truly know what it is like to be another person does not prevent me from trying, and there are certain methods that I can apply in order to do this. Understanding equid agency may be a step further away, but is nevertheless on the same scale. The strict dichotomy between humans and other animals (mirrored in a culture–nature and mind–body divide) that is so deep-seated in much Western thought is socially constructed – DeMello neatly traces it back to Aristotle, and certainly Descartes also played an important role in cementing it (2012: 36–41). Importantly, this dichotomy is hierarchical, with a perception of human superiority that spills over into a legitimization of human domination and mistreatment of other species.[2] Throughout history, and in many parts of the world today, very different classification systems and ways of seeing the world prevail, and often the line between human and nonhuman entities is blurred, if not non-existent (e.g. Morris 2000; Willerslev 2007). There is thus no inherent need or reason to maintain this hierarchical dichotomy, which is why the starting point here is the interaction itself and the assumption that both equids and humans actively engage in it.

1.2 Sources and terminology

In terms of the source material, three main lines of enquiry are used in this book: faunal remains, ancient texts, and iconography. For each, we are meet with very specific potentialities and challenges, and each contributes knowledge that is not accessible through other means. In the Bronze Age Near East, we are very lucky that the first great transformations in equid–human relations coincide with an intensification in written records and iconographic objects. These lead to a wealth of information, and the three lines of enquiry offer a rare luxury of being able to compare different records. Modern equine knowledge and ethology supplement and refine these ancient records.

Faunal remains

Animal bones constitute one of the most common finds at most archaeological sites of the ancient Near East. The compositions of faunal assemblages are incredibly revealing of human–nonhuman animal relations and social structures. Like pottery, the vast majority of animal bones come in fragmentary form and represent the waste of settlements. More rarely, complete or nearly complete animals are found, typically in non-habitation contexts such as tombs, temples or ritual deposits and, more rarely, in dumps. Animal bones, antlers, horns and tusks also form the basis of a wide range of tools, jewellery and other decorative items. Non-osseous parts of animal bodies were utilized to make products such as skin, leather, glue and various types of cords and strings. These organic items are very rarely preserved in the archaeological record of the Near East (with a few notable exceptions, like the extraordinary finds in the tombs of Jericho), where with luck we are able to note them through impressions in the soil. They are otherwise better known from texts and iconography, or found in adjacent areas like Egypt, where the dry conditions have preserved a broader range of material culture.

The bones bring us into direct contact with ancient equids. They are the physical remains of animals that lived and experienced the world 4000–5000 years ago, and who died in the vicinity (and sometimes because) of humans. Such remains provide us with a unique opportunity to become acquainted with the equids themselves: to determine their species, sex, age and aspects of lifestyle and roles performed when in contact with humans. Evidence from morphological and pathological studies can provide information about health and the activities an equid performed, for example indicating crib biting, bit wear or load carrying. Stable isotope analysis can help us understand feeding and the journeys of an individual, and aDNA studies are beginning to reveal information about parentage.

In practice, this potential information is rarely available, for a number of reasons. As with humans, many ancient equids come to us as anonymous tiny fragments or, even more frequently, not at all. In the faunal assemblages of the Near East, equid bones are found at many sites, but in fairly small percentages during the third and second millennia BCE. This is most likely because the faunal remains we collect consist primarily of food waste, and the consumption of equids declined substantially in the third millennium.

The collection and retention of faunal remains have not always been common archaeological practice (and in fact even today, are not always prioritized or consistently collected). Much information is thus lost to us. Potentially less damning, in the sense that future discoveries may help fill in gaps in research, is the unevenness of exploration, partly due to research interests and partly due to a real lack of sites. There are both chronological and geographical gaps. When we look at the distributional maps of faunal remains in Chapter 3 (also Appendix K), it would seem that equids disappear almost entirely from the southern heartland of Mesopotamia in the late second millennium BCE. This is certainly not the case; rather, it reflects a limited number of excavated sites with corresponding published analysis of the faunal remains. To repeat an oft-noted mantra in archaeology, this is an excellent example of absence of evidence not necessarily being evidence of absence.

Even with these challenges (and more will occur in the next chapters concerning the actual interpretation of the bones), faunal remains provide us with some of the most remarkable and tangible evidence for equid intervention in human lives in the ancient Near East.

Ancient texts

One of the greatest cultural achievements of humans, the invention of writing, is traditionally assigned to Mesopotamia.[3] Written records in the form of clay tablets are documented already in the second half of the fourth millennium, where we may even have the first examples of a type of equid being mentioned (Zarins 2014: 151–4, 259). In the third and second millennia, the form of writing was cuneiform, which was syllabic, but changed in style over the period. It was primarily impressed on clay tablets, which constitute the majority of sources discussed here. However, we also find inscriptions on a range of other objects, such as sculptures, buildings, reliefs and engraved on cylinder seals. By the second millennium, records were also made on wooden tablets with a wax surface, and possibly on some kind of parchment – unfortunately, these organic materials have not survived the conditions of the area.

The most important and prolific use of writing was for administration. Palaces and temples, but also certain individuals (usually private entrepreneurs of some kind) kept extensive records of their affairs down to the minutest detail. The archives of the Ur III period provide us with tablets in the hundreds of thousands, unfortunately mainly from looted contexts. They contain extensive information about the movement and counts of animals, people and goods. From them, we know much about the types of equids present, their ages, sex, some of their tasks, rations of fodder, and sometimes their health. We also learn that their skins were important, and that they could be fed to dogs belonging to the army. However, due to the very specialized purpose of the administration, there are many lacunas: they reveal little about breeding and daily management beyond pastures and fodder, and virtually nothing about training and behaviour.

Letters are another common and useful type of written evidence for equids. They are rarely specifically about equids, but often mention them as part of other concerns. The information must be extracted, but is no less valuable. The letters of the merchants at Kanesh/Kültepe are a fantastic and extensive record of donkeys carrying heavy goods over extremely long distances. The number of animals involved is astounding, and the correspondence reveals information about harnessing, prices, health and, to some extent, the treatment of donkeys. The Amarna letters represent exchange of goods on a completely different level, between wealthy rulers and vassals. Here horses, with their chariots, are elite prestige goods, highly valued and highly skilled.

A variety of other objects and types of written documents help in our endeavour to find our ancient equine companions. Scribal lists and practice tablets enumerate animals, workers and goods, literary compositions mention mythical and legendary equids, while fables refer to equid features (imagined or real); and 'manuals' offer fascinating insights into human–equine training and veterinary procedures to cure equine ailments. These are rare but hint at important aspects of which we would otherwise be entirely ignorant. They each present some very specific difficulties, which will be addressed with the relevant chapter.

As with the faunal remains, our written sources are extremely uneven. Some periods and areas offer almost no information, not only concerning equids, but in any capacity. Even in the record-rich Ur III period, the known archives all come from a fairly small geographical area of southern Mesopotamia (in particular, the sites of Drehem/Puzriš-Dagan and Girsu and, to a lesser extent, Ur, Nippur and Umma), although they do sometimes include interaction with sites and areas further afield. The representation in the earlier third-millennium records is better, with evidence also from northern Mesopotamia and Syrian sites, but the Levant remains unrepresented. We have a near reversal of this situation in the second millennium, where material from western sites such as Ugarit, Amarna and Anatolian Kanesh/Kültepe providing the bulk of the material, and southern Mesopotamia being disappointingly silent.

With the exception of the Kanesh/Kültepe archive, the majority of texts related to equids concerns activities of the highest tiers of society, and it is therefore a sad fact that we have limited information about the lives of low status equids. Like humans of similar low social status, their stories are harder to reconstruct, but much can be done with what the Kanesh archives provide, and Goulder has also shown that ethnographic work can provide important insights (2020; 2021; see Chapter 4).

Iconography

The visual representations of equids consist of figurines, plaques and inlays, seals and seal impressions, stelae, decorated vessels, and a few other specialized or unique objects. Large wall paintings or reliefs such as those known from Egyptian reliefs, Aegean palaces or from the Neo-Assyrian period are rarely preserved from the third and second millennium in the Near East, and none has yet been found to depict equids.

Much of the more detailed visual evidence also comes from elite contexts or are part of 'high end' products. For example, the famous Standard of Ur, while unlikely to actually have functioned as a military standard, is made of composite luxury materials (lapis lazuli, shell, limestone), was certainly made by a specialized craftsperson, and was found in a very wealthy tomb in the so-called Royal Cemetery at Ur (Figure 5.5; PG 779; Woolley 1934: plates 90c–93). The representations on this box-like object offer more detail about the equids, their wheeled vehicles and their participation in war in the Early Dynastic period than perhaps any other image. Seals and seal impressions are typically also primarily associated with high status individuals (rulers, royalty, high officials), as are many of the unique objects, such as for example rein rings topped by an equid figure, or a gold-covered dagger sheath from Byblos depicting an equid and rider.

The type of object most frequently found is simultaneously the one that would have been most widely accessible and the one least understood: the terracotta figurine. Anthropomorphic and zoomorphic terracotta figurines are found at almost every site, often in very fragmentary condition. Among these are hundreds if not thousands of equid figurines. However, they are often extremely schematic in their rendition and offer great challenges for identification. Even so, much information can be gained from them and, as we will see, some detailed studies moving beyond standard typologies have helped tease out aspects of species, gender and markings related to management and equipment.

With visual evidence, there is always a question of the extent to which it represents 'reality'. The iconographic record of the ancient Near East is abundant with supernatural beings, mythological scenes and hybrid creatures. Does that mean that we must dismiss all representations of equids as merely a figment of the imagination, not to be trusted for any kind of information? By no means. Whether or not individual images of equids refer to real, specific equids and/or specific events, the overall concept would be one recognized and understood by the viewer. In other words, we can be certain that the average person living in the Near East at the time would recognize that an equid was depicted, probably even the type of equid; the context and the specific type of equipment depicted would also be based on contexts where they might expect to see an equid, and on equipment actually used with them. Thus, while we should be careful not to assume specificity of event, we can be quite confident in inferring technology and the kinds of relations reflected in the images.

However, with this caution in mind, we do also know that many objects from the ancient Near East did refer directly or indirectly to real events – or at least events corroborated by other pieces of evidence. Thus, for example, we have the Stele of the Vultures, depicting a mix of supernatural beings and the king with his army, and with a text narrating the actions shown (Barrelet 1970; Winter 1985). More famous are perhaps Naram-Sin's stele depicting his victory of the Lullubi and Ashurbanipal's palace reliefs depicting battle against the Elamites. These are of course idealized renderings created by the victors, but these types of objects are nevertheless extremely useful sources for the kind of information that helps reveal equid–human relations in a variety of aspects, and this applies to all the iconography included here.

A final caveat that should be mentioned here concerning the visual record is that of unprovenanced and looted objects. Such objects are regrettably common and extremely detrimental not only to interpretation, but also to the heritage of the countries from which they were taken. These items are generally avoided in this study, although in a few instances reference is made to objects that have a particularly clear depiction of a specific aspect or element. As with the other types of evidence, iconography of equids is patchy both chronologically and geographically; again, this is likely just as much a result of the current state of the archaeological record as it is a representation of the presence or absence of equids. That said, there are indications that some regions specialised in the breeding and/or training of equids, as we will see in Chapter 7.

There is a large amount of material available to us concerning equids in the ancient Near East, and it amounts to a wealth of knowledge. But there are also large gaps in our knowledge – on many aspects of which all types of evidence are partly or wholly silent. Although frustrating, the gaps themselves are revealing, both of ancient lifeways and of our modern research. As we will see throughout, modern research from equine studies, ethology and zoology offers a valuable basis on which to interpret the ancient sources and the possibilities of equid–human encounters.

Terminology

The terminology concerning equids is far from standardized, and potentially quite confusing. Appendix A lists the modern equine-related terms used in this book, and I will therefore here only mention a few of the main ones. I use 'equid' as a general category referring to the animals of the *Equidae* family that appear in ancient Near Eastern history. The main species, the terms used to refer to each and their Linnaean equivalent are discussed in the next chapter. In all cases, gender and age qualifiers are the same for each species, qualified with the particular species when relevant. Thus, for example, donkey mare, hemione stallion and horse foal. I have chosen this scheme for simplicity, despite other terms also being in popular use, as for example jenny or jennet for a female donkey. When such alternative terms are in use, they are noted in Appendix A.

In referring to ancient terms, I follow Postgate (1986) in writing the Sumerian ideogram in capitals (ANŠE), the Sumerian phonetic value in regular letters (kunga$_2$, dusu$_2$)[4], and the Akkadian in italics (*imēru*); see also Appendix B.

1.3 The ancient Near East in the third and second millennium BCE

The Near East is a broad term applied in numerous ways. Here, the emphasis is on (Greater) Mesopotamia and the Levant, with occasional forays into Egypt, Anatolia and other regions of the eastern Mediterranean. Much has been and can still be said concerning equid–human relations in those areas (for Egypt, see e.g. the recent work by Turner 2021), but as each would require a book on its own, I have had to contend myself with brief mentions along the way. Similarly for the chronological span, which is based on the third and second millennia BCE (that is, the Bronze Age), with only short discussions where relevant of developments in the late fourth millennium at one end and early first millennium at the other.[5]

The Near East is famous for hosting early state formation, a process that began at least as early as the fourth millennium, but that continued through the third and second millennia. Many transformations and shifts in power and power relations occurred in the two millennia that are the focus of this book, and equids were both caught up in these changes and to some extent were a catalyst for them (for an overview of ancient Near Eastern history, see e.g. Van De Mieroop 2016). Donkeys were already long-distance travellers carrying goods in the late fourth millennium, facilitating contact between distant regions. In the third millennium, we see the rise of city-states in Mesopotamia, followed by the Akkadian 'empire', apparently the first instance in this area of a single person ruling over a larger territory. In the second millennium, we instead have powers of roughly equal dominance engaging in extensive exchange of goods, ideas and people: both diplomacy and warfare were common types of interaction. Equids participated in warfare in the third millennium with fairly heavy wheeled vehicles, but sometime around the middle of the second millennium, the light, two-spoked chariot, pulled by two horses, became popular and a necessary part of a successful army.

Prior to the late fourth millennium, the equid–human relationship was limited to that of the hunt. Throughout the third and second millennia, the complexities and developments in the relationship mirror and are part of the broader social, economic, ideological and political developments of the Near East. That is why this particular period is so exciting for understanding the role of equids and their interaction with humans. We see that equids began to act as workers, carrying burdens over short and long distances and helping to plough fields; they also carried humans and pulled wheeled vehicles, and took part in ceremonies, wars and hunting. Equids shared death with humans, both in the battlefield and on the road, and in physical mortuary spaces; some equids became part of human self-identity and symbols of prestige, while others were anonymous labourers paid little attention beyond the rations necessary to keep them working. The impact of equids on human lives and humans on equid lives is also reflected in management, including breeding, supplies of food and habitation space, veterinary care, tracking of movements and ownership, and mutual training. These many aspects of equid lives and their relations with humans are what will be explored in the following chapters.

2

Equid Species: Spirited Horses, Stoic Donkeys and Vigorous Hybrids

The first thing to consider is which equid species were present in the ancient Near East in the Bronze Age, and to what extent we are able to differentiate these species. The means of identification are of course dependent on the material available, and I will here examine in turn the current state of knowledge for faunal remains, iconography and texts. Despite these very different types of material and their individual challenges, the problems of identification are conceptually strikingly similar. Faunal remains, texts and iconography all contain specific markers that we may use to help identification, but in each case there is substantial fluidity and variation that complicate interpretation.

Making as precise identifications as possible is not simply an academic exercise. Although most or even all equid species may appear quite similar, there are in fact significant differences not only in appearance, but also in behaviour, temperament, physical requirements and ability and inclination to engage in specific activities. These features have implications for the kinds of relations that could take place between equid and human, including types of management, training, breeding and practical employment. It is therefore important to try to gain as accurate an identification as possible.

Having said that, we must also keep in mind that in some cases, equid species may indeed *not* have been differentiated, and that our Linnaean system of classification may not always map directly onto ancient concepts of animal/ world categories. This particularly applies to the iconographic and textual evidence. Thus, as we will see, there are instances when the broad category of 'equid' was used, and very deliberately so. In those instances, the precise species was not important – but this information itself is extremely useful for how we understand the ancient relations to and perceptions of nonhuman animals.

2.1 Faunal remains

It is here relevant to begin with a note on the history of the study of faunal remains from archaeological contexts – that is, the specialized field of zooarchaeology. It is now standard practice for most excavations to retain animal bones found during excavations (although it is still rare for all soil to be sieved for very small bones, so species such as fish, birds and rodents are likely to be underrepresented). This was not always the case, and especially early identifications were often made by excavators rather than specialized personnel – thus, for example, leading to the erroneous belief that the animals in front of the vehicle in tomb PG 800 at the Early Dynastic cemetery in Ur were donkeys (Woolley 1934: 74). Luckily these skeletons were among the osteological remains kept by Woolley and his team, and later re-examination by Robert Dyson Jr revealed them to be cattle (1960). The first detailed report on faunal remains in the Near East was published in 1941 by Max Hilzheimer on the material from Tell Asmar. Fortuitously, he took a particular interest in the equid bones from the site, 'The wild ass is unquestionably one of the most interesting animals of which remains were found at Tell Asmar' (1941: 2). Hilzheimer presented some of the earliest possible methods for distinguishing different equid species in the Near East, including a version of the so-called slenderness index.[1] These and other methods have proved useful, but far from bullet-proof. The identification of equid species is riddled with uncertainties stemming from a broad range in diversity and the possibility of hybridization, combined with minor discrepancies among expert identifications.

The species of equids believed to have been present in the Near East and surrounding areas are listed in the table below, with their Latin and common names.

Equus asinus – the domestic donkey – is by far the most common type of equid throughout the Bronze Age, although significant transformations begin around the turn of the second millennium, something which I will return to in more detail later. Donkey bones are very widely found in the Near East. *E. asinus* has now been proven through genetic studies to be the domestic descendant of *E. africanus* (possibly from two different sub-species: Beja-Pereira et al. 2004; Kimura et al. 2011; 2013). *E. africanus*, or the wild donkey, had its homeland on the African continent, but the exact limits of its distribution are still unclear.[2] The bones of the domestic donkey are difficult, if not outright impossible, to distinguish from *Equus africanus*, although this seems to become easier in the later part of our period due to significant differences in size (Grigson 1993: 645;

Table 1.1 *Equidae* in the ancient Near East. The species most relevant for this study are marked in bold, and have been identified with certainty in the Bronze Age faunal record

Latin name	Common name	Status
Equus asinus	**donkey**/ass	domesticated
Equus africanus	wild donkey/ass	wild
Equus caballus	**horse**	domesticated
Equus ferus	wild horse	wild
Equus hemionus	**hemione**/onager/Asiatic wild ass, half-ass	wild
E.h.hemippus	**Syrian onager**/hemippe/Syrian wild ass	wild
E.h.onager	Persian onager/onager	wild

2012: 188). At sites with phases in the fourth millennium and earlier, it can thus be difficult to ascertain whether we have domestic or wild donkeys, as is also illustrated by disagreement among experts.

Several species of equids have occasionally been identified at a single site. Thus, for example at the Late Uruk site of El Kowm 2 in Syria, both hemione and donkey are reported (Vila 1998; Helmer 2000). The donkey bones could not be categorized more specifically as *asinus* or *africanus*; the same applies to a number of other sites with late fourth millennium equid remains (see Chapter 3 and Appendix F). In most cases, there is no obvious difference in the distribution and treatment of donkey bones and other animals at these sites, suggesting that the remains found mainly represent food waste.[3]

The wild hemione can be divided into the subspecies *E.h.hemippus* (Syrian onager) and *E.h.onager* (Persian onager) that may be of relevance to the ancient Near East.[4] The Syrian onager is now extinct, and primarily known from a limited number of museum specimens (Bökönyi 1986: 312). The last known animal died in the 1920s in Vienna Zoo (Clutton-Brock 1992: 37). In the Bronze Age, its distribution may have extended throughout the Near East, but is more confidently identified in the area of the Khabur Basin. The Persian onager's homeland was further east in Iran, on the other side of the Zagros Mountains (where it can still be found, but is now endangered). There is as yet no conclusive evidence that it was present in the Near East. Bökönyi identified it at sixth-millennium Umm Dabaghiyah in Iraq (1986), but this was based on the assumption that the Syrian onager was a smaller animal (itself based on museum specimens and the last few surviving animals in zoos, which may well be smaller due to its later time period and life in captivity). Since no morphological or biometrical criteria are known to distinguish the two, Bökönyi's hypothesis has not been confirmed. It has been noted for e.g. fourth- and third-millennium Tell Brak that the faunal remains of hemione present are 'a larger animal than the modern *hemippus*' (Oates 2001: 286). In other words, either the Syrian onagers could be larger than we expect from known specimens, or the ancient distribution of the Persian onagers extended quite far west. The general consensus is that the remains we find in the Near East in the late fourth and third millennia belong to the Syrian onager rather than the Persian version, but this still lacks conclusive evidence.[5]

In the Bronze Age, horses occur as domestic *E. caballus*. More accurately, they are assumed to be domestic. Once again, no secure or consistently reliable criteria have been discovered that can distinguish between domestic and wild species on morphological or biometric grounds. This is in fact a lack that has caused a long and ongoing debate concerning when and where horses were first domesticated, a topic to which I will return briefly in the next chapter. Remains of horses are not uncommon at Neolithic sites in Anatolia and northern Syria (Grigson 2012), where they were hunted and eaten along with other wild animal species. It has long been thought that there was a hiatus between these Neolithic occurrences and the Bronze Age, and this hiatus was in effect used to distinguish between wild, hunted horses in the Neolithic and domestic ones from the Bronze Age (Bökönyi 1991: 129). This convenient division is complicated by reports of horse remains from layers dated to the fourth and third millennium in Anatolia, the Levant and Syria (Shev 2016). The status of these horses is still undetermined; Bökönyi believed the remains found at Late Chalcolithic sites in Anatolia to be from domestic horses, with the continued presence of horses at a site like Arslantepe from the late fourth millennium and throughout the Early Bronze Age (1991). However, as we shall see, the real impact of the horse was not until around the turn of the second millennium, and these were certainly domestic animals.

Much has been written and debated on how to distinguish between these species of equids based on zooarchaeological analysis (see Appendix D; Zarins 2014: ch. I). Zooarchaeological or faunal analyses use morphological and to some extent biometric criteria to identify animal species. There is a great range of variation, especially within *E. asinus* and *E. caballus*, and significant overlap between asinines and hemiones. This is perhaps best illustrated with the many breeds of modern horses. Consider, for example, the clear differences between a Shetland pony, a Shire horse and an Arabian. None of these breeds were the ones encountered in the Bronze Age Near East, and the variation is not quite so extreme, but it does provide an idea of how diverse equids can be within each species. Donkeys are also incredibly varied, and do not always conform to the stereotypical grey/brown with dark markings that is often presented today, although this may have been the most common.

The morphological characteristics are primarily based on the enamel patterns of teeth, general size (especially for horses), and postcranial remains, particularly the 'slenderness' of metapodials. Various other factors have been suggested for the skull and the postcranial skeleton. These features and their technical details are outlined in Appendix D, with comments and references for each relevant part of the skeleton. It is important to note that these criteria are *not* absolute: due to the great variety, for each criterion it would be possible to find exceptions. They thus suggest *tendencies* rather than hard and fast rules, and it is best to avoid applying them to single specimens. As noted by Zeder concerning dental remains, 'Positive species identification should be reserved for complete or nearly complete tooth rows only, and even then some reservations will likely be warranted. Isolated teeth can be typified as a collection, but are unlikely to serve as a secure basis for species identifications' (1986: 390).

Three main types of criteria are most widely applied: tooth morphology, general body size and the so-called slenderness index. General body size is perhaps the characteristic most commonly used in practice, and can with some confidence distinguish between horses (larger) and donkeys (smaller), at least in later periods when they were both clearly domesticated. However, this is not entirely reliable given the variation of each species, but more significantly, is less useful when wild species and hybrids are added to the mix. The slenderness index combines various ratios of postcranial remains, particularly the metapodials and, using a specialized formula, provides a mean typical for each species (as e.g. suggested in Groves & Willoughby 1981; Appendix D for details). This method seems to be a fairly good indicator, with the provision that there is overlap with some of the species.

Tooth morphology is a frequently applied indicator, but is compromised by overlap and significant variation, even within a tooth row from a single individual; further, age and wear affect enamel patterns, although these changes may not be significant until senility (Davis 1980: 291). Where at all possible, a combination of features strengthens the identification, but unfortunately this is not always possible. Enamel patterns as species indicator have recently been tested as a practical method by Katherine Twiss and colleagues, with a rather disheartening result. Seven zooarchaeologists employed some of the most common enamel criteria on ancient equid teeth. The identifications differed significantly, and the authors conclude that reports based on this method should not be accepted uncritically (Twiss et al. 2017: 301; see now also Chuang & Bonhomme 2018). A similarly damning conviction was already given by Groves and Willoughby in 1981: 'The belief that characters of the dentition (especially the cheekteeth) are completely diagnostic of species-groups in the Equine, is unfortunately, a myth: largely sustained, we suspect, by the wishful thinking of palaeontologists who often have nothing else to work with!' (1981: 341).

The slenderness index has not been tested to the same extent, but suffers from the disadvantage of requiring several parts of the skeleton of a single animal. In reality, it is very rare to have complete animal skeletons from an archaeological site. It is, however, a version of the slenderness index and biometrical ratios that has allowed Jill Weber to identify hybrids at Tell Umm el-Marra in Syria (2008; 2012; 2017), and she was only able to do this because not just one but around 25 complete or nearly complete skeletons were available for analysis.

Complicating matters: hybrids and domestication

Two factors complicate species identification: distinguishing between wild and domestic, and the possibility of hybrids. We have seen some criteria for distinguishing between asinines, hemiones and caballines do exist and can be applied, with some reservations. Hemiones are wild species, and although they may have been tamed to some extent by the Sumerians, they were never domesticated, and consequently there is no problem in their identification in that respect.[6] Donkeys and horses are another matter. The question of domestication will be explored in more depth in the next chapter; for now, it is merely relevant to note that morphological criteria have so far proved inadequate for providing evidence of domestication for horses, and is also insufficient for donkeys, at least in the first stages of domestication. Their identification thus has to rely on other data, including site and assemblage contexts, broader historical contexts, literary and textual sources, and any noticeable pathologies.

Given the overlap in variation of species, it is no surprise that recognizing hybrids constitutes an additional challenge. Mules and hinnies – crosses between horses and donkeys – are the hybrids best known to us today. There is evidence of their occurrence in the Bronze Age as well, but at least in the third millennium it seems that the more common hybrid was a hemione–donkey cross (the so-called kunga, see more below). With significant overlap in variation of donkeys and hemiones, their hybrids become very difficult to identify (some of this difficulty is illustrated by examples in Schubert et al. 2017, comparing morphological and genetic identification). They are suspected in a number of cases such as Abu Salabikh (Clutton-Brock 1986: 209) and Abu Tbeirah (Alhaique et al. 2021), but it was not until Weber's elaborate study of the Tell Umm el-Marra equids that they were identified with a fair degree of certainty.

Although it is easier to distinguish between horses and donkeys, with reasonably good criteria in place (see e.g. Wilkens 2003; Johnstone 2004; Hanot & Bochaton 2018), identifying mules and hinnies osteologically is still challenging. As Hanot and Bochaton note in their study, hybrids do not simply fall directly in between horses and donkeys, but can exhibit anywhere from 100 per cent donkey features to 95 per cent horse features (2018: 16). However, a good guide offered by those same authors is that if a specimen is less than 85 per cent of one of the species, it is very likely a hybrid (2018: 17).[7] This again means that single bones are not enough to make a discrimination, but that it is possible with more extensive assemblages or skeletons. So far, the oldest fairly secure identification of a mule/hinny comes from a first millennium context (Uerpmann 2003: 551).

Other hybrids would have been possible, but so far have very little evidence. Based on morphological and biometric criteria, Gilbert suspects horse-onager hybrids at Godin Tepe (1991). Iconographically, these would probably be indistinguishable from other hybrids, but we have little knowledge of their typical physical characteristics. If they were recorded in the texts, their designation has not yet been detected; however, there are several equid-related terms as yet not entirely understood, as we will see below. Any hybrid breeding involving *E. africanus* has not been suggested, but would be equally difficult to differentiate from other hybrids.

Ancient DNA

Zooarchaeological analysis is not the only way of identifying animal bones, and aDNA methods have now been developed to be able to recognize equid species (Schubert et al. 2017). The 'Zonkey' method presented by Schubert and colleagues is able to identify not only the different equid species, but also first generation hybrids (F1), including distribution of parent aDNA. This is very recent, and has therefore only been attempted to a very limited extent for any remains from the Near East (Schubert and colleagues tested it on Byzantine and Roman mules, and identified one female hemione from southwestern Iran dated to the Chalcolithic, 2017: 155). At Abu Tbeirah, mtDNA has identified the remains of one equid as *E. hemionus* for at least one of the parents and another as *E. asinus* for one parent (Alhaïque et al. 2021), but this is so far the only result from the Near East for our period.

2.2 Textual sources

Equids occur in Sumerian and Akkadian cuneiform sources throughout the third and second millennia, but signs depicting equid heads can be found already in documents from the fourth millennium (Zarins 2014: 151–7). There is a large range of words and phrases referring to different species and types of equids, with important shifts and additions over the two millennia. I will here concentrate on the most commonly occurring and important versions; more details, variations and discussion can be found in Appendix B. The basic Sumerian logogram is ANŠE. The sign itself is a schematized equid head, and it is earlier versions of this head that are found on proto-cuneiform tablets from Jemdet Nasr and Uruk in the late fourth millennium (Falkenstein 1936: no. 49; Postgate 1986: 200; for early third-millennium versions, see e.g. Burrows 1935: pl. 13).[8]

ANŠE could mean either simply 'equid' or more specifically 'donkey', depending on the context. In administrative records, ANŠE could be used in a summary fashion, recording a total number of the various types of equids under the one broad type (e.g. P217280). This system already informs us that equids were conceptualized in a manner similar to ours today: that the species were differentiated, but ultimately belonged under a single category of animals, that of equids. In other words, the ancient folk taxonomy in this case seems to correspond quite well to our modern Linnaean system of classification.

In order to further determine the type of equid referred to, ANŠE could be followed by one or more qualifying signs. These qualifiers can relate to species, but also a number of other features, such as age, sex, function and feeding. As suggested by Zarins, a good indicator that a qualifier refers to species rather than some other feature is whether it occurs with other qualifiers, such as both males and females, and a range of age groups (Zarins 2014: 151, 163).

Besides ANŠE, our most commonly mentioned equid actors in the third millennium are ANŠE.ŠUL.GI (also written ANŠE.DUN.GI[9]), ANŠE.LIBIR (dusu$_2$), ANŠE.ZI.ZI, ANŠE.EDIN.NA, and ANŠE.BAR.AN. Much has been written about the meaning of each of these terms (see e.g. *CAD*; *RLA*, 'Pferd, A.I', 'Maultier'; Salonen 1956; Gelb 1955: 246–7; Maekawa 1979a; 2006; Postgate 1986; Zarins 1986; and most recently, the detailed discussion by Zarins 2014: Ch. III, based on his earlier 1978 study). There now seems to be general agreement that these terms in fact refer to equid *species* (this has not always been the case – see detailed notes for each term in Appendix B). Broadly speaking, there is now also consensus concerning the meaning of at least some of these terms. Thus, ANŠE.ZI.ZI is translated as (domestic) 'horse'. It occurs in the Ur III administrative documents, and is replaced in the Old Babylonian period with ANŠE.KUR.RA (*sisûm*). ANŠE.EDIN.NA ('equid of the steppe') is translated as 'onager' (or, as I prefer, 'hemione'), with the Akkadian *serrēmu* having the same meaning, although it is only rarely attested in the second millennium.

The trouble starts when we get to ANŠE.ŠUL.GI, ANŠE.LIBIR and ANŠE. BAR.AN. Their interpretation has rather serious implications for how we understand equid–human relations in the mid- to late third millennium, and it is therefore worth delving into the issue a little deeper here. ANŠE.ŠUL.GI was probably replaced with ANŠE.LIBIR (= dusu$_2$) after Early Dynastic IIIB (Maekawa 1979a: 42). Maekawa and Postgate understand this as the common domestic donkey (Maekawa 1979a; Postgate 1986), but Zarins insists that it rather designates the horse (2014: 165–9 and throughout). The crux of Zarins' argument relies on the assumption that ANŠE by itself means donkey, and that variation and imprecision in the form of several words (or at least, signs) for the same concept would be unlikely. This is a valid point when applied within a single document, or in some cases even archives limited to a specific site and period. However, as we have seen, ANŠE could certainly mean both equid in a generic sense, and donkey in a specific sense.

As Maekawa further points out, ANŠE.ŠUL.GI and ANŠE do not occur in the same texts at Lagash, 'no equid named anše may be distinguished zootaxonomically from the ANŠE.DUN.GI and the ANŠE.BARxAN' (1979a: 36). In the extensive Ur III archives, ANŠE.LIBIR / dusu$_2$ was primarily in use at Drehem (Puzriš-Dagan): currently, of the 313 texts mentioning dusu$_2$ recorded in the BDTNS, 88.8 per cent come from Drehem, where the use of anše on its own as 'donkey' rather than 'equid' is also rare. Another 8 per cent come from Girsu, and 1.6 per cent from Umma. Although it could be argued that this reflects a focus on horse-breeding at Drehem, in this case the distribution seems more likely to reflect variation in local scribal conventions. Such local conventions are known in relation to other aspects of the Ur III archives (Molina 2016). More importantly, the substantial numbers of ANŠE.ŠUL.GI and ANŠE.LIBIR do not concur with all other evidence, which indicates that horses were extremely rare before the Ur III period (and we already have the ANŠE.ZI.ZI meaning horse), and even then they were far from common. It thus seems much more likely that these terms all refer to the common domestic donkey.

ANŠE.BAR.AN (anše kunga$_2$) has convincingly been argued to be a hybrid, based on the fact that a later version of the same cuneiform sign (ANŠE.ŠU$_2$.AN / ANŠE.ŠU$_2$.MUL = *parûm*) referred to a horse–donkey cross (Salonen 1956: 74–5), and that ANŠE.BAR.AN, in contrast to other equids, never occur as parents in the texts, an absence expected for a sterile animal (Zarins 1978: 13; 2014: 174). Although Maekawa continues to identify ANŠE.BAR.AN as the (Persian) onager (1979a; 2006; 2018), the main disagreement between scholars concerns what type of hybrid was meant. The texts strongly suggest that ANŠE.LIBIR females could be mothers of ANŠE.BAR.AN (e.g. Zarins 2014: 174, 271–2), so we can say with some confidence that donkeys acted as one of the parents. The later Akkadian *parûm* is a horse-donkey cross (*RLA*, 'Maultier', §2), but given the low numbers of horses present in the third millennium, Postgate's argument that ANŠE.BAR.AN initially referred to a donkey–hemione cross which later retained the meaning of hybrid, but of different species, is the most appealing (1986: 200).

The main species of equid in the late third millennium are neatly recorded in Ur III archives, which also provide an indication of which were most common, as for example in P127971 from Drehem/Puzriš-Dagan (see also P126669, P127972):

38 anše si$_2$-si$_2$ [horses]
360 anše eden-na [hemiones]
727 anše kunga$_2$ [hybrid equids]
2204 dusu$_2$ [donkeys]

The corresponding Akkadian terms used primarily in the second millennium are more secure in their identification. So we know that *imērum* should be translated as donkey, *agālum* likewise (not common; possibly more specifically referring to a riding donkey), *serrēmu* as hemione (not attested before *c.* 1500 BCE[10]), *sisûm* as horse, *parûm* as mule/hinny, and *perdum*, *kūdanum* and *damdammu* probably also some kinds of hybrids.

In the second half of the second millennium, two other languages, both also using the cuneiform script, record equids in our area: Hittite and Ugaritic.[11] The texts concerning equids (mainly horses) are not numerous, but they do add valuable aspects not mentioned elsewhere, or only mentioned in passing. Hittite uses the same ideograms as those found in Sumerian and Akkadian discussed above to refer to donkeys, horses and mules/hinnies (*RLA*, 'Pferd', A.II); hemiones and kunga$_2$ hybrids are apparently not recorded. Ugaritic was a West Semitic language used at the site of Ugarit (Ras Shamra) on the western coast of

Table 1.2 The most common ancient terms for equid species and the translations used in this book (for the more detailed version, see Appendix B)

Sign(s)	Sumerian	Akkadian	Translation	
ANŠE	anše	*imērum*	donkey, equid	
ANŠE.ŠUL.GI		*agālum?*	donkey	
ANŠE.LIBIR	dusu$_2$	*agālum*	donkey	
ANŠE.EDIN.NA	anše-edin-na	*serrēmu*	hemione	
ANŠE.BAR.AN	anše-kunga$_2$	*parûm*	hybrid equid (donkey x hemione; Akkadian mule/hinny)	
ANŠE.ZI.ZI	anše-si$_2$-si$_2$	*sisûm*	horse	
ANŠE.KUR.RA		*sisûm*	horse	

Syria. It is only present in the archaeological record from the fourteenth century and until the city was destroyed in the early twelfth century; it primarily uses an alphabetic writing system. In Ugaritic, we find mention of donkeys (*ḥmr, atnt, ʿr, pḥl*), horses (*śśw/śśwt*), and mules/hinnies (*prd, kdn*) (del Olmo Lete & Sanmartín 2003). As with Hittite, hemione and kunga$_2$ hybrids do not occur in the records. Some of the terms for equids, and those related to equids, may be loan words (Watson 2011), which may imply an origin for the concepts themselves.

2.3 Iconography

Depictions of equids in the ancient Near East appear on seals and seal impressions, tablets, plaques, vessels, stelae, inlays and other decorative elements, and as figurines. The most common depiction in the Bronze Age are figurines and seals or seal impressions. For the Near East in this period, we do not at this point have large surviving wall paintings or reliefs that include equids – as for example occur in New Kingdom Egypt or the many elaborate palace reliefs of the Neo-Assyrians.

Figure 2.1 Images of modern a) *E. hemionus hemippus* (after Antonius 1929, photo by Conrad Keller), b) *E. asinus* at The Donkey Sanctuary in Sidmouth (photo by the author), c) *E. caballus* in their paddock on a warm summer day in Denmark (photo by the author).

The relatively small media of the extant objects are not particularly conducive to species identification; nevertheless, it is clear that at least in some cases, an effort was made to convey specific features. Given the visual nature of these objects, the most obvious manner of identification is to use the physical characteristics of equids, as has indeed been the case for most studies, whether explicitly or implicitly so. The physical attributes typical of each species that may be of relevance to the objects that survive are summarised in the table below, and modern versions of the main species can be seen in Figure 2.1. A more detailed overview can be found in Appendix C.

Physical characteristics may seem straightforward, but in practice this is far from the case. They lead to a rather impressive range of interpretations. One example will suffice for now. The famous Standard of Ur, which we will return to many times over the course of this book, depicts teams of equids in front of wheeled vehicles. These equids have been identified as pretty much every possible equid species present in the Near East at the time: donkeys, onagers/ hemiones, horses, and donkey–hemione hybrids (for a review, see Zarins 2014:

Table 1.3 The main physical attributes of the main equid species (see Appendix C for more details)

Physical attribute	Horse/*E. caballus*	Donkey/*E. asinus*	Hemione/*E. hemionus*
Ears	short	long	short to long
Mane	hanging; can also be upright; long and thick	thin and scruffy; upright	upright, 'clipped' appearance
Forelock	present, hanging	absent or very thin	absent or very thin
Head and neck	small compared to body; long neck	large compared to body; short neck	large compared to body; short neck
Tail	long and full from the base	tufted at end; mid-length	tufted but full from halfway down length; mid-length
Body	curved back	straight back	straight back
Chest	broader	narrower	narrower
Legs	long-legged	short-legged	long-legged
Markings	can have white legs or facial markings	often dorsal and shoulder stripe	dorsal stripe

128; also van Buren 1939: 29; Maekawa 1979a: 46; Clutton-Brock 1992: 68–9). This range of identifications is a healthy reminder that interpretation can be very subjective, and that analysis of visual representations require caution. It forces us to think about how ancient peoples conceptualized, categorized and represented their world. This includes considering the possibility of categories that do not necessarily correspond directly with those we use today.

The main physical features that may help identification receiving attention in the iconography are the mane, tail and ears (Recht 2018: 65). Horses usually have a hanging mane, short ears and a full tail; donkeys have a thin, standing mane, long ears, and a tufted tail; and hemiones have a thin, standing mane, long (Persian onager) or short (Syrian onager) ears and the tail is tufted but quite full roughly halfway down. When excited, horses may lift their tail (sometimes accompanied by snorting), which is reflected in the visual representations; donkeys may instead 'wag' their tail, but this would be more difficult to render in a static image, and has not so far been detected. To a lesser extent, we may also examine the general shape and proportions of the body, and presence/absence of markings, but these seem to be less reliable if used on their own.[12] Donkeys and hemiones have large heads, short necks and fairly flat backs, while horses have smaller heads compared to the body, placed on a long, high set neck and with a curved back. Horses and hemiones can have long legs compared to body size, and hemiones can be particularly slender.

As with the faunal remains, it is possible to find exceptions to nearly all of the characteristics listed here and in the appendix – some horses have standing manes and fairly large heads, and hemiones can appear remarkably caballine. Also in common with the fauna is the fact that it is the hybrids who present the greatest challenge, precisely because they are crosses that mix the features of both parents. In general, hybrids tend to mostly take after the mother, although head and tail may rather resemble the father (Clutton-Brock 1992: 45). It is also the mother that at least to some extent determines the size of the offspring, and for this reason, mules tend to be bigger than hinnies.

In many depictions of equids, the features listed here are not detailed enough (or have not been preserved) to provide conclusive identification to species level. This may at times simply be because no specific equid species was intended (analogous to when anše was used in texts to simply mean 'equid'). The majority of cases may rather be a matter of our inadequacy and lack of greater context in order to recognize the species. Most likely, an ancient observer would fairly easily be able to determine which animal was depicted, based on known emic reference points. Our best option is then to combine physical attributes as they are rendered with artistic traditions and contexts.

2.4 Temperament, behaviour and agency

Although an equid may be physically suitable for intensive interaction with humans, it may not have any particular interest or inclination for such socialization. Equids have individual temperament (what we may refer to as 'personality' in humans, and what I here also call *personhood*), but there are also general characteristics pertaining to each species. These are important precisely because they have bearing on what activities each equid species was willing to perform for or in conjunction with humans, and how much effort would be needed in the training process. I will therefore examine the characteristics of the equid species here in turn, insofar as they are known, and with due allowance for individuality and personhood.

Horses

Due to modern equestrian interest, our knowledge of caballine biology and ethology, and possible ways of interaction are highly advanced. With the right knowledge and experience, the horse–human relationship can involve extremely complex activities and fine-tuned communication. At its most delicate, a small muscle flexion or shift in weight of a rider can transmit the intention of stopping, turning or changing pace; the same minute tension or shift in the horse may alert the rider to specific surroundings or intentions of the horse. Today, this is perhaps best illustrated by modern horse–rider combinations achieving incredible athletic feats in for example dressage, showjumping and eventing. But the same concept can be extended to the past, and to activities not limited to riding or direct contact. Donkeys and hybrids may also be able to maintain similar communication, although the high level of sensitivity and quick reaction may be more prevalent with horses and mules.

Horses have a flight-fight instinct, which means that they react to pressure and danger differently from donkeys. They will attempt to physically remove themselves from the situation that is causing discomfort. If seriously spooked, a horse may run amok in an uncontrolled manner where all communication lines have been shut down – indeed, this is one way in which we may call horses 'spirited'. It is this running instinct and quick reaction that is exploited in the horse–human relationship, and what is likely to make horses more desirable companions in certain events, as for example when facing or escaping a formidable foe on a battlefield. If the relationship is well-developed and both human(s) and horse(s) are well-attuned to each other, it could be extremely effective; if not, the flight instinct and lack of communication could have disastrous consequences for all involved.

Horses have comparatively wide hooves set at a lower angle than donkeys. This makes navigating uneven terrain more difficult, but allows for great speed over flat or undulating spaces, and is also very useful for high impact. Today, this feature is taken advantage of especially in racing and showjumping; in the past, the possible speed must have been particularly appealing.

Donkeys

Compared to horses, donkeys are quiet and stoic. Donkeys will put up with a high level of pain without showing external signs of it, or only very subtle signs.[13] This is a challenge for owners and veterinarians even today, because by the time a donkey shows signs of pain, a disease can often be so far advanced that it is too late to treat (Minero et al. 2016; Evans & Crane 2018). The signs usually consist of the donkey being even quieter than usual, perhaps isolating itself and lacking appetite; in order to detect that something is wrong, it is often necessary to know the usual behaviour of the individual donkey. The stoicism is also part of why donkeys have appealed so strongly to humans, because it means that they accept the relationship and requests made by humans with little outward objection. They carry heavy burdens and travel long distances, and will not stop until or unless seriously ill.

Donkeys have a reputation for being stubborn. This 'stubbornness' is actually an expression of fear or discomfort, where they may, in the first instance, 'freeze', and subsequently begin to react by kicking, biting or pushing. One of the main behavioural contrasts to horses is that donkeys tend to have a fight-flight instinct, compared to the horse's flight-fight instinct (Burden & Thiemann 2015: 377; Navas González et al. 2016: 80; F. Burden, pers. comm.). In other words, donkeys will often choose to fight first, perhaps as a result of living in small groups, where flight is not always the most efficient defence (Evans & Crane 2018: 11). This has the consequence of the donkey being 'an animal less inclined to panic than the horse' (Burden & Thiemann 2015: 377), potentially avoiding some of the dangerous situations that the more nervous nature of the horse may provoke. However, it has been suggested that the same trait can mean that equids more inclined to react with flight are easier to train (Navas González et al. 2018).[14]

A related trait is that donkeys, in contrast to horses, are territorial animals, and thus will protect their lived space. In the interaction with humans, this potential aggression against other species can cause problems (Burden & Trawford 2006), but can also be an advantage, for example when donkeys act as guardians of other animals (Dohner 2007; Nichols 2019[15]). Donkeys form lifelong (non-sexual) companionships or 'pair-bonds' (Murray et al. 2013). These bonds are so strong that separation can cause serious stress and a condition known as hyperlipaemia, which can be fatal (Evans & Crane 2018: 11, 89–95). Bonding of this kind is also known among horses, but perhaps not with the same strength or longevity (McGreevy 2012: 126–7).

Donkeys require less feed than horses, and can more easily thrive on steppe and bush vegetation.[16] Some of the most commonly recorded cereals in the Near East, barley and wheat, are in fact considered particularly suitable for donkeys, while these are harder for horses to digest. Donkeys can go for longer without water, although this does not mean that they do not require the same amount as horses (Burden & Thiemann 2015: 378). Their narrow upright hooves are well-adapted for difficult terrain, but less suitable for pure speed on long and fairly flat surfaces. These traits mean that donkeys are particularly good for long-distance trade and transport, which would often include navigating uneven and mountainous terrain, and limited access to highly nutritious fodder.

The straight back and comparatively short, low-rise steps of donkeys make for a much more comfortable ride over long distances. The lower-set withers and narrower shoulders mean that the riding position and balance is very different from that with horses, and in some cases this may be reflected in the rider being seated much further towards the rear of the donkey's back. The difference in physical build of horses and donkeys also result in the same tack not fitting equally well on both: ideally, it should be specifically developed and adapted for each species. As we will see, this can be detected in the ancient material, where there was both experimentation with types of tack and adaptation to species.

Hemiones

Information concerning hemione behaviour in relation to humans is much harder to come by, partly due to limited interaction beyond hunting, and partly due to their extinct or endangered status. The data we have primarily concern their behaviour and social structures in nature, and relate to the Persian onager, *E.h.onager* (e.g. Klingel 1998; Tatin et al. 2007). In common with donkeys, hemiones are mostly territorial.

The zoologist Otto Antonius carefully observed equid species in the Schönbrunn Zoological Garden in the 1920s to 1940s and reported his findings in *Der Zoologische Garten* (1929–44). This includes a paper on the zoo's one male Syrian onager, with supplementary information from museum specimens (Figure 2.1a; Antonius 1929). Antonius describes this hemione as small, barely one metre withers height (as seems also to be the case for a museum specimen), 'avellaneous' in coat colour, without shoulder stripe, with short ears, 'glorious big and fiery eyes' (1929: 24), and nostrils apparently bigger than horses', flaring up when excited. It took long strides, and the sound it would make is described as a short donkey bray. The stallion met by Antonius was fiery, ready to fight by biting and kicking, and attempts to habituate it to a halter and lunging had to be abandoned.[17] The difference from the Persian onager is in the coat colour and length of the ears.

It is unfortunate that Antonius was only able to observe this single live animal, and almost impossible to disentangle this particular hemione's individual encounter with and response to human interaction from anything that may be typical of Syrian onagers. Overall, it seems to have reacted more like a donkey than a horse, choosing fight over flight, perhaps even going so far as to being offensive (Antonius 1929: fig. 5 shows the hemione apparently attacking the metal bars of its enclosure by biting, with a human on the other side). How typical this behaviour is, is difficult to assess, since his early history is not related (he arrived from Aleppo as a gift when two or three years old), and his first encounters with humans may have been thoroughly unpleasant.

Other sources emphasize the speed of hemiones. Henry Layard, during his travels in the Middle East, notes that 'in fleetness they equal the gazelle; and to match them is a feat which only one or two of the most celebrated mares have been known to accomplish' (as quoted by Hilzheimer 1941: 2–3). This is corroborated by Xenophon in his *Anabasis*, 1.5 [2], 'As for the asses, whenever one chased them, they would run on ahead and stop – for they ran much faster than the horses – and then, when the horses came near, they would do the same thing again, and it was impossible to catch them unless the horsemen posted themselves at intervals and hunted them in relays. The flesh of those that were captured was like venison, but more tender'.[18] Hemiones may have made for a more comfortable ride, similar to donkeys: Groves and Willoughby note that they 'have a noticeably easier, and faster, gallop than any horse' (1981: 346). However, a third-millennium text from Abu Salabikh known as *The Instructions of Shuruppak* suggests that hemiones did not have a high level of endurance, advising against buying one as it would only last until the end of the day (Biggs 1974: 60, line 48). Beyond temperament, this could go some way towards explaining the preference for donkeys as working animals.

Mules and hinnies

Beginning with what we have most knowledge of due to modern practices, we can say that mules and hinnies, unsurprisingly, display features from both parents. Very generally speaking, hybrids tend to mostly take after the dame, and it is the dame that has the most influence on size, although the offspring can outgrow both parents. A hybrid may also primarily resemble its mother in temperament since that is the species it is brought up with (Svendsen 2009: 101). Mules, with their equine dame, tend to be bigger than hinnies; they often have the body of a horse with the extremities of a donkey, while hinnies often have the body of a donkey with the extremities of a horse (Travis 2004: 1–2).

Hybrids may display what is known as 'hybrid vigour' or 'heterosis'. Hybrid vigour is the accentuation of qualities from both parents – Svendsen describes the mule as possibly 'exhibiting the sure-footedness, stamina and stoical nature of a donkey combined with the vigour, strength and size of a horse' (2009: 105). Thus, for example, hybrids may have a taller withers height than both (although within the limits provided by the dame), be strong with a high level of endurance and capacity to withstand harsh conditions, and it may be that other qualities, such as speed or intelligence, could also be accentuated (Travis 2004: 4). In experiments with horses, donkeys and mules, the latter carried out the (visual) task given with significantly more efficiency than both its parent species (Proops et al. 2009). Another experiment testing spatial problem-solving abilities of the same species, with the addition of dogs, also saw mules performing the best (Osthaus et al. 2013). Hybrid vigour may thus extend to cognitive abilities and constitute an important advantage in the training process.[19] Such studies have not yet included hinnies, so it is not known how they would rank; we also do not have information about wild species or the effects of domestication on cognition.

Kungas and other hybrids

Crosses between domestic donkeys and hemiones presumably also display a mixture of features from both parents, and if the same principles apply as for mules and hinnies, it may very well be the case that the offspring took mostly after the dame. This is surely amplified if the foal is brought up with its biological mother. Few modern examples are known. Antonius describes a Persian onager stallion who impregnated three donkey mares (1944: 3–6). Unfortunately, one mare died during pregnancy, and the second one gave birth to a stillborn foal. The third, Julietta, gave birth to a colt named Florian, and the year after, to a filly named Loisi. In appearance, they were both a mix of the features of their parents, the body being more donkey-like than onager, and both with quite slender limbs (more so the mare). Florian is described as 'dark mouse grey' in coat, with Loisi a darker colour; both had the usual lighter colour around the eyes, muzzle, belly and inside the legs, and Florian had a shoulder and dorsal stripe. Their temperament was very individual: while Florian was tame and accepted the halter, Loisi was more feisty, attempting already at two weeks old to escape her stall. Antonius describes the Persian onager stallion serving the donkey mares as cautious in his behaviour towards them (1944: 6). Nevertheless, he was evidently successful in a number of instances, demonstrating that breeding programmes involving wild species are not wholly unrealistic for ancient Mesopotamia, if requiring extra care, time and knowledge.

No crosses or donkeys with Syrian onagers are described, although Gray mentions one being born in London Zoo in 1883 (1954: 48). The information we have suggests that kungas, assuming they were *E.asinus* × *E.h.hemippus*, like mules and hinnies, took traits from both parents and may have displayed some level of hybrid vigour. This could mean an animal capable of great speed, of gracile build with excellent endurance, and potentially with some challenges in temperament. These could be partially mitigated by an upbringing with domestic donkeys and by interaction with humans from an early age.

Looking back at the advantages and disadvantages of the temperament, behaviour and physical attributes of the different equid species in interaction with humans, a combination of all the most desirable traits would indeed make for a most magnificent animal. It can therefore be no surprise that they were so highly regarded in the ancient Near East.

Mares, stallions and geldings

Overall, male and female equids do not display significant sexual dimorphism. Horse stallions may have a slightly different distribution of muscle mass and carriage of the neck. Behavioural differences between mares and stallions can occur, in particular when mares are in heat and/or stallions in the vicinity of mares in heat. In such situations, equids may be less attentive to communication from humans. Similarly, stallions may in general be less attentive, and are more likely to bite both humans and other equids. However, one must here once again take individuality into account, and ranges in temperament both in species and breeds. A variety of responses to forceful behaviour of equids have been devised by humans, and castration of male animals is one of them. Castration practices in the Near East will be discussed in Chapter 9. Here, we can note that geldings are usually more attentive and less confrontational than both stallions and mares. This likely applies to all the equid species appearing in this book. Today, horse stallions are typically only kept as stallions if they are also breeding studs, and manuals on donkeys and mules/hinnies recommend gelding as soon as possible to ensure they are 'manageable' (e.g. Svendsen 2009: 102; The Donkey Sanctuary 2016: 31).

Interacting with humans

Equids are sentient, social and intelligent beings. These features all form the basis of the possibilities of equid–human relations. Equids learn. They can learn what humans might consider both good and bad skills or habits (The Donkey Sanctuary 2016: 21). Some skills are fairly easily learnt, while others require much time and expertise. This applies to humans and equids alike, and we can thus characterize such interaction as co-training, where there is a real back and forth between the two species. That is not to say, of course, that the training is always equal or symmetrical, or that both parties enjoy the entire process.

Horses use visual input for at least initial identification of other animals, and other senses add to this if the first input is not sufficient (McGreevy 2012: 44). Horses can also visually recognize individual human faces. What is more, they also recognize and remember individual facial expressions, and differentiate between their meanings (Smith et al. 2016; Proops et al. 2018). The studies carried out on this were with horses, but the same is likely to apply to at least domestic donkeys. The ability to make such specific identification, and to retain them, would reinforce personal relationships between human and equid, and the equid may be more or less interested in the interaction based on previously noted facial expressions of a human. This tallies well with known special bonds between individual humans and animals.

For all the equids participating in this book, understanding and detecting intention and agency are a matter of careful study of and attention to detail. Equine body language can be very subtle, but no less forceful or significant than that of humans. A swish of the tail, a flick of the ear, shifting of hooves, the flaring of nostrils, a lowered neck: these are just a few of the ways in which an equid expresses itself and its mood. We have noticed these traits today, and many who work with equids on a daily basis are experts at reading the tell-tale signs (Waring 2003). We are not alone in this. The people of the ancient Near East knew their equids, and when we are lucky, we can detect their engagement with and observations of equids in the surviving bones, texts and material culture. Throughout this book, I will examine these signs, and the knowledge of the specific physical traits and temperament of the equid species will help us to better understand the interactions. These interactions, it is important to reiterate, are dynamic and *two-way*: humans recognize equid behaviour and intention, but equids are also capable of recognizing human behaviour and intention, and react accordingly.

Listing all known behaviours and their significance here would take several books on its own (and indeed already has), so I will confine myself to only bringing up those relevant to the ancient material as and when we encounter them. For those interested in delving further into this topic, a list of suggested literature can be found at the end of Appendix C.

Beginnings, History and Distribution

3.1 First encounters and 'domestication'

In zooarchaeology, domestication is 'customarily defined as the controlled breeding of plants or animals by humans, [but] the real distinctiveness of domestication lies in the fact that it involves ownership and thus results in a completely different level of human commitment than does hunting' (Levine 1999: 19–20). The term has become central in archaeology because it supposedly marks a great change in human history. This change is associated with a greater degree of sedentary lifestyles and increased control or management of natural resources (including animals) by humans. By extension, it can also lead to greater social complexity and hierarchical structures. For nonhuman animals, this usually means that they are kept within supervised spaces and selectively bred. Over longer periods of time, morphological and genetic changes take place in the domesticated species of both plants and animals. Animals often become smaller, and the skull may shorten in some species; other changes depend on individual species.

The zooarchaeological definition is thus, on the face of it, fairly straightforward, but a closer examination reveals both methodological and conceptual challenges (see also O'Connor 2000: ch. 13 for an excellent overview of the discussion, differing views and problems, and Smith 1987 for the valued meaning of domestication). For equids, the skull does not seem to change, and the criterion of decreased size is unreliable. The elaborate debates on horse domestication in the Eurasian steppes make it clear that it does not apply to horses (Levine 1999: 13; Olsen 2006). For donkeys, difficulties have been noted with finds from Abydos in Egypt, dated to *c.* 3000 BCE. Here, the donkeys were wild or intermediary between wild and domestic based on metacarpal measurements, but pathological evidence suggests that they had been carrying heavy loads (Rossel et al. 2008), and thus were more likely domesticated. It is suggested by the researchers that for donkeys, size decrease is instead a late indicator of domestication (Kimura et al. 2013).

Human–nonhman animal relations are in fact much more complex than a simple domestic–wild dichotomy. Concepts such as 'tame', 'feral', 'hybrid', 'semi-wild', 're-wild' and irregular or seasonal interaction and 'self-domestication' reflect some of the complexities, but still do not cover all the types of interactions that can occur, and scholars working on human–nonhuman animal relations are now advocating moving beyond these categories (see e.g. Harris & Hamilakis 2014; Lescureux 2019). This certainly also applies to equids in the ancient Near East, where we know that wild species (hemiones) were caught and at a minimum participated in breeding programmes with (domestic) donkeys. Looking at modern practices in Ethiopia and Burkina Faso, Goulder reports the frequent supplementing of herds with wild equids, along with entire herds being left to themselves for long periods of time, and intermittently being captured and (re)integrated into human spaces and interaction (2020: 52). All of these complicate identification into wild/domesticated categories, both osteologically and genetically.

In zooarchaeological practice, 'domestication' is a primarily technical term, but due to its impact in human history it also becomes associated more broadly with social hierarchies, progress and 'civilization'. The move to more sedentary lifestyles, aided by animals, is associated with a higher level of civilization, as perhaps most famously expressed in Gordon Childe's work (e.g. 1958). Even today, there is a lingering prioritization of permanence over mobility (exacerbated in archaeology by permanence being more easily recognized in the record), and a marginalization of mobile groups. The term thus has an added conceptual baggage with colonial and modern Western value judgements. In this book, the focus is less on identifying 'domestication' and more on the types of interaction and equid–human relationships that are implied by it and other related terms. The varieties of interaction can have anything from a minor to an enormous impact on the lives of both human and animal. For example, 'domestication' (and taming) involves humans imposing limitations on another animal, and in particular robbing it of choice of movement and feeding (McGreevy 2012: 16–18). Keeping a live equid within human-occupied or dominated spaces entails controlled pasturing, fences and possibly even stabling – with huge differences in the impact on equid lives in each of these. Type and time of feeding is controlled largely by humans, although equids may attempt to push back by escaping or starting to eat, chew or bite things that were not intended for this. Choice of when to rest is also limited, and on a social level, equids may not be allowed to decide which companion(s) to spend time with. All of these factors may have psychological consequences and influence the behaviour of equids

(McGreevy 2012: 18–23). Some equid behaviours can be understood as an expression of resistance, of the equid pushing back or attempting to negotiate its relationship with its human(s) (Recht 2019).

These and other interactions that may fall under the categories of domestication, wild and so on are the focus throughout this book, but the concepts themselves will only be applied to a very limited extent. However, some of the methods developed for identification are useful for detecting interaction more broadly; and establishing methods of detecting interaction are of course crucial to the current endeavour.

3.2 Detecting interaction

The discussion concerning the time and place of first domestication(s) of equids is interesting in terms of social, political and economic developments in the Eurasian steppes, and in the possible implications for the spread of horses and related technologies. However, its main relevance for the theme of this book is in the attempts to identify equid–human interaction based on archaeological remains. A number of methods or possible methods have been developed in order to address the question of domestication, and while shifting the focus specifically from this concept, we may test these same methods on material from the ancient Near East. What follows is thus an outline of some of the suggested methods, and to what extent they have been or could be applied to the ancient Near East, along with other means of detecting equid–human interaction of any kind.

Faunal-based markers of interaction: Assemblages

When equid bones are found in anthropogenic contexts, we have an indication that some kind of interaction has occurred. Detailed specialist study of the bones can help further determine the type of interaction, along with other information about the life and death of an animal.

Identifying equid remains as coming from wild or domesticated animals can provide some parameters to the kinds of interaction taking place. The most common morphological change in domesticated animals is one of decrease in size but, as we have seen, this is not a very useful marker for equids. Equid bones may also be identified as wild or domestic based on the date of the context or site in which they were found. If a site is dated to a period long before any known animal domestication, it is assumed that all animal remains are from wild specimens. This is a fair assumption until we reach periods of contention or where the status of a specific species is in question – as indeed is the case for the early suggested horse domestication in the Eurasian steppes. A pertinent example of this logic for the Near East can be illustrated with the distribution of *E. caballus* remains in Anatolia, where there is an apparent gap at the end of the fourth millennium until the mid-third millennium; remains before this are believed to come from wild animals, and those after primarily from domesticated ones (Arbuckle 2018: 53). Experts express disagreement over the status of the fourth-millennium remains (Grigson 2012: 191–2), illustrating that the date of a site or context is not enough on its own to determine the type of equid–human interaction that took place, at least not for the periods under discussion in this book. The geographical region of a site may also be used to argue for or against domesticated animals being present, based on the known distribution of a wild species. In the Levant, this logic has been applied with the assumption that no wild populations were present in the fifth or fourth millennia, but this distribution is no longer certain (Grigson 2012: 186).

A somewhat related method is that of examining the overall composition of the faunal assemblage from a site or a more limited context. The hypotheses mentioned in the following that are based on these kinds of analyses have been neatly outlined by Levine (1999). The make-up of an entire assemblage may provide a clue: if all other animal remains can be confidently identified as belonging to wild species, there is a strong possibility that also the equid remains are from wild animals, and that we are therefore likely dealing with a prey–predator relationship. This is particularly the case if there are no signs of differential treatment of equid versus other animal bones. Conversely, it has been argued that the occurrence of equid remains with domesticated species suggests that they also should be seen as domesticated.

The age and sex distribution of the remains could also serve as an indicator. It has been suggested that a majority of mares indicates domestication, while an equal number of males and females indicates wild animals. However, in the wild, horses would tend to live in groups of mares, young and one male.[1] Another suggestion is that an occurrence of old animals indicates wild, but old animals are less likely to survive that long in the wild, whereas when part of a long-term equid–human interaction, they would be kept at least for as long as they are able to fulfil their function. In fact, we do find equids of quite advanced age in the faunal assemblages of the Near East, and there is evidence that in other equid-based societies such as that of the Pazyryk Scythians, even horses no longer able to perform were cared for and perhaps even highly honoured as 'elders' (Argent 2010; 2016).

The parts of the skeleton present may also be revealing of relations. If an assemblage mainly consists of meat-rich elements, it may represent consumption. 'Kill sites' or butchering areas are sometimes identified by the presence and absence of certain skeletal elements – that is, animal bodies may be cut up and undesirable parts left behind where they were killed, and the hunters or butchers only bring back selected parts. Such sites can be found at varying distances from settlements, but are more commonly a feature of early prehistoric periods, when hunting was a more predominant source of meat. A high percentage of head and foot elements could suggest such a scenario, but may also indicate skinning; in some places, the hide with skull and foot bones were hung and displayed to mark significant spaces. 'Hoof-and-head' deposits are known from northern Europe and the Eurasian steppes (Robertson-Mackay 1980; Anthony 2007: e.g. 406–7), and may also be represented at Tell Umm el-Marra (Weber 2012: 167) and in Tell Banat North Monument A (Porter et al. 2021). The presence of complete or nearly complete articulated skeletons is a clear sign of non-consumption or any other postmortem use of equid bodies. In those instances, we must therefore look elsewhere for their significance for humans: for this, see especially Chapter 8.

Cutmarks, chopmarks and gnawing provide another avenue for clues about equid–human relations, and in particular about the use of equid bodies and body parts after death. Cutmarks can indicate butchering for meat and/or skinning – in rare cases, they can even hint at a cause of death, depending on their location and type of bone they are found on. Cutmarks are not often recorded on equid remains from the Near East; along with their low frequency in household waste assemblages, this is taken to mean that they were rarely or not eaten. Only a few sites report cutmarks on equid bones, as at Tell es-Safi (Greenfield et al. 2021), Tell Tuqan (Minniti 2008), Tell Jemmeh (Wapnish 1997), Afridar (Kansa 2004), Khirbet al-Batraway (Alhaique 2008), Lachish (Croft 2004: 2284–6), Tell Brak (Weber 2001) and Abu Tbeirah (Alhaique 2019: 424–5), and in some of these cases we seem to be dealing with wild equids most likely hunted for their meat, as in the late-third-millennium levels at Tell Mashnaqa (Vila 2006) and Tel Halif (Zeder 1998: 112–13). At Tell Umm el-Marra, a large percentage of hemione bones in some areas of the site, and the cutmarks present on them, reveal evidence of an extensive leather-working industry in the late third millennium and Middle Bronze Age (Nichols & Weber 2006). It should be noted here that bodies and body parts can be used for much more than food or hides/leather. For example, tools, decorative items, strings and ropes, glue and fuel can all be made from parts of the animal body. These are mostly invisible in the archaeological record of the ancient Near East, but some are mentioned in texts (e.g. as kuš še-gín, glue, or sa, sinew), and there are rare examples of bone tools identified as made from equid bones at Tell Halawa (Meyer & Pruss 1994: 272, nos. 8–9, figs. 91–2, pl. 31), Tell Asmar (Hilzheimer 1941: 2–20), Nippur (McMahon 2006: 39, pl. 132.6) and Tell Umm el-Marra (Nichols & Weber 2006: 48–9). Finally, it should also be noted that an absence of cutmarks in itself does not equate to an absence of any of the above-mentioned uses.

Since gnawing is rarely attributed to humans for equid remains, it hints at a fascinating human-mediated equid–carnivore relationship. While rodents and other animals may feed on various animal bone waste, the few examples of gnawed equid bones reported from the Near East are consistent with dogs, as at Tell es-Safi (Greenfield et al. 2021), Tell Brak (Weber 2001: 348), Tell Jemmeh (Wapnish 1997), Afridar (Kansa 2004), Lachish (Croft 2004: 2284–6) and Abu Tbeirah (Alhaique 2019: 424–5). This could mean that one of the uses of dead equids was as fodder for other animals, as is also documented in cuneiform tablets (Tsouparopoulu 2012; 2013; for equid–dog relations, see also Tsouparopolou & Recht 2021).

Faunal-based markers of interaction: Pathologies

A variety of pathologies have been put forward as evidence of equid–human interaction, with equids engaging in ploughing, pulling wheeled vehicles (and sledges), and load-carrying (humans and goods). These centre on the skull (teeth), spine and lower legs, and many markers have been developed to address the question of domestication but will here be discussed in terms of what they may reveal about equid–human relations. It should be noted that the majority of research on modern pathologies is focussed on horses (especially thoroughbreds) due to the interests of extensive equestrian/horse-racing industries, and it is unknown to what extent the results can be extrapolated to other equids.

Skull and teeth

Starting with the skull, the marker most commonly referred to is that of bit wear. The use of a bit can mean that an equid was ridden or that it pulled a wheeled vehicle, both of which imply very close relations between humans and equids, especially since they involve a significant amount of training and ongoing communication. Bits could also be used for ploughing or simply leading an equid, but this appears to be rare, and largely unnecessary (Goulder 2020: 80). The use of a bit can cause wear on the corner of the lower second premolar, also referred to as 'bevelling'. This is well-documented for horses from Iron Age northern Europe, where the wear is significant and quite clear (see e.g. Kveiborg 2017: chapter 4). It is also one of the main arguments used for the early domestication of horses in the Eurasian steppes (e.g. Anthony & Brown 2003; Anthony 2007: 212–13), but the evidence and method are a matter of some dispute, in particular since bevelling has been identified on non-working animals and can be caused by malocclusion with the upper second premolar (see e.g. papers in Levine et al. 2003; Bendrey 2007a; Levine 2012). Bits today are most often made of metal, but other materials also exist, and may have been used in the past even before metal bits occurred. The above-mentioned studies suggest that bit wear can also be caused by other materials, but with a lesser degree of wear than metal (Anthony & Brown 2003).

A second type of bit wear on the lower second premolar has been suggested by Bendrey (2007a) to occur on the anterior edge. In his study, he also detected this on a few specimens of unworked equids, but the patterning on these was slightly different, and never reached so deep as to expose the dentine. Finally, a type of pathology that can occur as a result of the use of a bit is exostosis or 'bone spurs' on the diastema (the section between the incisors and premolars on the mandible). These are reported in modern horses engaging in various disciplines (Cook 2002). To date, this type of pathology has not been identified on Near Eastern specimens, but is present on Iron Age horses from Denmark (Dobat et al. 2014: 197) and the UK (Bendrey 2007a). Based on Bendrey's studies, it is the most reliable criterion, since none of the specimens of unworked horses examined exhibited exostosis beyond his level 1, while all specimens with a level 2-4 of exostosis or loss of diastema came from working animals (in a 0-4 grading system: Bendrey 2007a). Both of these methods, along with evidence of bevelling, has been applied to remains from Botai in order to support the argument for early horse domestication in the Eurasian steppes (Outram et al. 2009). Both have also been dismissed by Levine as 'deeply flawed' due to inappropriate modern proxies for the ancient horses of Botai (Levine 2012). In any case, it should also be noted that bit wear on teeth or the diastema need not occur at all, regardless of the type of bit used, which again means that its absence does not prove an absence of the use of bits. Possible bit wear has been suggested for donkeys from Tell Brak (Clutton-Brock 2003), Abu Salabikh (Clutton-Brock 1986) and Tell es-Safi (Greenfield, Shai et al. 2018) in the third millennium, and at Tell Yelkhi for a donkey dated to the Old Babylonian period (Postgate 1986: 203). In all cases, the wear is minimal, and other causes cannot be entirely ruled out; the wear could also be explained by organic bits (e.g. bone, leather or rope). The wear that might be caused by lip/nose rings has not yet been studied in detail, but is suspected for some specimens of the Tell Umm el-Marra equids (Weber, pers. comm.).

Crib-biting is when an equid sucks in air by biting on its crib, stall sections, tethering poles or any other nearby feature. It is usually associated with long periods of confinement, and possibly caused by boredom or stress. The behaviour is well-known in modern horses (Wickens & Heleski 2010) and also occurs with donkeys (Navas González et al. 2016: 81). Notching, fractures or excessive wear on the incisors of equids have been interpreted as indicators of crib-biting (Bahn 1980), but have also been detected on wild horses (Rogers & Rogers 1988). It must therefore be used with caution as a marker of stabling. Notching on incisors has been detected on several donkeys from Akkadian levels at Tell Brak (Clutton-Brock & Davies 1993; Clutton-Brock 2003).[2]

Spine

Load-bearing, from carrying either a rider or goods, may cause spinal pathologies such as spondylosis/'kissing spines', spondylarthrose and compression/inclination of the neural spine (Peters 1998: 159–60; Clutton-Brock 2003; Rossel et al. 2008: 3718–19). The vertebrae may remodel, fuse and/or compress, potentially causing some pain, stiffness and lameness, but not necessarily incapacitating the individual animal. The cause of such pathologies can, but need not, be load-bearing. It can be related to age and other as yet not well-understood conditions or causes – some are known from unbroken horses and from wild *Equidae* that have had no contact with humans (see e.g. Rothschild et al. 2001; descriptions in Henson 2018). These criteria are therefore indicative rather than conclusive, but gain strength when combined with other factors or when several individuals from the same site display similar pathologies, as with the case of the donkeys found at Abydos. Damage to vertebrae is reported for one of the donkeys from Tell Brak (Clutton-Brock & Davies 1993; Clutton-Brock 2003).

Lower legs

A number of pathologies may also occur on the lower limb bones that can be caused by strenuous training, load-bearing, traction, or restriction of movement, including osteoarthritis (in particular what is commonly known as 'bone spavin') and periostitis (Peters 1998: 160–1). Bone spavin causes ossification or fusion of the tarsal joints (Farrow 2006: ch. 15; Boswell 2015) and should therefore be visible in faunal remains of those parts. It has been associated with strenuous activity in all modern equestrian disciplines, but has also been detected in young horses not yet broken in (Hartung et al. 1983; see also Bendrey 2007b). Periostitis or 'bucked shins' is associated mainly with young horses whose bones have not yet fully finished forming and adapting to intense training, particularly on hard ground (Brokken 2015). As a result, an additional layer of bone can form at the point of stress, which can also be visible osteologically. Additional possible pathologies have been reported for cattle used for traction (e.g. Cupere et al. 2000; Bartosiewicz 2008); these may also apply to equids but, as noted by Greenfield, 'such pathologies may arise from conditions unrelated to traction' (2010: 41). Pathologies possibly related to traction are reported on donkeys from Tell es-Safi (Shai et al. 2016), and exostoses on the hoof core have been used to argue for load-bearing on another donkey from ancient Tell Brak, with the bone growth thought to occur due to riding or pulling a vehicle over hard ground (Clutton-Brock & Davies 1993; Clutton-Brock 2003: 126).

Traumas and injuries, cause of death

Evidence of trauma, injuries, fractures and so on on animal skeletal parts may be indicative of a range of human-nonhuman animal relations. Groot (2008) has identified three types of fractures: pathological, stress and fatigue fractures, as we have seen examples of above, and acute fractures. The latter can have either healed or killed the animal. If healed, this may suggest that the animal was cared for by humans and nurtured back to health. If the animal instead died from the injury, we have cause of death, whether intentional or accidental. There are very few acute injuries on animals reported from the ancient Near East. In the vast majority of cases, we do not know how equids died or were killed. Even though they featured in sacrificial practices, and their complete bodies were used to mark sacred space, skeletal evidence of the cause of death is missing. Only a few examples from the Levant have suspicious damage to or missing vertebrae, or a severe twisting of the head (e.g. Greenfield et al. 2021), but these may have occurred postmortem. This is in contrast to the extensive mortuary horse sacrifices of the later Saka Scythians, where blunt force trauma to the skull is frequently reported as the cause of death (see e.g. Kashkinbayev 2013; Kosintzev & Samashev 2014).

Iconographically-based markers

Iconographic evidence of interaction is most obvious when equids are depicted as ridden or pulling a wheeled vehicle. But there are also more subtle markers, such as minor harness elements or pieces of gear, for example in the form of genital straps on figurines (see Chapter 9). The very existence of images of equids is a type of interaction, albeit one that may be far removed and indirect – the craftsperson may have personally observed the equid (and in some cases, specific details do suggest this), have been told by someone else what it should look like, or copied from other images. In all cases, some kind of relation is implied, but the nature of it must be inferred from each individual piece or assemblage of pieces.

Epigraphically-based markers

Detecting equid–human interaction in texts is in some ways fairly straightforward. Since most texts documenting equids are administrative records, their very mention implies some kind of interaction. Many of these merely record lists of animals, in the hands of a certain official or herder, or being transferred to someone/somewhere else. While more detailed information may be limited, even such records provide us with insights concerning management and number of animals, clearly within anthropogenic social and economic structures. Even the non-administrative texts that include equids, such as fables or mythological compositions, refer to interaction between humans and equids. Sometimes these are indirect, and often reveal observation of equine behaviour, either in 'the wild' or in their reaction to humans.

Equid gear, provisions, spaces and equid-derived products

Equid–human interaction can be represented by gear specifically designed for use with equids, including harness and tack elements, and wheeled vehicles or parts thereof. Some caution is required here in that some elements may also be used with other animals (in particular cattle), so a stronger case can be made if they are found in association with equids. Equid gear is in fact rarely recovered from archaeological contexts because it was mainly made from organic elements such as leather and plant fibres. However, rare examples of bits, saddle bag parts and chariot parts have been discovered, primarily from Levantine contexts.

Provisions and/or spaces for equids could include stables, training arenas and 'race tracks', stalls, tethering poles, troughs, and water and food supplies. These are extremely difficult to identify purely on archaeological grounds, and spaces designed for equids are likely to be placed outside the main urban areas. Nevertheless, such places have been suggested in a few instances, as for example at third-millennium Tell Brak and late-second-millennium Ugarit, as will be discussed in Chapter 7.

Finally, primary and secondary products derived from equids hint at the uses of the equid body. We know from the textual records that equid skins were kept, but these have not preserved. Equids could also provide meat for consumption and milk for dairy products, as reported from organic residue analysis of ceramics from Botai in the Eurasian steppes (Dudd et al. 2003; Outram et al. 2009), but there is as yet no evidence of the consumption of equid-dairy in the Near East. The only type of equid-derived product detected so far are a few tools made of equid bones, but this in itself is a fascinating aspect and suggests that at least in some cases, equid bodies were fully exploited for resources. Animals living in or passing through spaces inhabited by humans can leave their marks in the form of footprints, in particular if walking over wet clay (and as we might see today with prints on asphalt). For example, a tablet from Ur bears the wonderful traces of paw prints (Ur III, Penn Museum Object no. B16461), and at the Temple Oval at Khafajeh, 'foot'-prints of cattle, sheep, dogs and humans were found in a courtyard (Delougaz 1940: 81). To date, these marks do not include those of equids,[3] but equids have instead been detected through the presence of herbivore dung, as in the Tell Brak 'caravanserai' (Oates & Oates 2001: 44).

3.3 Historical and geographical overview

(See also Appendices F and K)

Equidae

Wild equids were present in the ancient Near East long before our story begins. Figure 3.1 shows a map of the geographical and chronological distribution of sites with faunal remains of any species of *Equidae* (Appendix K; see also Bollweg & Nagel 1992 for a catalogue and chronological timeline). Until the fourth millennium, the majority of osteological finds of equids represent hunted and eaten animals, which also means that they sometimes constituted quite large parts of an assemblages – as for example at Tell Zeidan (Grossman & Hinman 2013), Umm Dabaghiyah (Bökönyi 1986), Shams ed-Din Tannira and Yabrud (Uerpmann 1986). The maps also clearly show a much greater concentration of equid remains in Syria/northern Mesopotamia and the Levant than in the entire area of modern Iraq during all periods. This, however, almost certainly reflects

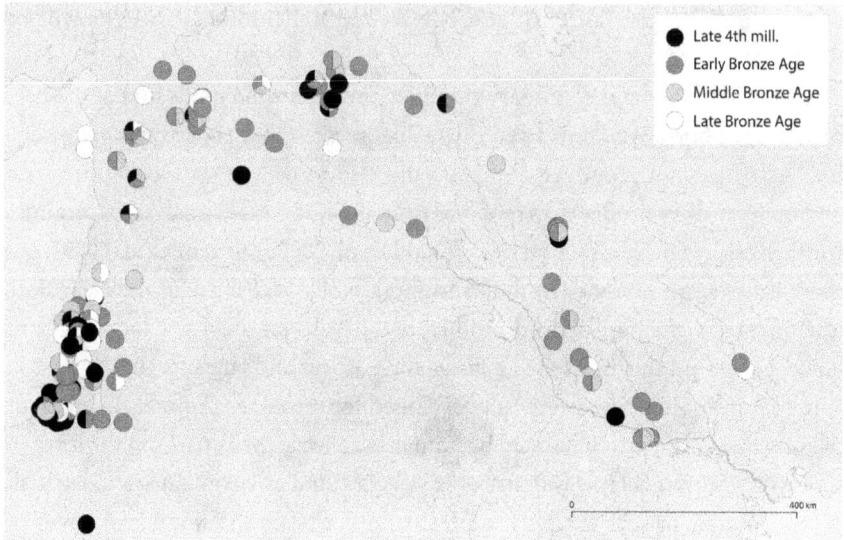

Figure 3.1 Distribution of sites with *Equus* remains.

unevenness in our research more than it does ancient realities. Syria and the Levant has been much more intensively investigated in terms of zooarchaeological studies (and in more recent times, when such studies are more common), and with much more information from second millennium sites. Detailed faunal reports simply do not exist for many of the major southern and central Mesopotamian sites. It is thus extremely important to keep this state of research in mind when interpreting the maps. We know from other types of evidence that this absence of known faunal remains does not equal an absence of equids in those parts of Mesopotamia.

In the following sections, each of the main species of equids in the ancient Near East will be discussed in terms of the distribution geographically and chronologically. The discussion of the faunal remains is based on identifications made by zooarchaeologists, but the caveats and potential pitfalls associated with this should be kept in mind (see Chapter 2 and Appendix D); similarly for the iconography and textual evidence, which are based on our current state of knowledge. In all cases, hybrids are the most challenging to identify.

Hemiones and donkeys

E. Hemionus was a wild equid that was hunted for its meat and skin but, from at least the third millennium, also captured alive and tamed enough to be part of

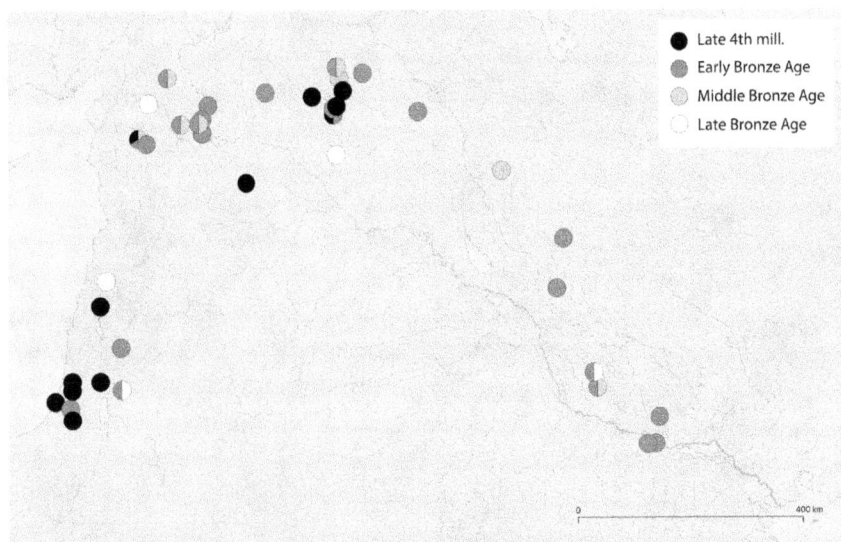

Figure 3.2 Distribution of sites with *E. hemionus* remains.

breeding programmes.[4] Unsurprisingly, hemiones are found in fourth-millennium levels at a number of sites in Syria and the Levant (Figure 3.2). In the third millennium, they are much more common, including in Mesopotamia; this corresponds well with their increased importance in the textual evidence and breeding to make kungas. In the second millennium, they continue to be identified at some sites, but were superseded by horses as parents of hybrids.

E. africanus is the progenitor of domestic donkeys, and donkeys appear to have been first domesticated in northern Africa by at least 3000 BCE, perhaps as early as 7000–6000 BCE (Kimura et al. 2013). The genetic research on mitochondrial DNA suggests that two different sub-species of African wild donkey were domesticated about 5000 years ago (Beja-Pereira et al. 2004; Kimura et al. 2011; 2013). The two may or may not have been connected in time and space, and it is possible that there were several locations of domestication, and the southern Levant has been suggested as another one (Milevski & Horwitz 2019). Evidence from Africa suggests that morphological differences between wild and domestic donkeys were initially minimal and therefore difficult to distinguish. This is exemplified by ten *E. asinus* skeletons found at Abydos with strong evidence of having carried heavy loads (either from riding or transport of goods), but which otherwise morphologically are a better match with wild donkeys (Rossel et al. 2008). The Abydos donkeys may represent an early phase of domestication. Regardless of their original place(s) and time of domestication,

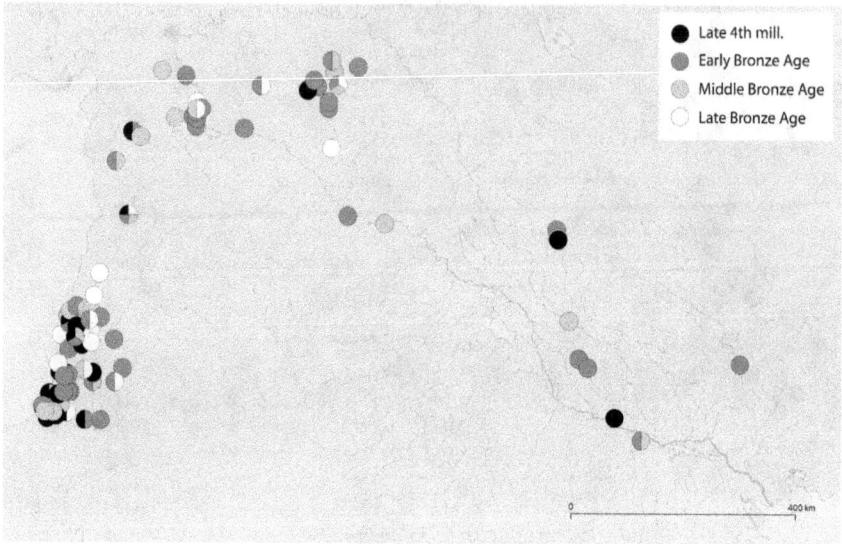

Figure 3.3 Distribution of sites with *E. asinus* remains.

donkeys spread throughout the Near East and Egypt quite quickly in the late fourth and early third millennia (Figure 3.3). They were probably the most ubiquitous equid throughout the third and second millennia, and very likely present at every site throughout the area (Grigson 2012: 189), despite our somewhat patchy zooarchaeological record.

Schematic signs of equid heads occur on tablets from the late fourth millennium found at Uruk, Jemdet Nasr and Susa (Potts 2014; Zarins 2014: 152–4), but determining their exact species is more challenging. Those on a tablet from Uruk (Zarins 2014: 259), with their markedly long ears and erect manes, are most likely donkeys (unless we consider Persian onagers a possibility). Those on the Susa tablets instead have short ears and erect manes, which would suggest Syrian onagers (Potts rules out this option based on the thick neck of some variants of the pictogram, and instead thinks they are either horses or donkeys; 2014). The equid sign then appears at Ur in Early Dynastic I ('Archaic' texts), and Zarins considers the sign for ANŠE to refer to donkeys from this early period onwards (2014: 161–2).[5] As with the faunal records, donkeys are common in the written sources throughout the third and second millennia.

Hemiones (EDIN.NA, without the ANŠE) occur in the written sources already in Early Dynastic I-II, associated with skins (Postgate 1986: 199), and continue to appear throughout the third millennium, in particular in the Ur III records. The hemione then disappears from the records until the mid-second millennium (where it occurs as *serrēmu*); this again likely reflects its decreased importance as a parent of hybrids but does not mean that it was no longer present at all – as the faunal record also demonstrates.

Horses

Where and when horses were first domesticated has been and remains a heated question, in particular in scholarship of Botai and related cultures in the Eurasian steppes as this is considered the most likely contender (Anthony et al. 1991; Anthony 2007; papers in Levine et al. 1999; 2003).[6] One of the main challenges, as we have seen, is that we cannot refer to dimorphic distinctions between wild and domestic horses, and must therefore find alternative means of determining their status. Debates over the archaeology and faunal analyses have been joined in the last two decades by stable isotope and genetic studies (e.g. Orlando et al. 2009; Outram et al. 2009; Warmuth et al. 2012; Orlando 2015). Although the archaeological and zooarchaeological evidence for horse domestication in the Botai region in the fourth millennium or even earlier remains circumstantial and somewhat open to interpretation (Levine 2012), the status of those horses as domestic is now often assumed (e.g. Gaunitz et al. 2018). The latest genetic research has not been able to identify the progenitor of modern domestic horses (Fages et al. 2019),[7] nor has the progenitor of ancient Near Eastern horses been detected.

Whatever the conclusion to the discussion of the role of horses in the Eurasian steppes, it does not seem that those events had any immediate impact on conditions in the Near East. In the Near East, horses were present in the late fourth millennium in parts of the Levant, western Syria and Anatolia (Figure 3.4). There has been much debate about whether these remains represent wild or domestic horses (Bökönyi 1991; Grigson 2012: 191–2 with further references; Shev 2016; Arbuckle 2018: 53). There is instead general consensus that the *E. caballus* remains from the third millennium belong to domestic horses. Along with a spread east, there seems to be a continuity, but in fact most of the faunal remains of horses in the third millennium come from very late in the millennium (including those at Nippur, Selenkahiye, Tell Mozan and Tell Munbaqa) and are only represented by very few bones at each site.[8]

In written sources, the sign associated with horse, ANŠE.ZI.ZI (Appendix B), is first attested very rarely in a few Early Dynastic IIIB and Old Akkadian documents. A cylinder from Nippur, perhaps dated to the Early Dynastic IIIB period, mentions 'anše zi-zi hur-sag', translated as 'mountain horses' (P222183, column 14, line 10). Anše zi-zi occurs in an Old Akkadian administrative tablet

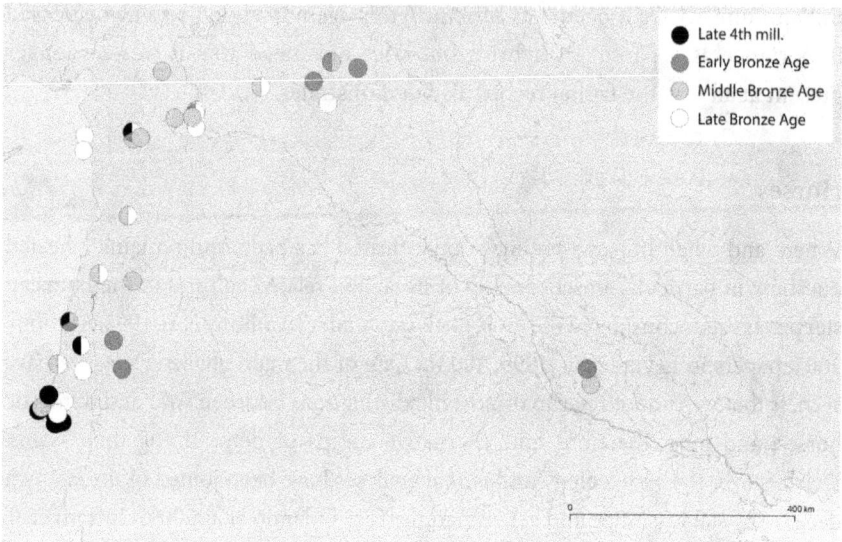

Figure 3.4 Distribution of sites with *E. caballus* remains.

from Girsu (P217016, obverse, line 5), and anše si$_2$-si$_2$ in an Old Akkadian composite text which is rather a literary composition (P462081, surface a, line 63'). The term becomes more frequent in the Ur III administrative texts, where it was recorded at Girsu, Drehem, Umma and Ur, along with in Šulgi A (ETCSL, 'A praise poem of Shulgi (Shulgi A)'). The written sources thus agree quite well with the limited faunal evidence, placing the spread of the (domestic) horse in the late third millennium, with only sporadic appearances earlier in the millennium. In the second millennium, horses slowly increase in importance, which is reflected in both the faunal and written records (as ANŠE.KUR.RA/*sisûm*). As mentioned above, the gaps in the faunal evidence from the area of modern Iraq should not be understood to mean an absence of horses, since the written records make it clear that horses were present, and even something of a specialty of the Kassites in the mid- to late second millennium.

Hybrids: kungas and mules/hinnies

Due to the uncertainties involved in morphological identification of equid crosses, there are as yet no entirely secure examples from the faunal record. However, the mid- to late-third-millennium equids from the Elite Mortuary Complex at Tell Umm el-Marra, identified as donkey–hemione hybrids by Weber (2012; 2017) are good candidates. They first appear in the cuneiform records in

Early Dynastic III at Ebla as anše kunga₂ (ANŠE.BAR.AN; Postgate 1986: 201), and become more common in the Ur III records at the end of the third millennium.

Kungas appear to have been superseded by a new cross in the second millennium, mules or hinnies (*parûm, kūdanum, damdammu, perdum*), but this hybrid may already have overlapped with kungas in the Ur III period (see Appendix B). A single equid bone from Tall al-'Umayri is the only example of an identification of a mule/hinny from the third or second millennium in the ancient Near East (EBA III, Peters et al. 2002), although mules are also claimed to be present in the assemblage of Selenkahiye (Ijzereef 2001), and suggested for several other Syrian sites (Buitenhuis 1991).

Iconography

In the iconography, we are hard pushed to differentiate hemiones, donkeys, horses and hybrids, partly due to intraspecies variability, and partly due to the highly stylized manner of much of the visual evidence. Methods of identification rely on the physical characteristics outlined in Chapter 2 and Appendix C. When these are not sufficient, their date and iconographic context may provide further hints. Apart from the tablets with equine heads, fourth millennium depictions of equids are rare, and often not well provenanced.[9] Exceptions are impressions from two stamp seals from Tell Brak, dated to the Late Chalcolithic. One shows lions attacking what may be an equid (Figure. 3.5a; Emberling & McDonald 2003: 18, fig. 22.3). The hunting context suggests a wild equid; the thick neck and short ears would imply horse rather than hemione. The second motif has a standing quadruped with a smaller quadruped beneath its belly, perhaps a mare with her foal (Figure 3.5c; McMahon et al. 2007: 164, fig. 15c), but further definition of species is not possible. Some of the Levantine figurines carrying burdens (Chapter 4, Figure 4.1) probably date to the late fourth millennium; from the broader context and the burden carried, they are thought to be donkeys.

An early-third-millennium painted sherd from Susa (Figure 3.5b; Mecquenem 1943: 87, fig. 72.11, 97, fig. 77.2) probably depicts hemiones (tufted tail, short ears, no contact with humans), while the many scenes of wheeled vehicles and equids of the mid- to late-third millennium show kungas and donkeys (tufted tails, ears either long or short; hemiones excluded given their unlikely use as traction animals; see also Chapter 5 and figures therein). Donkeys continue to appear in the iconography of the second millennium on plaques and seals, as figurines and in various other media, but there are no unambiguous examples of hemiones or hybrids.

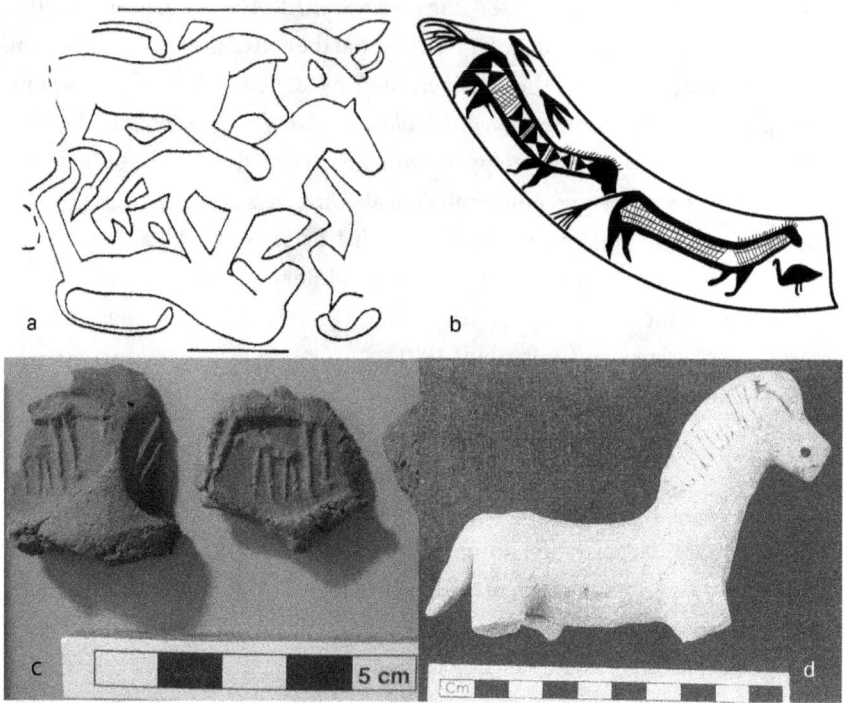

Figure 3.5 Early visual representations of equids:

a) Sealing from Tell Brak. Stamp seal, TW-1903, 12013, TB 21070, Late Chalcolithic (after Emberling & McDonald 2003: fig. 22.3). Courtesy of Helen McDonald and Geoff Emberling, drawing by Helen McDonald.
b) Painted sherd from Susa, Tomb 322. Early Dynastic (drawn after Mecquenem 1943: 77.2).
c) Sealings from Tell Brak. Stamp seal, Late Chalcolithic (after McMahon et al. 2007: fig. 15c). Courtesy of Augusta McMahon.
d) Terracotta figurine from Tell es-Sweyhat. 8.2 × 12.7 cm, c. 2350–2250 BCE (after Holland 1992–93: fig. 6). Courtesy of the Oriental Institute of the University of Chicago.

A shell inlay from Susa, perhaps dated to Early Dynastic II-IIIA may depict a horse or a hemione (Figure 9.4), but the earliest unambiguous representation of a horse is a figurine from Tell es-Sweyhat, dated to the Akkadian period (Figure 3.5d). Unusually for a figurine, its full tail is clearly rendered, and its hanging mane unmistakable, made with applied strips of clay. Impressions of the seal of Abbakala dated to Ur III could depict a horse, as suggested by Owen (1991; see also Figure 6.1d).[10] Horses are the ridden animals on most of the Old Babylonian plaques discussed in Chapter 6 (Figure 6.3). Equids associated with chariots and other wheeled vehicles in the second millennium are often depicted with raised tails: these can be confidently identified as horses (Figure 5.9b-d, f). An equid figurine dated to the Akkadian period from Tell Chuera has a thick, lifted tail and a prominent mane (erect or flowing), and this could also be an early example of a horse (Moortgat 1962: 18, fig. 12f; possibly associated with a model of a wheeled vehicle).

With this general overview of the methods of detecting interaction and the chronological and geographical distribution of each equid species, we can now have a closer look at the evidence for the various types of equid–human relations in the ancient Near East. We start with one of the oldest, that of equids as beasts of burden.

Equids Changing History I: Caravans and Transport of Goods

4.1 Beasts of burden

Beyond humans hunting equids for meat and other resources, the first more intimate type of interaction between humans and equids in the ancient Near East is reflected in the recognition of equids as effective carriers of heavy or bulky material. This is much more than a trivial realization. The impact would have been substantial, widespread and long-lasting (Milevski 2011; Greenfield et al. 2012; Shai et al. 2016; Mitchell 2018). In most parts of the Western world, the industrial revolution and invention of the automobile have made equids as beasts of burden largely redundant, but even as late as the First World War, horses, donkeys and mules participated (and died) en masse (in the hundreds of thousands, The Donkey Sanctuary 2019). In other parts of the world, including much of the African continent, donkeys in particular continue to play a crucial role in the everyday lives of many people (Meutchieye et al. 2016; Goulder 2020; 2021; see also www.thebrooke.org/our-work).

When Sherratt proposed his model of the secondary products revolution, he observed the impact of equids both as pack and plough animals (1981; 1983). For the Near East, there has been an increased recognition among scholars of the importance not only of long-distance transport of goods, but also of local or short-distance everyday transport. As Mitchell writes concerning long-distance transport: '[t]hroughout the Bronze Age the large-scale movement of goods by land between Palestine and Egypt, Afghanistan and Syria, or central Turkey and southern Iraq would have been inconceivable without [donkeys]' (2018: 79).

Transport can occur on water where rivers or oceans provide access, and on land, humans and other animals can be used as beasts of burden. However, donkeys have the advantage of being able to carry heavier or bulkier loads over longer distances, for longer periods of time, with minimal guidance and through difficult terrain, and are comparatively low maintenance in terms of water and fodder.[1] They would thus have been crucial in solidifying and expanding trade in key materials such as copper and other metals, although the evidence demonstrates that much more than metals moved around during the Bronze Age of the Near East. Besides tin, copper, silver and gold, the commodities carried include textiles, wool, various types of grain and flour, oil, water, ropes, bitumen, salt, precious stones, and vessels (see e.g. Michel 1996: 403–5), not to mention the donkeys themselves being sold off at the end of the journey. Importantly, however, and often overlooked, donkeys made a massive impact not only on long-distance trade, but also on local and regional levels, in the day-to-day lives of people at all levels of society.

Some of the first evidence of equids carrying goods comes from the Levant in the form of small terracotta figurines (Amiran 1985; Ovadia 1992; Hizmi 2004). The figurines begin to appear towards the end of the fourth millennium and beginning of the third, in EB I-II, possibly even at the end of the Chalcolithic. They show a quadruped animal which is in most cases fairly undiagnostic, but is identified as equine based on the lack of horns, overall body shape and type of tail that would suggest for example sheep, goat, cattle or dog, along with a comparison with figurines clearly depicting other types of animals (Figure 4.1). It is not possible to identify more precisely which type of equid was intended purely based on the features of the figurines. The figured animals typically carry either a pack (or saddle bag) or a pair of containers, one on each side of the back or withers.

The figurines are primarily found in the Early Bronze Age at Levantine sites, but are also known from Mesopotamia. The containers carried are generally quite large compared to the equid. If this scale reflects reality, it suggests very heavy burdens. The fact that the containers are all closed shapes indicates that they likely contained a liquid such as water, oil or wine, although grain cannot be ruled out. We still have limited understanding of the use or function of zoomorphic figurines in the ancient Near East, but it is perhaps worth noting that in these examples the (miniature) containers carried by the equids are faithfully rendered and fully functional. The pack or saddle bag is harder to understand, but was probably used for solid items such as textiles or even boxes or skins containing smaller objects. They could also be saddles for riding, but this type is never depicted with a human burden, nor is there breakage to suggest a rider once existed.

From the Royal Cemetery of Ur, we have the only other type of iconographic representation of an equid as a pack animal as part of the inlay of a 'wardrobe chest' (Early Dynastic III, PG 800, Woolley 1934: 80, pl. 94). In this case, the

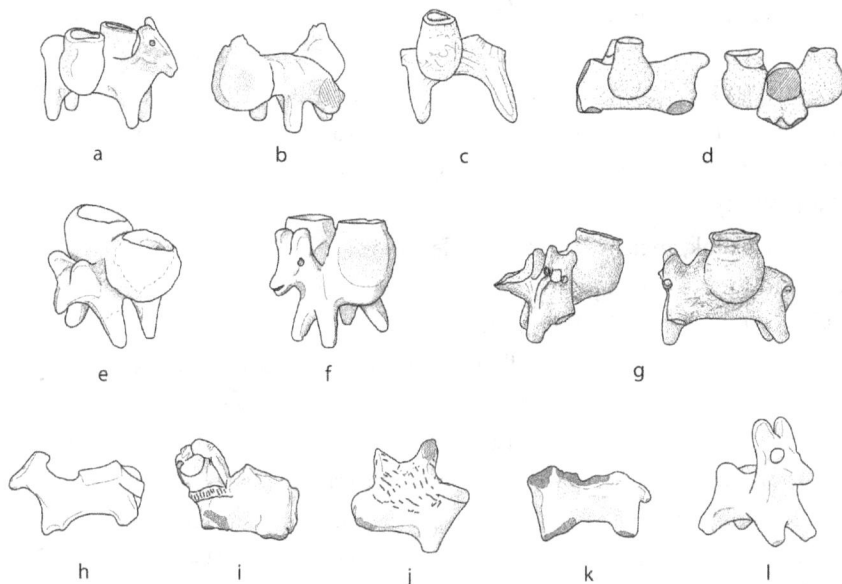

Figure 4.1 Selection of terracotta equid figurines carrying packs:

a) From Bat Yam, tomb cave. 9 × 6.5 cm, EB I (drawn after Ovadia 1992: fig. 4).
b) From Azor, Tomb 60. L. *c.* 6.5 cm, EB I? (drawn after Hizmi 2004: photo 4).
c) From Tel Dan. L. *c.* 6.2 cm, EB II-III (redrawn after Greenberg & Porat 1996: fig. 4.3).
d) From Hirbet ez-Zeraqon, lower city House B1.3. 4.3 × 2.3 cm, EB II (redrawn after Al-Ajlouny et al. 2012: no. 1).
e) From Giv'Atayim, Burial Cave 1. 8 × 7.4 cm, EB I (drawn after Ovadia 1992: fig. 1).
f) From Azor, burial cave. 9.5 × 7 cm, EB I (drawn after Ovadia 1992: fig. 2).
g) From Tel Rosh Ha'ayin. L. *c.* 9.7 cm, EBA (redrawn after Eitan 1969: fig. 3.1).
h) From Khirbet el-Makhruq. L. *c.* 8.5 cm, EB II-III (drawn after Hizmi 2004: photo 1).
i) From Habuba Kabira. X:237, L. 6 cm, EBA (redrawn after Strommenger 2017: pl. 179.11).
j) From Tell el-Abd. TA 93:257, 5.7 × 6.9 cm, EBA/MBA (drawn after Finkbeiner 1995: pl. 4.g,j).
k) From Uruk, Area K/L 12/13. W17193 - VA-L12 b4, 6.5 × 4 cm, Early Dynastic (drawn after Wrede 2003: pl. 31).
l) From Emar. MSK.74.595, Louvre AO 26903, 6.10 × 3.30 cm, LBA (drawn after collections.louvre.fr/ark:/53355/cl010118240).

equid appears to be a donkey (although the ears are fairly short); it is also clearly marked as a stallion. The piece is not entirely preserved, but we can see a quite large, soft object slung over its back, indicating yet another type of pack, possibly containing textiles.

Textual evidence from the third millennium referring to pack donkeys is scarce. Zarins mentions a possible early example in a Jemdet Nasr period tablet from Uruk which lists twelve KASKAL.ANŠE, where KASKAL may mean 'road' or 'travel', and these could therefore be caravan donkeys (2014: 199, tablet IM 23435). An Early Dynastic III text from Shuruppak has donkeys going to Kish (Zarins 2014: 199), which may also refer to caravan donkeys. Towards the end of the third millennium, a literary composition from Girsu includes references to pack saddles being lifted onto and copper being strapped to donkeys (P431182, lines 353–5).

At Tell Brak, ancient Nagar, in modern-day Syria, a large complex in Area FS dated to the Akkadian period has been interpreted as a 'caravanserai' (Oates & Oates 2001; Oates 2003). The structures include a temple to Šakan (a deity closely associated with equids, especially hemiones), reception rooms, storage areas, a large court, and facilities that might have been used for the needs of equids, such as a possible trough in one room and a tether in a courtyard, also associated with herbivore dung. Similar way stations where caravan donkeys could be housed are thought to have existed at Tell Beydar (acting as a connection to Tell Brak/ Nagar: Sallaberger 1996a) and Tell es-Sweyhat (Holland 2001–02).

The entire FS Area complex at Tell Brak was deliberately filled in and 'ritually closed' with a number of deposits that involve at least eight donkeys (see also Chapter 8). Although not specifically describing or depicting pack animals, several texts found in the temple refer to equids, and images of equids are known from the site in the form of a substantial number of terracotta figurines and seal impressions (Oates 2001; 2003). There is thus no doubt that Tell Brak was a hub for equine-related activities, and the combined evidence from Area FS strongly suggests that donkeys lived there, perhaps in transit or while waiting for their next assignment. Zooarchaeological analysis (Clutton-Brock & Davies 1993; Clutton-Brock 2003) of the donkey bones from this area indicates pathologies of the hooves and teeth that could be caused by the carrying of heavy goods on hard surfaces and crib biting (which in turn is a sign of stabling or confined space). As noted in Chapter 3, however, this evidence should be used with great caution, as other factors could also cause such pathologies.

Another set of ritual burials of donkeys in the third millennium comes from the Levantine site of Tell es-Safi. I will return to the ritual aspect of these in Chapter 8, but it is here relevant that these donkeys have also been interpreted as valuable in relation to merchant and caravan activities, especially between Egypt and the Levant (Greenfield, Greenfield et al. 2018, who also note that a landowner in Dynasty 4 Egypt is recorded as having over 760 donkeys, testifying to a large-scale industry). Stable isotope analysis of the teeth of one of these donkeys is consistent with an upbringing in Egypt, and arrival in Tell es-Safi not long before its death (Arnold et al. 2016).

The early second millennium

The early second millennium is famous for its trade between Assur and Kültepe-Kanesh in central Anatolia (Larsen 2015). Kültepe (ancient Kanesh), an Assyrian 'colony' or *kārum,* has yielded over 23,000 tablets recording business activities between the two settlements, along with a network of at least twenty-five other *kārums* and trading stations (*warbartum*) in Anatolia (Veenhof 2013: 36). They testify to an enormous and extremely elaborate trading system that not only spans the 750 km distance (as the crow flies) between Assur and Kanesh, but also much further afield into, for example, Afghanistan and Iran to the east, and Dilmun in the south. Caravan activities and pack donkeys (ANŠE.GU$_2$ / *anše ša biltim*) in this period are also known from records from, for example, Mari, Chagar Bazar (e.g. van Koppen 2002; Heimpel 2003) and Tell al Rimah (Dalley et al. 1976; Dalley 1977), but the greatest bulk and most information come from the Kanesh letters, which are therefore the main focus here.

The trade involved primarily the movement of textile and tin to Kanesh and other settlements across the Anatolian plateau, in return for silver and gold back to Assur (with a range of other goods also documented). The tablets found at Kanesh record the transactions and concerns of private merchants, although with the involvement of the local palaces, which would extract taxes and had first buying privileges on certain items. Typically, we see an arrangement where one family member in Assur sends goods to another family member in Kanesh to sell there. The related family members are especially fathers, sons and brothers, but female members of the families are also sometimes involved. We only have the letters from Kanesh – their equivalent in Assur has not been discovered. Much has been written about this correspondence (e.g. Larsen 1967; 1976; 2015; Veenhof 1972; 1997; 2013; Dercksen 1996; 2004; texts published in the *Ankara Kültepe Tabletleri* volumes), but crucially for the discussion here is the role of donkeys in these activities. The goods were carried by donkeys in caravans (*ellatum*[2]) along a route that was over 1000 km long (Larsen 2015: 175). Setting off from Assur in the morning,[3] each donkey would be fitted out with a saddle cloth, a pack saddle and a 'top' bag. The bags would contain textiles and tin as the main goods, the total weight of which is thought to be around 75–90 kilograms (Dercksen 1996: 61). Additionally, the donkeys sometimes had to carry some provisions for the journey itself, including a small amount of fodder, taxes and tolls for along the route, and personal items of the accompanying humans. The equipment seems to have been kept with the donkeys, and was sold with them.

The pack saddle and extra bags were made of organic materials which are not usually preserved in the ancient Near East. Metal buckle-like objects have been found at Tel Haror, associated with a complete donkey skeleton, dated to MB III (*c.* 1700–1550 BCE). The excavators have suggested these might have been parts of saddle bags (Bar-Oz et al. 2013). The donkey was also found with a metal bit in its mouth, which was almost certainly not used for pack donkeys, but is rather for use with a chariot. It may be that several roles of working equids were amalgamated into this one ritual deposit, combining pack (donkey) and chariot (horse) into one.

Returning to the Kanesh documentation, it seems that merchants may have grouped their donkeys into shared caravans, with each merchant sending two or three donkeys. Caravan numbers of up to 300 are mentioned (in a text from Mari: ARMT 26/2 432). However, this number is very unusual, and a more common size is likely to have been about 20; the largest caravan attested during the Level II period consisted of 34 donkeys (Barjamovic et al. 2012: 77). They were accompanied by hired 'pack masters' (*kaṣṣārum*) and 'drivers' (*sāridum*), who would be responsible for the animal and goods along the way. Usually, the ratio would be roughly 1:1 for the number of humans and donkeys.

The journey is believed to have taken about six weeks one way, with an estimated coverage of twenty-five kilometres a day (Dercksen 2004: 255); since the roads were often blocked from December to April, travelling was seasonal, and could thus be made twice a year. It could be a difficult and dangerous journey, both physically in carrying heavy loads, negotiating the terrain and enduring heat, but also due to political unrest and in risking attacks from robbers (Barjamovic 2011: 26–33). Many donkeys perished along the way, with recorded mortality rates as high as 75 per cent (Dercksen 2004: 263). The cause of death is not noted in these records, so we cannot say if it was due to neglect, exhaustion, injury, sickness, maltreatment or other factors; there is also no indication of whether the loss was felt outside economic concerns. The dangers of travelling through the countryside and through certain regions are hinted at – for example, 'I did not have the silver sent to you with the travellers who were mugged. When the road opens, I will have it sent to you' (CCT 3, 26a, as translated in Barjamovic 2011: 43, who provides further examples of problems with roads closed due to weather or unrest). Another example comes from Mari, where Ili-iddinam, a messenger of Yasmah-Addu, was accompanying a caravan that included horses and a donkey (P273030; Meier 1988: 75). The company was attacked by bandits, who took the equids and killed Ili-iddinam, although some of the others escaped.

Along the route there were 'inns' where caravans might stop for the night, with the letters demonstrating that a fee needed to be paid for the stay. Some of these have been identified, along with their fees and possible geographical locations, by Barjamovic (2011: 34, 36–7). These inns may have provided both food for the human personnel and fodder for the animals, and illustrate some of the economic and social impact the caravans must have made throughout the landscape.

Donkeys have a very high level of endurance, and can often be left at night to find their own forage. However, it seems that either not enough time was allowed for the donkeys to find their own food, or not enough could be found, because we frequently hear of fodder being bought or brought for them, along with a concern that they should be fed. A letter written by a man called Imdīlum illustrates this nicely:

> Thus (says) Imdīlum, speak to Anāni, Aššur-idi and Amur-īlī: 20 half-packs of *kibšum*-type 8 half-packs of *upqum*-type, 16 top-packs belonging to me, 1 top-pack of the pack masters, 1 of Anāni, 1 of Aššur-idī, in all 3 top-packs belonging to you, – you must not load any other *qulqulum*-package on the donkeys, – and 15 black donkeys, the eight of you are the donkey drivers. Why is it that I constantly hear that you have added 13 bags with your *qulqulum*-bags to my top-packs and thus are maltreating my donkeys and making me angry? Please take care to feed the donkeys; do not be sparing with fodder. Do not add anything to my top-packs and your *qulqulum*-bags. Put the silver which I gave Amur-īlī for his expenses en route in one of the half-packs and guard it well. If you notice that there is any unruly one among the donkeys, sell it and add 2 or 1 shekels of silver to its proceeds and buy a fine donkey ... Take Pūšu-kēn's donkeys back from the paddock.
>
> TC 1, 16. Translation in Dercksen 2004: 281

Dercksen writes that fodder in the form of straw was usually bought before leaving Assur, at half a shekel of silver per donkey (2004: 266). Straw is extremely bulky, and it seems that it was transported in accompanying wagons (*eriqqum* – for a selection of texts mentioning these wagon loads, see Barjamovic 2011: 44–8). Even with these, it is likely that further fodder had to be purchased during the journey. Pack donkeys from Chagar Bazar are recorded as fed with barley (van Koppen 2002: 24); this would have been a much more practical item to transport over long distances. There is no mention of the provision of water in the texts, which probably means that access was not really a problem. There are, however, occasional references to the donkeys being allowed or not allowed to rest at the end of a journey (Dercksen 2004: 267; Larsen 2014: no. 540). The rest would have been needed, and seems to have been the norm in all but urgent circumstances; we also hear of donkeys being left in a 'paddock' (see below) or with a herdsman in order to recover (Dercksen 2004: 261). The items that would be sent back to Assur, silver and gold, were much more compact and fewer donkeys were thus needed for the return journey. The donkeys were bought in Assur at a price of 16–17 shekels of silver, and could be sold in Anatolia for a profit, at 20–30 shekels of silver (Dercksen 2004: 260), suggesting that donkeys were less common there (at least the particular type preferred by the Assyrian merchants).

Donkeys need minimal guidance and happily follow each other in file without much interference. Bridles would be entirely unnecessary (nor do any of the figurines wear such), although it may be useful with a simple halter for the lead donkey or when navigating paddocks or urban landscapes. It is also likely that, having travelled the route once or twice, individual donkeys would remember it. The high number of human personnel accompanying the donkeys is thus a bit surprising, and must be related to the packing and guarding of the goods more than ensuring that the animals act as desired. Given the taxes and tolls extracted, both in Assur and Kanesh, and along the route at key sites, bridges and so on, we may expect attempts to circumvent some of these expenses. Sure enough, the letters even mention smuggling and hint at special tracks used by smugglers (Barjamovic 2011: 139, 162 n. 553, 169–80). Goulder reports how the memory of donkeys is utilized for smuggling in various parts of the world today, with the animals undertaking journeys unaccompanied by humans (2020: 117) and bringing the smuggled goods to the desired destination. In the Kanesh letters, there is no indication of awareness of the intelligence and memory of donkeys in this regard, or any hint that it was taken advantage of (although perhaps we should not expect such activities to be recorded, even in private archives).

The donkeys were kept in and bought from a *gigamlum*.[4] This is usually translated as 'paddock', although 'donkey farm' may be a more accurate term, since they appear to be fairly organized and certainly more than a simple field in which to put donkeys. A 'paddock' near Kanesh is mentioned in Imdīlum's letter, and another one near Assur is also known (TC 2,7; Veenhof 1972: 2). We do not know if these institutions bred and trained donkeys themselves, or if they collected them from smaller-scale breeders in their vicinity. A combination of the two is perhaps the most likely scenario. For the carrying of goods, the donkeys would not need much training, but had most likely been at least tested before being sold to merchants. A few texts do refer to 'unruly' donkeys who did not appreciate their task (e.g. TC 1, 16; Veenhof 1972: 2 n. 7; see also Chapter 9).

It is extremely difficult to quantify the number of animals taking part in these procedures, but it must certainly have been substantial and breeding would therefore have required a certain level of systematization. Although caravans with as many as 300 donkeys are rare in the texts, they hint at the extent of the network, and it is also worth remembering that this is only one trade route among many at the time (even if the longest linear one), and with many further locations even within Anatolia. Only very rarely do we hear of problems in the supply of donkeys (Dercksen 2014: 69), so the breeding programmes must have been largely successful.

The donkeys in the letters are often described as black (*ṣallāmum*), as also mentioned in Imdīlum's letter above.[5] This would appear to refer to a particular breed, presumably tending to have a dark-coloured coat. They were the preferred breed, and this may have been because they were larger than others, because donkeys described as 'fine' were 'of tall stature and small teeth' (Dercksen 2004: 260). However, they may simply have been most widely available and/or possess other qualities making them particularly popular for caravans. The reference to small teeth is enigmatic – Veenhof suggests an animal eating little, and Dercksen a relation to age (Dercksen 2004: 260). Donkeys probably started their life as working animals around the age of three, but we lack information about working-life expectancy. Donkeys are the only equids mentioned as beasts of burden in the Assur-Kanesh caravans.[6] Mules and horses are recorded in other contemporary sources (Dalley et al. 1976: Text 85; Durand 1988: 123; Michel 2004: 192),[7] but donkeys were by far the most common pack animals throughout the third and second millennium. The caravan donkeys are rarely qualified with male or female, most likely because this was generally not considered important since there is little difference in their strength or endurance.[8] Female donkeys in caravans occur only in a few Kanesh letters (Dercksen 2004: 260, n. 683), and in a letter where a caravan was diverted from Emar to Qatna (BM 97130; Zarins 2014: 201).

The remains of these unsung heroes of the Kanesh-Assur trade have not been discovered,[9] so we know little about the imprint their hardships may have made on the bones themselves, other ways of dying, or uses of dead donkey bodies (see also Chapter 8). Pathologies possibly related to load-bearing have only been recorded for some of the third-millennium donkeys from Tell Brak (Clutton-Brock & Davies 1993; Clutton-Brock 2003). However, the Kanesh documents do provide direct and indirect hints of the kind of life led by a caravan donkey. The estimated burdens of up to 90 kilograms is a rather heavy one for animals that were perhaps 1.10–1.15 metres high at the withers, to be carried all day for six weeks.[10] An Old Babylonian proverb suggests that caravan donkeys did not always enjoy their task and provided some resistance: 'Into a plague-stricken city one has to be driven like a pack-ass' (ETCSL Proverbs collection 256, 21–2; see also Chapter 9). The implication here is of course also that physical measures were taken to coerce pack donkeys into moving and to continue moving. One text specifically commands that donkeys should not be rested at the end of a journey but immediately sent on (Larsen 2015: no. 540) and, as we saw above, donkeys died en route (see also P360684 for another letter mentioning this). That said, the records of provisions, feeding and rest at 'inns' do suggest that in most cases the donkeys were provided at least a minimum level of care.

Local transport

Donkeys had an enormous impact on long-distance trade and transport, but it is very likely that their impact on everyday lives at a local level was at least as significant. In her recent book on this topic, Jill Goulder employs studies of the role of donkeys in parts of Ethiopia and Burkina Faso, demonstrating their importance as working animals (2020). Local transport (defined as no longer than a return journey that can be made within a single day) includes movement of people and goods, such as water, grain, fuel, straw, building material and so on. All of these activities would be very relevant in the ancient Near East on a daily basis, and it is fairly safe to assume that donkeys performed similar tasks. Various arrangements can be suggested. Some private individuals or families may have owned a single donkey used for all sorts of activities throughout the day; other individuals might have borrowed or 'rented' the donkey for a specified time, perhaps helping with seasonal agricultural activities or in building works. It is also possible that villages or small communities shared a limited number of donkeys. Unfortunately, the nature of our material (see Chapter 1) means that these types of local, non-palace/temple activities are largely invisible (for regional exchange networks in the Early Bronze Age Levant, see Milevski 2009).

However, some of the material may provide indirect evidence for the involvement of donkeys in local transport and the working routine of people and animals outside the elite sphere. For example, an Early Dynastic IIIB text from Girsu mentions how, if a worker owns a donkey, he can sell it to his supervisor for a reasonable price (Zarins 2014: 199, text no. 20). This is a testament to local trade, but one might also wonder what role a donkey would have for a worker – one likely scenario being that it could be a useful aid in everyday tasks. In practical terms, the containers depicted on the Early Bronze Age terracotta figurines in Figure 4.1 (see also Appendix G), with their large size and suggestion of liquids, would perhaps be more suitable for short journeys than a long trek across the desert. They would, for example, be particularly useful for local and daily transport of water or grain.

That private persons could employ donkeys in this manner is recorded in several law codes. In Hammurabi's code no. 7, guides are set for buying a donkey, and in nos. 244 and 269, a donkey can be hired, in one case to thresh (Harper 1904: 18, 85, 93); the hiring of a donkey is also mentioned in the *Laws of Eshnunna* and in Middle Assyrian law (Pritchard 1969: 162, no. 10, 195, no. 152). These examples verify that donkeys could be bought and hired by private individuals, and that at least one of their functions was for agricultural help. While the law codes only mention men, we may take note of Goulder's observation that the presence of donkeys in the context of less wealthy households may have been particularly empowering for women (2021).

4.2 Trade and exchange of equids

As we have seen in the Assur-Kanesh trade, donkeys not only transported goods, they were themselves part of the goods sold at the end destination. In the third millennium, Tell Brak, ancient Nagar, was apparently famous for its equids, in particular kungas (Oates & Oates 2001; 2003). Letters from Ebla record how they were procuring equids from Nagar (Archi 1998), and as noted in the discussion above, a possible 'caravanserai' has been identified at Tell Brak, along with a number of complete donkey skeletons. Another letter records that the spouse of Isharbeli brought two horses (anše-zi-zi) with her to Girsu (P217016; Zarins 2014: 207). High officials and rulers also gifted equids to each other, as noted in several other tablets from Girsu, where, for example, the spouse of the governor of Adab gives equids to Baranamtarra, the spouse of the governor of Lagash (P221416; Zarins 2014: text no. 15). A king of Nagar also gifts a kunga to Ibbi-zikir, a minister to the king at Ebla, for his involvement in a conflict with Mari, while another Ebla letter mentions 159 kungas and one donkey sent as part of a royal dowry (Archi & Biga 2003: 18, 28).

Another famous collection of correspondence involving long-distance trade is the so-called Amarna letters, dated to the fourteenth century (Moran 1992; Rainey 2014). Discovered at the site of Tell el-Amarna, Akhetaten's new capital in Egypt, they represent a rather different kind of exchange. The letters can be divided into two main types: those between the king of Egypt and rulers of other regions in the eastern Mediterranean (including Babylonia, Assyria, Hatti, Mittani and Cyprus); and those between the pharaoh and his vassals, especially from various sites in the Levant. The former type is particularly relevant here,[11] and both types will be discussed in the next chapter in terms of the use of chariots. The correspondence between rulers reflects equal relations, with the protagonists addressing each other as 'brothers'. They exchange goods, especially luxury goods, but also women, as a means of establishing diplomatic relations. The exchange is phrased very differently from what we see in the Kanesh archives, where there is a clear and open focus on trade for profit. The Amarna Letters instead constitute 'gift exchange', meaning that the consignments sent ostensibly work as gifts but with an explicit expectation of a return gift. Often the goods desired in return are even specified. The letters are, along with spectacular discoveries such as the Uluburun shipwreck, excellent representations of the 'international spirit' that was the Late Bronze Age of the eastern Mediterranean.

As can be gathered from the regions involved, goods, people and animals travelled over vast distances. Some distances could – and even had to – be traversed by sea and rivers, but over land donkeys were as important as previously. The journeys could still be dangerous endeavours (possibly even more so, given the high value of the items being moved), and the letters record how caravans and envoys required guards. There is otherwise much less information about the practical aspects of this trade because of the diplomatic nature of the letters (not being a business archive), so the number and type of donkeys involved are not known, nor are there indications of how they were treated or to what extent they accepted their participation.

The goods that were exchanged included horses and chariots, and it is very clear that both the horses and the chariots were expensive luxury 'goods' in this context. For example, *EA* 22 lists four beautiful horses, a chariot covered in gold and harness and bridle elements of gold, silver, ivory and precious stones (Moran 1992: 51–61; see Chapter 5 for selected quotation). Since this 'gift exchange' was not explicitly predicated on profit, the closest we get to prices are the values listed in this letter. They are not strictly prices, but a way for the sender to brag about the size of the gift (and the expected return gift). The horses and chariots were considered extremely valuable, regardless of how the value given here should be divided. The letters do not specify what roles the horses and chariots exchanged in this manner played once reaching their end destination. Given that they were dealing with live animals, they could not simply be stored away for later use. They therefore imply that appropriate facilities, technology and specialized personnel were available; with their high quality and level of training, the equids are unlikely to have simply been put to pasture and left to fend for themselves.

The harness elements listed in the letter above were decorated to levels so extreme that they are likely to have been impractical, in some cases even limiting the efficiency of some elements. This, combined with the relatively low number of horses recorded in these types of letters (the highest being ten teams of horses), demonstrates that these particular sets of horses and chariots were primarily intended for display rather than engagement in battle, or at most represent the horses and chariot of the ruler. They were exchanged purely for their own sake, rather than as a sort of incidental part of other transactions, as appears to be the case for the donkeys of the Assur-Kanesh trade.

In the Late Bronze Age, records of trade in donkeys and horses have been found in various archives from Ugarit, for example from the Houses of Rap'anu and Urtenu (Malbran-Labat & Roche 2018: 255). These are commercial transactions, although gifts including equids do also occur, for example between Ugarit and Hatti, and horses were traded between Anatolia and Egypt, perhaps through Ugarit (Loretz 2011: 155–6). Donkeys were still being used as pack animals in caravans (e.g. RS 18.115) – we mostly hear of them between Ugarit and their Hittite lords, but they certainly would have travelled throughout the Near East.

The value of equids

As far as can be gathered from the various sources, equids were the most valuable animals of the ancient Near East. But this statement covers a great range based on aspects of space, time, species, physical features, health, age, demand and other factors that we are not at present able to determine. Prices of equids are recorded in the tablets in quite a number of cases, but the evidence is uneven, and although similar units were used, it would be unwise to directly compare prices in late third-millennium Mesopotamia with those almost 1000 years later in the Levant.

Throughout, donkeys appear to have been the least expensive, and probably the most numerous. For the third millennium, Zarins notes ranges of about 2 to 7 shekels of silver (for ANŠE, ANŠE.ŠUL.GI and ANŠE.LIBIR) (Zarins 2014: 201, 203, 216). This corresponds to 600–2400 litres of barley. The only other equid we have a recorded price for in the third millennium is the kunga. This animal could be very expensive, with prices ranging from 11 to 30 shekels of silver in the southern Mesopotamian archives (Zarins 2014: 16), but as high as 300 shekels of silver in the tablets from Ebla (Archi 1998). We do not have records of the prices of horses in the third millennium, and if hemiones were traded, they also do not occur as such. It is possible that the latter were mainly kept at certain specialized breeding sites, procured through hunting rather than through trade with other sites.

From the first half of the second millennium, the Kanesh archives also mention prices of various goods, services and the caravan donkeys. As we saw above, in Assur, the donkeys could be bought for 14 to 17 shekels of silver, while in Kanesh, they were sold for 20 to 30 shekels of silver (Dercksen 2004: 260). For comparison, a female slave also cost about 20 shekels of silver, while 1/3 shekel of silver could get you 100 loaves of bread (Barjamovic 2014: 14). Horses were certainly also traded, but we do not know their price. Horse-donkey hybrids (*perdum*) were about four times as expensive as donkeys (Michel 2004: 192–3).

The Late Bronze Age is the heyday of horses (and the true chariot), and both were very expensive. Prices recorded at Ugarit and elsewhere have been neatly compiled by Heltzer (1978: 17–52, Table 1). In Ugarit, horses could cost from 35 to 200 shekels of silver (a horse mare is also recorded as selling for 30 shekels of silver and a large bronze vessel); in Kassite Babylonia, we have a price of 50 shekels of silver, and in Nuzi about 30 shekels of silver. For donkeys, prices are noted at 15 to 30 shekels (Kassite Babylonia), 6 2/3 shekels (Nuzi), 4 to 8 shekels (Hittite empire), and 10 to 30 shekels of silver (Ugarit).[12] For another comparison, Pardee notes that a sheep would cost about 1 shekel of silver, a young bull 10, and an adult bull 17 shekels of silver (2000: 223–4), and Heltzer provides an elaborate list of prices of goods at Ugarit, along with comparisons to other important areas (1978: Table 1 and 2).

The documents that mention prices of equids are business or administrative records, akin to modern receipts. As such, they do not explain why a kunga cost 11 shekels of silver in one instance, and 300 in another. We can surmise that the factors mentioned above, such as time, location and demand, were part of the equation. The quality of the individual animals may also account for some of the differences. For example, the preferred 'black' donkeys of the Assur–Kanesh caravan trade are likely to have been more valuable than other sorts. Elsewhere, white, 'fine' and swift animals are noted as particularly desirable (see Chapter 9). Individual temperament and skill level are also likely to be reflected in the value of equids.

As we will see in the discussion on ownership (Chapter 7), donkeys could be owned by individuals of almost all levels of society, while hybrids and horses appear to be much more restricted in their socially stratigraphic distribution. They were and are expensive animals to breed and train, and require an elaborate infrastructure that implies a certain level of wealth and specialized workforce.

4.3 Mobility and routes

All of this illustrates the immense mobility of equids. With the exception of migratory animals, they probably travelled further and more extensively than any other nonhuman animals. Donkeys and boats were the main means of long-distance travel, along with carts and other wheeled vehicles in some instances. Equids could also be transported on boats. This is perhaps most obvious in records of the horses being sent by the king of Cyprus to the king of Egypt (*EA* 37),[13] but is also implied in texts as early as the Akkadian period (Zarins 2014: 199).

Some of the known journeys travelled by equids involved in gifting, trade and caravans are marked on the map in Appendix K5. The journeys are shown in direct lines since the exact routes are not known for each, but we can be certain that they were much longer, in some cases thousands of kilometres. In the third millennium, the trade in kungas between Tell Brak/Nagar and Ebla is well documented, and surely they also travelled to southern Mesopotamia, where considerable trade and gift-giving is recorded between the cities of that region. Donkeys that were probably part of caravans travelled between Egypt and the Levant, as has recently been demonstrated by stable isotope analysis of donkey teeth from Tell es-Safi (Arnold et al. 2016), and is supported by Egyptian wall paintings showing donkeys coming with 'Asiatics' (Newberry 1893: pl. XXXI; cf. Cohen 2016; Mourad 2020). In the first half of the second millennium, the long route between Kanesh and other Anatolian settlements and northern Mesopotamian cities has been studied in detail and many of the possible paths tracked (see e.g. maps in Michel 2004; Barjamovic 2011; Atici 2014). The longest journeys recorded are perhaps those in the Amarna letters, which also involve horses travelling by boat. Since these movements consists of fine horses being gifted, there can be no question of a relay system; the horses must each travel the whole length of the route.

But equids did not only travel as pack animals or as trade goods. They were part and parcel of violent encounters already from the third millennium and travelled both short and long distances to engage in battle. A famous example of this is the battle of Qadesh in 1274 BCE, when the Egyptian army, including a large chariotry contingent, set out on the long journey to Qadesh on the Levantine coast, where they fought the Hittite army. Those who survived the battle and were fit enough had the good fortune to repeat the distance on the journey back home. The many requests in the Amarna letters for horses and chariots to the king of Egypt from vassals in the Levant further demonstrate that the journey was not unfamiliar to the horses of the Late Bronze Age. Beside the equids trained for and engaging in battle, the pack donkeys make their appearance again. They are recorded as accompanying armies, carrying their provisions, as for example in Old Babylonian tablets from Mari, where donkeys carry grain and flour for the army (Heimpel 2003: 402–3, 454; see also ARM 26, 521–2).

Yet another aspect of battle is the aftermath of collecting the spoils. When conquering foreign cities, equids were captured as booty and brought back to the home city, which could involve journeys both long and short. On the 'peace' side of the Early Dynastic Standard of Ur, we see equids (probably donkeys) being taken as part of the booty (Figure 5.5), and donkeys are on a list of booty on an Ur III tablet from Drehem (Lieberman 1968–69). Equids taken as booty may even be 'repurposed', as when the king of Mittani sends horses 'from the booty of the land of Hatti' to the king of Egypt in *EA* 17 (Rainey 2014). In a battle at Megiddo, the Egyptian king also reports capturing horses and chariots, which presumably then travelled back to Egypt (Pritchard 1969: 237).

Equids were thus extremely well-travelled and associated with both commoners in helping with daily tasks, with private merchants, and with royalty and other high-status individuals. Donkeys especially interacted with the first two groups, while hybrids and horses were often more highly valued and part of elite identity.

Equids Changing History II: Chariots and Traction

5.1 Ploughing

Another aspect of the working lives of equids was as traction animals, helping with ploughing, threshing and harrowing. Cattle are perhaps better known for performing these tasks, partly due to Sherratt's focus on them in his model of the secondary products revolution (1981; 1983). In the textual material of the ancient Near East, one of the first qualifiers associated with equids is as plough animals. If the term GIŠ.ANŠE is to be understood as plough donkeys, they already occur in the Jemdet Nasr period (Zarins 2014: 189). They then re-appear in the Early Dynastic III period, usually with the term 'anše apin'. Some of the numbers of equids indicate extensive and systematic use that would certainly not have been new to the Early Dynastic III period. For example, a tablet from Abu Salabikh records barley fodder for 180 plough donkeys (anše apin) and 150+ plough donkeys helping with harrowing of the field (P010420; Zarins 2014: text no. 5), while another tablet from Fara/Shuruppak has 256 plough donkeys (P010979; Zarins 2014: 189).

The equids working as plough animals were fed barley, and allocations of fodder are one of the main topics of the tablets (see Chapter 7). The numbers involved further substantiate a highly organized system that also required the production and sharing of large amounts of grain with animals. It seems that donkeys were the main equid engaging in farming activities, but kungas are also associated with ploughs, or the plough team leader (saĝ apin) or a farmer (engar). The working plough equids could be both male and female, although there may have been local preferences.[1] Male equids seem to have been most common as farm helpers based on extant records, but this is difficult to substantiate since we are not dealing with complete records; in many cases, the sex of the animal is not specified. The equids worked in teams. The teams probably consisted of two or four individuals, but in most cases, the tablets simply use a term for 'team' (e.g. bir$_3$).

Only textual records provide evidence for equids as plough animals. They do not occur as such in the images of farming activities (which are in any case rare[2]), nor has this activity been recognized in faunal remains. This is not surprising, since the skeletal remains of these equids, engaged as they were in low-status activities, are unlikely to be represented in most faunal assemblages. Until or unless we locate depositions of equids working as farm helpers, there is little chance of detecting pathologies caused by their working lives. Another point worth repeating here is that all the written evidence concerning ploughing comes from either palace or temple archives. Thus, they reveal little about private or smaller town/village farming. However, as demonstrated by Goulder (2020), we can assume with some certainty that donkeys were important in the daily endeavours of private individuals, with mechanisms in place similar to those for pack animals. Depending on the means of the individual farmer, donkeys may have worked either on their own or in teams, and may have been hired or shared within a community.

Donkeys continued to act as plough animals in the second millennium, but we no longer have the corresponding administrative archives that record these activities. Instead, law codes such as that of Hammurabi provide hints, for example with no. 269, in which a donkey may be hired to thresh (Harper 1904: 93).

The equids were under the care and supervision of the plough team leader and/or farmer. With an experienced plough driver, a donkey would only need a little training to be an efficient agricultural helper, while it may be more challenging and less efficient with a person with less experience. As Goulder has observed in the modern use of donkeys in parts of Africa, they may even be left on their own as semi-wild through most of the year, and then recaptured and retrained when needed for the agricultural season (2020: 52). This has the advantage of a long period of minimum caring or management requirements, and such a practice could also have been in place in the ancient Near East. It is also possible that they could have been performing other duties during these periods.

5.2 Wheeled vehicles and means of communication

Much has been written about chariots and other wheeled vehicles in the ancient world. The topic can – and has – taken up entire books by knowledgeable experts. The work of Joost Crouwel and Mary Littauer (e.g. Littauer & Crouwel 1979; 2002) has been influential in Near Eastern studies.[3] Their contributions can hardly be underestimated, and much of what follows is strongly based on this

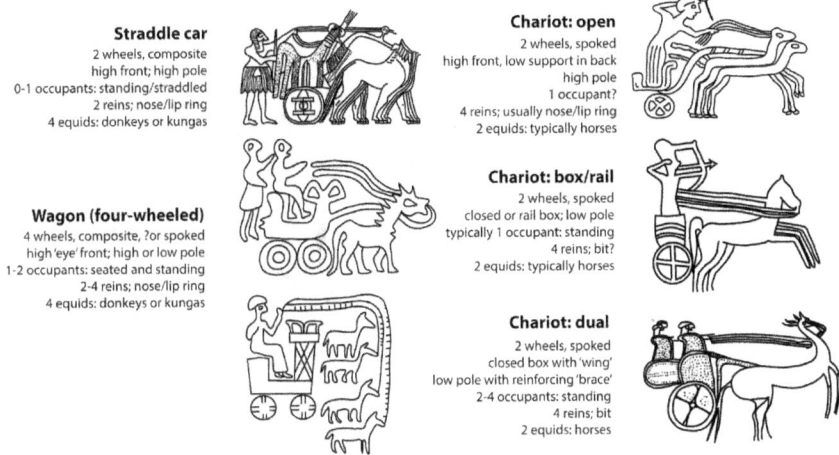

Straddle car
2 wheels, composite
high front; high pole
0-1 occupants: standing/straddled
2 reins; nose/lip ring
4 equids: donkeys or kungas

Chariot: open
2 wheels, spoked
high front, low support in back
high pole
1 occupant?
4 reins; usually nose/lip ring
2 equids: typically horses

Wagon (four-wheeled)
4 wheels, composite, ?or spoked
high 'eye' front; high or low pole
1-2 occupants: seated and standing
2-4 reins; nose/lip ring
4 equids: donkeys or kungas

Chariot: box/rail
2 wheels, spoked
closed or rail box; low pole
typically 1 occupant: standing
4 reins; bit?
2 equids: typically horses

Chariot: dual
2 wheels, spoked
closed box with 'wing'
low pole with reinforcing 'brace'
2-4 occupants: standing
4 reins; bit
2 equids: horses

Figure 5.1 Types of wheeled vehicles and their most typical characteristics (drawn after Woolley 1934: pl. 181b, plaque from Ur; Rova 2012: fig. 10, no. 61, seal impression from Tell Beydar; Frankfort 1939b: pl. XLn, Old Assyrian seal, reversed; Porada 1948: no. 971, cylinder seal, reversed; Yon 2006: no. 8, cylinder seal from Ugarit; British Museum 1896.0201.10/C338, amphoroid chariot krater from Episkopi-Bamboula, Cyprus).

earlier research. Some repetition is inevitable (and necessary for a proper treatment of the topic), but my focus here is on what the wheeled vehicles reveal about equid–human relations. The first thing to note is the modern terminology used. 'Wheeled vehicles' may not be the most elegant of terms, but it does accurately reflect the general category that covers quite a variety of contraptions used for transport in the ancient Near East.[4] The word 'chariot' is sometimes used in this same, broad sense, but strictly speaking refers to a specific type of light, spoked vehicle that is particularly suitable for e.g. warfare and hunting.

Three main types of vehicles are depicted with equids, using the typology developed by Littauer and Crouwel (1979; for a full and detailed typology of wheeled vehicles based on terracotta models, see also Bollweg 1999): 'straddle cars', '(four-wheeled) wagons', and 'chariots' (Figure 5.1; see also Appendix H).[5] Each of these will be discussed in turn, along with their communication systems and chronological implications.

Straddle cars

Straddle cars are two-wheeled vehicles which appear in the iconographic record in the Early Dynastic II period, and do not seem to survive beyond Early

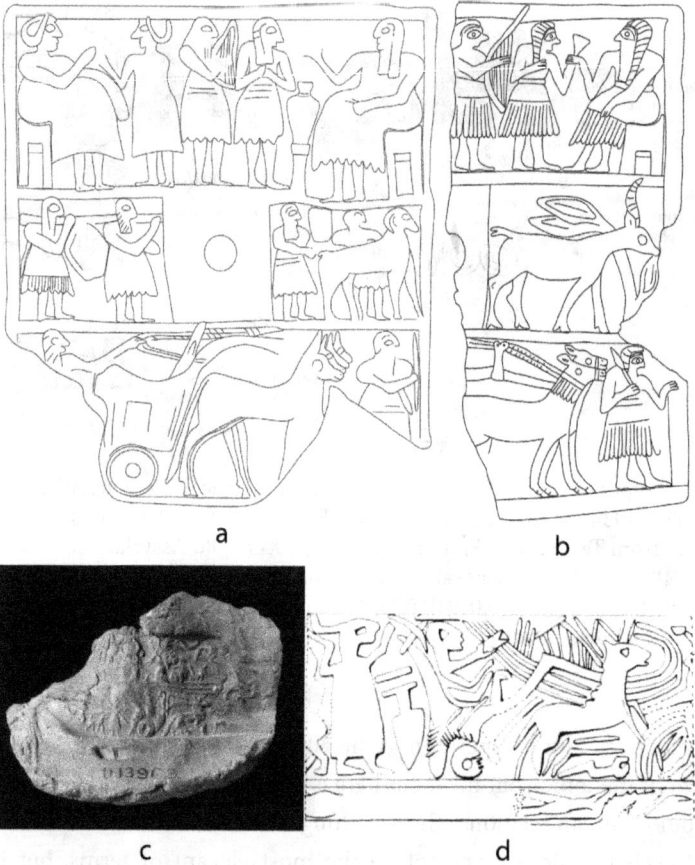

Figure 5.2 Depictions of equids and straddle cars:

a. Limestone plaque from Tell Agrab, Shara Temple. Ag. 35:668 / A 18073, 22 ×
   25 cm, Early Dynastic II (drawn after Frankfort 1943: pl. 65).
b. Limestone plaque from Khafajeh, Sin Temple VIII. Kh. V 35, H. 23 cm, Early
   Dynastic II (drawn after Frankfort 1939a: pl. 108).
c. Clay sealing from Ur. U. 13963 / BM 1930,1213.407, H. 7 cm, Early Dynastic III.
   © The Trustees of the British Museum.
d. Seal impression from Abu Salabikh, Ash-Tip. 6G76:457 AbS 1656, Early Dynastic
   III. Courtesy of J. N. Postgate.

Dynastic III. Only a few examples are known, and several of these are on
limestone plaques of nearly identical compositions (Figure 5.2a-b). Other
examples come from seal impressions and a unique copper model from Tell
Agrab (Figures 5.2c-d; 5.3). Straddle cars usually have a high front, a high curved
pole and two composite disc wheels.

Usually, one person stands straddled over a central 'seat', but could presumably also be seated. The standing position would allow for greater control and manipulation of balance, and would be suitable for higher speed. However, only the seal and seal impressions (Figure 5.2c-d) actually depict equids at a gallop or canter, while the plaques show walking equids. The plaques do not have drivers in the car itself; rather they walk behind, or perhaps next to, the box.

The plaques and the model have four equids pulling the vehicle; in two-dimensional media, this is sometimes shown by depicting one equid in profile and the remaining ones in outlines behind. Two examples instead show two and three equids (Figure 5.2a-b). On the glyptic material, the number of equids is difficult to determine (two or three seem to be depicted, but they may be shorthand for a full four-equid team). One of the earliest texts with an association of equids and wheeled vehicles (ᵍⁱˢGIGIR), an Early Dynastic IIIA tablet from Fara/Shuruppak, mentions a team of three equids (P010701; cf. Zarins 2014: text no. 6).

Based purely on the physical characteristics as rendered, these equids were certainly *not* caballine. The short ears could suggest hemiones or kungas, while the shoulder stripe on the plaques from Khafajeh and Ur (Figure 5.1 straddle car; Woolley 1934: 376–7, pl. 181b.) suggests donkey; placed in the context of what we know about the equids in this early period, it is most likely that they are either domestic donkeys or kungas. The equids on the plaques have an overall body shape that is strikingly un-equine at first glance, but examination of the details reveals that they are indeed equids (especially in their type of tail, ears and lack of horns). One possible conclusion that could be drawn from this is that the craftsperson was not personally familiar with or had themselves observed equids, but had simply been told to change certain elements in a rather superficial manner. Another closer look at the details suggests a more complex scenario that involves a strong artistic tradition not easily shaken. For example, the neck and head of equids are placed in a higher position than other quadrupeds, and the ears placed differently, not having to make space for horns. These elements are accurately rendered on the plaques, and represent the kind of detail that is more likely to originate from firsthand observation than from secondhand descriptions; they continue as such throughout the third and second millennia. Even though we may debate the species of these equids today, ancient viewers almost certainly knew exactly what was being depicted.

The straddle car has one central pole which is either straight or curves upwards before descending at the withers of the equids. The equids create power through the shoulders with what Spruytte calls the 'neck-yoke system' (1983: 14). This system was probably adapted from what was used with cattle, which have a much

Figure 5.3 Copper model of straddle car with four equids and one driver, from Tell Agrab Shara Temple. Ag. 36:150, H. 7.2 cm, Early Dynastic (drawn after Frankfort 1943: plates 58–60).

stronger shoulder section. It is perhaps not the most amenable to equids, but a shoulder-collar variant is used today and in recent times, especially for pulling heavy loads and at a fairly steady pace. Our most detailed representation, the model from Tell Agrab, shows the use of a single yoke placed on and perpendicular to the pole, and spanning the shoulders of the two pole equids, with the other two equids as outriggers (Figure 5.3). On the plaques, short tassels are attached to the collar; whether this is functional or decorative is unclear.

Communication with the equids took place through reins and with the aid of a goad or whip; it also seems that they were sometimes led by a person walking on foot. The reins ran through a rein ring to a nose/lip ring or to a noseband. The rein ring would prevent the reins from getting tangled, and offers some extra leverage for the driver against the pull of the equids. A rein ring further allows for the crossing of reins, which may have been used with chariots. Usually, a total of two reins are depicted for the team of four equids: one rein for each of the two pole equids (i.e. the two central equids, on either side of the pole). With this system, steering would presumably be through pulling one equid right or left, and relying on the others to follow. Equids do respond in this manner to the movements of their companions, but reaction time would be rather slow, and the nose/lip attachment would be inefficient. Only in the model from Tell Agrab is the use of the lip ring clear, while its use is inferred on the plaques (the presence of a noseband, as in Figure 5.2b, does not preclude use of the lip ring). A goad or whip can be used for speed, but also for navigation, with equids learning to turn right or left based on a tapping on the hind quarters; vocal cues may be used in a similar manner.

Wagons (four-wheeled)

The four-wheeled wagon, also called battle wagon or battle car (Figures 5.4 and 5.5), is depicted on numerous seals and seal impressions primarily from the Early Dynastic III and Akkadian periods (Figure 5.4b-g; see also catalogue of glyptic material in Jans & Bretschneider 1998), but also continues in the second millennium as represented in a smaller amount of glyptic material (Figure 5.4h). Additionally, the Early Dynastic III period provides us with one of the most famous objects from ancient Mesopotamia, the so-called Standard of Ur, which depicts equids on one side (the 'Peace' side), and equids and four-wheeled wagons in action on the other side (the 'War' side) (Figure 5.5). Comparable but less well-preserved inlay elements come from Mari (Figure 5.6a-b, A1), and the well-known 'Stele of Vultures' also depicts a wheeled vehicle, either a two or a four-wheeled wagon (Littauer & Crouwel 1973; Winter 1985). A Scarlet ware vessel from the Diyala region (probably Khafajeh), dated to Early Dynastic I-II, demonstrates the early origin of this type of equid and wheeled vehicle combination (Figure 5.4a), with an apparent peak in popularity in the Early Dynastic III-Akkadian periods.

The four-wheeled wagon is very similar to the straddle car, but instead of two has four composite disc wheels. It has a high front, usually with two gaps at the top that resemble the famous fourth-millennium 'eye' idols of Tell Brak. The sides have low panels or side screens, although these are not always depicted. One or two occupants are depicted. When there are two occupants, one person, the driver, sits or stands in front, while the other one perches behind, always standing, and frequently rendered as smaller in stature. This second person holds on to the shoulder of the driver, and may not only be transported and/or part of a unit, but could also act as ballast, helping keep balance, especially at higher speeds or if attempting to turn, and may also have been crucial in helping prevent the wagon from hitting the equids in moments of slowing or stopping, especially since no backing element is evident. In any case, they are in a position where they could quickly and easily jump off the wagon and potentially directly engage in other activities, such as a battle; on the Standard of Ur, they are armed with javelins or spears.

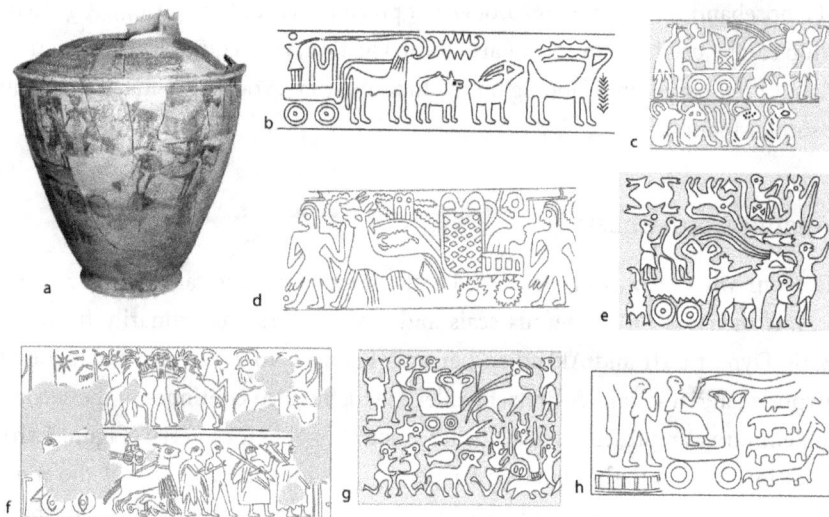

Figure 5.4 Depictions of equids and four-wheeled and other wagons:

a. Painted ceramic jar from Khafajeh. BM 123293, H. 34 cm, Early Dynastic II-III.
    © The Trustees of the British Museum.
b. Seal impression from Tell Chuera, Kl. Antentempel. Early Dynastic? (redrawn after
    Moortgat-Correns 1988: fig. 11).
c. Seal impressions from Tell Brak, Area AA 1070, Room 23. TB 13010 / A3000:4:71 /
    A3000:4:67 / A3000:4:71, Early Dynastic III-Akkadian (redrawn after Oates et al.
    2001: fig. 313.2).
d. Seal impression from Uruk/Warka. W 24278, Early Dynastic II? (redrawn after
    Bollweg 1999: fig. 180).
e. Seal impression from Tell Beydar. Composite, Early Dynastic III (redrawn after
    Rova 2012: fig. 7, no. 55).
f. Limestone cylinder seal from Ur, Tomb PG 1236. U. 12461 / BM 122538,
    H. 4.5 cm, Early Dynastic III (drawing of modern impression after
    BM 122538).
g. Seal impression from Tell Beydar. Composite, Early Dynastic III (redrawn after
    Rova 2012: fig. 12, no. 62).
h. Seal impression from Nuzi, house of Tehip-tilla, *c.* 1450 BCE (drawn after Porada
    1947: no. 977).

Most frequently, the four-wheeled wagon is depicted with four equids, as for
example shown in outline on the Standard of Ur. Many of the seals and seal
impressions only show one equid, but multiple reins alert us to the presence of
teams of four, a convenient artistic shorthand for the miniature medium.
However, there are also instances of three and possibly even five equids
(Figure 5.4a). The equids are always placed next to each other (rather than in
modern quadriga, where there would be two in front and two behind), and

Figure 5.5 The Standard of Ur from Ur, Tomb PG 799, 'War Side' (top) and 'Peace Side' (bottom). BM WA 121201, H. 20.3 cm, shell, lapis lazuli and red limestone, Early Dynastic III. © The Trustees of the British Museum.

an uneven number of equids would thus create an imbalanced team, since a single pole was still used. The extra equid may therefore in these cases be a reserve. The same species of equid occur as with the straddle car. Whenever the tail is rendered in detail, it is tusked, ruling out horses. The mane on the equids on the Standard of Ur is erect, as is the forelock; the Mari inlays are all rendered in the same style. The ears are either short or long – those with particularly long or accentuated ears are probably donkeys, while the remaining ones could be hemiones, donkeys or kungas. Again, based purely on the iconography, it is not possible to be certain, but the unlikelihood of hemiones being tamed to perform such a complex task speaks for kungas in those with short ears.

Interestingly, on the Standard of Ur, the equids are marked as stallions (in contrast to those with the straddle car, which appear to be gender neutral – see also Chapter 9). This is otherwise rarely done – only seal impressions may also depict male equids, but with bovine-like rather than equine genitalia. Based on this, it is therefore unwarranted to assume that stallions were preferred or the most common draught animal for four-wheeled wagons. Nevertheless, in the Standard of Ur the marking of the gender of the animal was clearly meaningful and important.

Communication was, as with the straddle car, done through two reins for the four (or two) equids, running through a rein ring to a lip/nose ring. Actual rein rings closely corresponding to what can be seen in the iconography constitute some of the few surviving elements of wheeled vehicles from the ancient Near East. A number of rein rings from Early Dynastic II-III have survived; these were also used with cattle, and could be topped by a figure, such as the famous silver and electrum example from Ur with a donkey or kunga (Figure 5.7a; cf. Figure 5.4f, where the figure is also depicted on top of the rein ring). Other examples with equid figures on top come from Tell Ahmar and Kish (Watelin & Langdon 1934: pl. XXV.1,4; Thureau-Dangin & Dunand 1936: pl. XXXI.7; further examples in Braun-Holzinger 1984; Dolce 2015). In many cases, the reins are shown as leading to the lip of the equid (not the mouth as for a bit), while in the inlays from Mari and on the Standard of Ur, the contraption is rendered in more detail. It appears to consist of the ring in the lip, attached to a bar, akin to a modern twitch, and the reins appear to in turn be attached to this. Twitches are a short-term means of restraining an equid and forcing calm by tightly squeezing its upper lip (Ali et al. 2017). This method is today highly contested, and certainly longer periods of use can cause damage. The twitch itself can have many forms – anything that will keep the tight squeeze can work, even using a hand could work. It is possible that the bar depicted was designed in such a way that a pull on it or the ring would have an effect similar to a twitch, essentially relaxing and presumably slowing the pace of the equids. Even without the bar, a lip ring could have worked in this manner, going some way towards explaining the use of this otherwise not very effective system of communication.

Some of the equids wear bridles consisting of a headstall, a noseband and sometimes a browband (Figures 5.6, 5.8), with or without a muzzle. Muzzles are also rendered on a number of third millennium figurines (Figure 5.8b-c). The important detail to note is that the noseband is broad and placed very low on the nose, in one case even covering the nostrils of the equid. This would both impede breathing (which may prevent an equid from running too fast) and prevent the equid opening its mouth too wide. Both the low and broad noseband and a

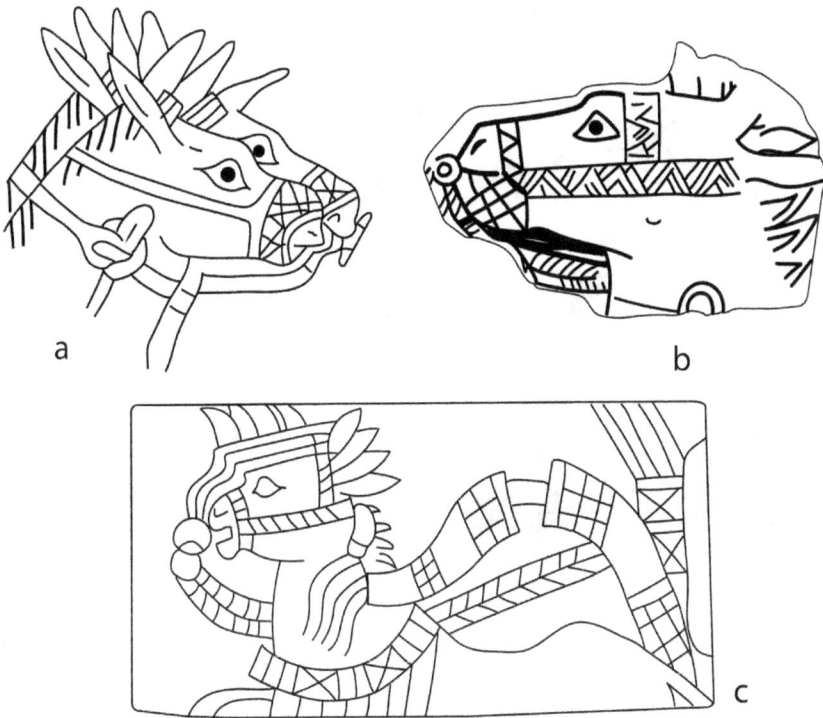

Figure 5.6 Depictions of equids on inlays:

a. Inlay from Mari, Ishtar Temple A. Early Dynastic IIIA (drawn after Parrot 1956: pl. LVIIb).
b. Inlay from Mari, Ninnizaza Temple. Early Dynastic IIIA (drawn after Parrot 1967: pl. LXV.2467).
c. Shell plaque/inlay from Nippur. No. 6N-169 / 6N-233 / Chicago Oriental Institute, Early Dynastic II-IIIA (drawn after Zarins 2014: fig. 2.63).

muzzle would prevent an equid opening its mouth too much and/or biting. These bridles are thus a technological measure adapted to equine behaviour, most likely to curb biting and internal bickering; the latter being even more common among stallions, and the measure is therefore particularly apt for the images of teams of four stallions (see also Recht 2019).

More detailed representations depict long tassels attached to a neckband. The tassels hang loosely over the front and shoulders of the equids. They appear to have become a standard part of the ensemble. If made of leather, they may have provided some minimal protection for the equids, but they may equally have been associated with the social status of the animals, marking them as 'chariot equids'. Finally, the inlays from Mari are fragmentary, but probably belong to

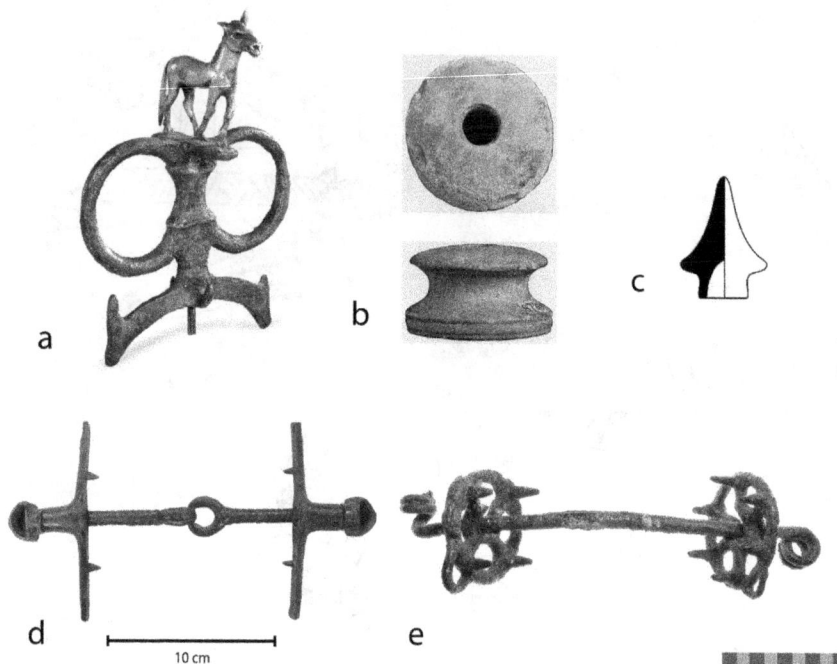

Figure 5.7 Equid equipment:

a. Silver and electrum rein ring from Ur, Tomb PG 800. U.10439 / BM 121348, H. 13.5 cm, Early Dynastic IIIA. © The Trustees of the British Museum.
b. Stone and ivory pommels from Nippur. CBM 8730 and 8727, H. 3.5 cm and 5.2 cm, Kassite (after Hilprecht 1893: pl. X.22-23).
c. Calcite finial from Ugarit, village centre, D1a/3 UF 586. RS 83.5226, H. 3.9 cm, Late Bronze Age (redrawn after Caubet 1991: fig. 1).
d. Metal bit from Tell el-Amarna. Ashmolean 1933.1209, Late Bronze Age (photo by the author). Courtesy of the Ashmolean Museum, University of Oxford.
e. Metal bit from Tel Haror, Sacred Precinct. Specimen IAA # 2009–951, The Israel Museum, Jerusalem, MB III, *c.* 1700/1650–1550 BCE. Courtesy of Guy Bar-Oz.

teams like those on the Standard of Ur. They depict a band and a knot tied around the neck of the equids (Figure 5.6a-b, A1). This would appear to be a safety mechanism, akin to modern quick release tugs or snap shackles. Dangerous situations can quite easily occur with wheeled vehicles, and the equids can get trapped and injured. A quick release tug can be pulled in one fast movement to loosen the harness and detach the equids. The presence of this mechanism implies a long period of experimentation with and use of wheeled vehicles, not to mention accidents with equids. It also implies that measures were taken to try to ensure the safety of the animals, whether for economic or sentimental reasons, or a combination thereof.

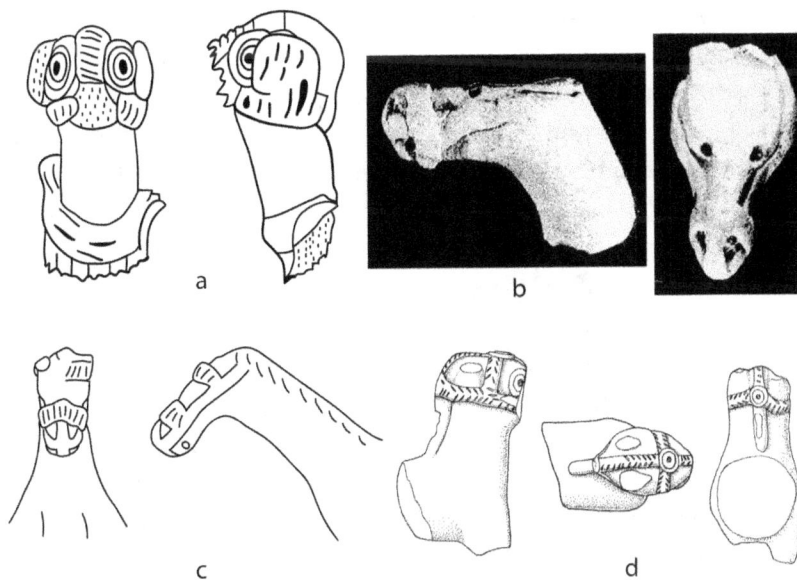

Figure 5.8 Terracotta figurines with equipment:

a. Terracotta figurine from Selenkahiye. SLK 67–642, H. 4.5 cm, Ur III (redrawn after Liebowitz 1988: pl. 24.4).

b. Terracotta figurine from Tell Mozan, Unit A2, f119. A2q251.1, Akkadian. Courtesy of The International Institute for Mesopotamian Area Studies.

c. Terracotta figurine from Tell Brak, Area SS 502, Level 4, Phase M. Reg no. 3134 / TB 10076, 6.5 × 8.4 × 4.3 cm, Akkadian (redrawn after Oates et al. 2001: fig. 489).

d. Terracotta figurine from Tell Halawa, Q1e:57 layer 3bc. ID no. 80Q180 / Museum für Vor- und Frühgeschichte Saarbrücken, H. 7 cm, c. 2500–2000 BCE (after Meyer & Pruss 1994: fig. 37). Permission of Halawa Expedition.

Chariots

The true chariot is a light, spoked, two-wheeled vehicle designed for speed, and typically pulled by two horses (Figures 5.1; 5.9; 5.10, A2). The chariots usually consist of a small box with just enough space for two occupants, the box being either a rail or covered with leather, textile or wood, sometimes richly decorated. We are very fortunate that complete examples of this type of chariot have been preserved in Egyptian tombs, and we therefore know more about this than any other type (see most recently Veldmeijer & Ikram 2018). Two other types of chariots occur in the iconography. One appears to be open, with a high front, perhaps a development from the four-wheeled wagon (Figure 5.1); these are not always easily distinguishable from those with a full box, and the remaining elements seem otherwise similar. Another type is the dual chariot, so named because of its two side 'wings' (Crouwel 1981: 63–70). This is an Aegean type, exclusively found on objects from that region. Typically, they are depicted on so-called chariot kraters, which were exported to the eastern Mediterranean, including Cyprus, and with 83 examples (sherds and complete vessels) so far reported in the Levant. These vessels have been discussed in detail elsewhere (Recht & Morris 2021), and since they are imports, they are not included in what follows, except to say that they are an excellent illustration of the spread of the horses-and-chariot motif and ideology in the Late Bronze Age (see below).

When the species can be identified, the equids pulling chariots are horses. They nearly always come in pairs of two, but there are examples of teams of three (Figures 5.9d, 5.10a). Teams of three appear to have been rare, but horses in threes are also listed as such at Middle Bronze Age Chagar Bazar (Gadd 1940: 31). In the earliest representations of the open type chariot, from Kültepe/Kanesh, communication with the equids was still through a lip ring, with one or two reins for each equid (Figure 5.9a). A seal stylistically dated to the Late Bronze Age also appears to depict this system (Porada 1948: 131, no. 971). These are rare occurrences. In nearly all other instances, we see teams of two equids/horses and a communication system of two reins for each animal. The two reins would greatly improve navigation compared to the single rein. They would be attached through a rein ring on the yoke to the bridle. The Egyptian chariots give us a good indication of what the yoke looked like, and stone yoke pommels and finials that would have been attached to it have been found at various sites in the Levant and Mesopotamia (Figure 5.7b-c).[6] These objects are not extremely characteristic or immediately recognizable as chariot parts, and it is therefore possible that they also occur at other sites but have not yet been identified as such.

The bridle would allow for much greater precision and better timing than the lip ring. The reins could be attached either to the lower part of the cheek straps, where they meet the noseband (essentially the equivalent of a modern bitless bridle), or attached to a bit. Both systems would be quite efficient, and both are used today for riding. For chariots, bits may offer a faster response in the equid due to a greater and harsher pressure. Most iconographic representations from the Near East do not actually depict the bit, but contemporary images from Egypt do. Actual metal bits have been found at a number of sites (Figure 5.7d-e),[7] although the amount is disproportionately low considering the number of horses and chariots mentioned in the texts. Two main types are known (Littauer & Crouwel 2001), demonstrating ancient experimentation and negotiation between human and equid. One is a straight bar with circular cheekpieces or bit guards on either side, sometimes studded (Figure 5.7e). This

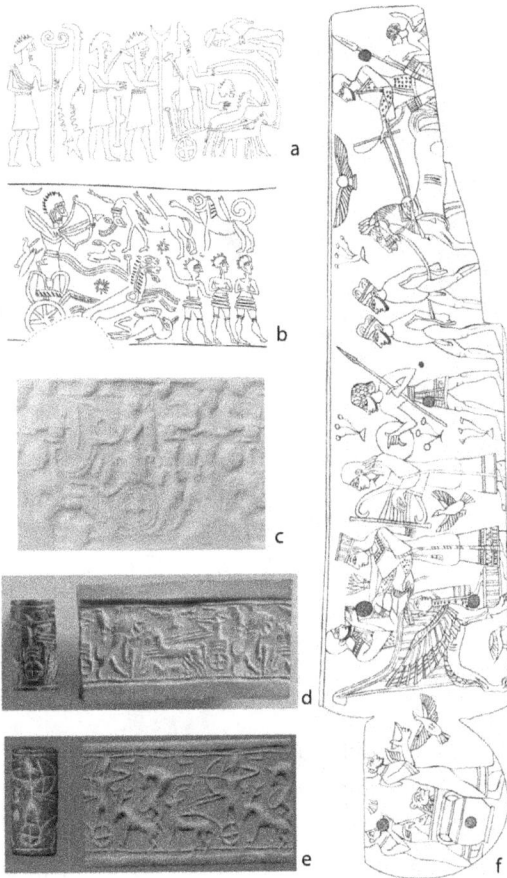

Figure 5.9 Depictions of equids and chariots:

a. Cylinder seal impression on clay tablet from Kanesh. Metropolitan Museum of Art 66.245.17b, 20th–19th centuries BCE. Drawing courtesy of Metropolitan Museum of Art.

b. Hematite cylinder seal. Département des Monnaies, Médailles et Antiques, Bibliothèque Nationale, Paris 1980.292.34 (drawing of modern rollout after P502725).

c. Modern impression of stone cylinder seal. Ashmolean 1920.25, H. 2.3 cm, 1900–1700 BCE (photo by the author). Courtesy of the Ashmolean Museum, University of Oxford.

d. Steatite cylinder seal from Ugarit. RS 4.021 / Louvre Museum AO 15772, H. 2.2 cm, Late Bronze Age. Courtesy of Musée du Louvre (collections.louvre.fr/ark:/53355/cl010140539).

e. Serpentine cylinder seal from Ugarit. RS 8.325 / Louvre AO 19162, H. 2.3 cm, Late Bronze Age. Courtesy of Musée du Louvre (collections.louvre.fr/ark:/53355/cl010143924).

f. Ivory furniture inlay from Megiddo. PAM No. 38.780; b 2005, *c*. 1150 BCE (after Loud 1939: pl. 4.2). Drawing courtesy of of the Oriental Institute of the University of Chicago.

Figure 5.10 Gold bowl from Ugarit, near temenos wall of Temple of Baal. Louvre AO 17208, Dm 18.8 cm, Late Bronze Age. Courtesy of Musée du Louvre (collections. louvre.fr/ark:/53355/cl010141976).

would be considered a harsh bit today. The cheekpieces prevent the bit passing into or through the animal's mouth when only one rein is pulled (in order to turn); the studs add additional pressure (and pain!), with the potential outcome that the equid might respond more quickly. The disadvantage is that the equid may instead decide to resist this painful bit, causing delay and disruption, and the bit and studs may cause damage to the equid's mouth. The other type of bit is composed of two parts connected in the centre (Figure 5.7d). Two bars serve as cheekpieces, again sometimes with studs, and with the same function as the bit with a single straight mouthpiece.

The two reins are a game changer in terms of manoeuvrability. We do not have surviving three-dimensional models that provide a bird's-eye view of how the reins were arranged, but most likely, they were arranged as is common today, with the two right reins (one for each equid) in the right hand of the driver, and the two left reins in the left hand. We still also see the use of a whip for communication, and we may surmise that vocal cues were used. Some drivers appear to have been extremely skilled daredevils: in some images, the reins are tied around the waist of the driver, while they are actively shooting a bow, the horses at full gallop. Steering from this position would not be as efficient as with the hands, but probably not impossible, using movement of the hips for steering, combined with vocal cues and very well-trained horses. It is, however, an excessively dangerous feat. If the driver should lose balance even slightly or something on the ground rattle the chariot, or if the horses spook, the driver could easily fall off, and could end up in a scenario like that of Achilles dragging Hector behind his chariot. It would, in other words, require highly trained and skilled horses and driver, a well-built chariot, and a good bit of luck. This may be exactly the reason that Egyptian wall paintings tend to show the pharaoh or other elite persons in this position; of course, this does not mean that such persons often actually engaged in such activity.

Found with the preserved Egyptian chariots were auxiliary reins (or 'cheek rowels'; Littauer & Crouwel 1985: 84). One of each of these would be placed on the outside of each horse. They consist of a rod with a studded disc placed centrally. The edge of the disc, with the studs, would hit the horse's neck when the opposite rein was pulled, causing pain and urging faster turning.[8] This harness element is not depicted in the images from the Near East, so may not have been used there. Two other elements that may have an Egyptian influence are occasionally depicted: a rug with pendant tassels, covering the body of the horse, and a poll plume, placed on top of each horse's head (Figures 5.9e; A2; for plumes, see also Egyptian scarabs found at Levantine site in Keel 2010a,b). These are both decorative elements designed to enhance the visual impact of the entire ensemble.

Other harness elements and archaeological evidence of wheeled vehicles

A few additional harness elements deserve attention here because they reveal technological and equine knowledge. Several of these are related to safety. Blinkers are a part of the bridle, placed so as to block the hind view and part of the side view of the equid. Equids are highly reliant on visual stimuli. They have a broad field of vision, almost 350 degrees, with only a blind spot to the rear, and a narrow angle directly in front for about two metres (McGreevy 2012: 37–45, for horses; Navas González et al. 2016: 99, for donkeys). The blind spots are easily accommodated by a slight turn or tilt of the head. The vision is directly downwards along the nose, so that in order to see things directly in front, the equid needs to raise its head and nose. With these features, an equid can detect predators approaching from almost any direction. At the same time, sudden movements or activity behind the animal may cause it to lose attention or even panic and bolt or freeze, depending on species. This is potentially very dangerous when hitched to a wagon or chariot, and the blinkers (also found in the written records as ᵏᵘˢIGI.TAB.ANŠE/*naplastum*) thus help prevent accidents.[9] A number of terracotta figurines from the third millennium have applied blinkers (e.g. Figure 5.8a), and blinkers are depicted in Late Bronze Age chariot scenes (Figures 5.9f; A2). They are primarily used with wheeled vehicles, since there is not the same risk of extensive damage when riding or handling from the ground, and it is therefore probable that the figurines were part of chariot teams.

Another feature which helps prevent injury to the equids is a backing element. A backing element would prevent the vehicle from rolling forward and hitting the equids when they stop or slow down (Brownrigg 2019: 88). We find this element on non-glyptic representations of chariots, especially from Ugarit (Figure 5.10, A2; also Figure 5.9f), where the 'girth' strapped around the stomach of the horses would prevent the yoke and all its accompanying elements from slipping over the neck of the equids. How this problem was solved with earlier types of wheeled vehicles is a bit of a mystery. It may be that the backing element was not depicted, or in the case of the four-wheeled wagons, hidden beneath the tassels. The yoke would rest against the neck of the equid, and provide some resistance, but in itself, this was probably not enough, and there would be a risk of yoke and collar slipping over the neck and heads of the equids. The high curved poles seen with straddle cars may be an attempt to address this problem, since the angle against the neck of the equids would provide greater resistance. As mentioned above, for the four-wheeled wagons, it may also be explained with the 'extra' small person that we frequently see depicted behind the driver of wagons: this person may have had the responsibility of both providing ballast and counter-pull when the wagon was slowing down and stopping. This would also explain why they are sometimes shown either stepping down/up or immediately behind, but on the ground, even appearing to hold on to the back (Figure 5.4c,g).

Wheeled vehicles were made primarily of wood, with parts of leather, wool/textile, and small metal parts such as rein rings, nails and linchpins.[10] Various parts of wheeled vehicles are documented in the late third-millennium texts from Ebla (Conti 1997); these hint at an important industry, and a fairly standard 'kit' associated with wheeled vehicles and their draught animals. There are also later texts listing elements of wheeled vehicles, as for example in a Late Bronze Age text from Emar with objects made of wood, including what is translated as a chariot seat, the pole of a chariot, footboard of a chariot, socket of a chariot, pivot of a chariot, peg of the pivot of a chariot, cross-beam of a chariot, chariot body, peg of a chariot body, chariot yoke, chariot wheel, peg of a chariot wheel, cart, pivot of a cart, cart wheel and nail of a cart wheel (P271301). Another text from Emar lists leather (kuš) objects that include equid harness elements: bridle, collar, blinkers, reins, handle of reins and unspecified bridle parts (P271483); some rein rings have been discovered (e.g. Figure 5.7a).

Wood and leather are rarely preserved in Mesopotamia, and no complete wheeled vehicles or harness sets have been found. From Early Dynastic III tombs at Ur and Early Dynastic II tombs at Kish, wheels and traces of wheels of the four-wheeled wagon type were found (Watelin & Langdon 1934: pl. XXIII.1; Woolley 1934: pl. 33; Gibson 1972: 83–6).[11] These correspond quite closely to the iconographic representations, and harness elements in the form of collars, rein rings and reins were also preserved, primarily because they were made of metal or covered in precious materials (Woolley 1934: plates 34–5[12]). None of these elements were directly or certainly associated with equids, and the vehicles appear to rather have been pulled by cattle – there is no doubt that this was the case at Ur, while the stratigraphy of the Kish 'Chariot Burials' is rather complex, with both cattle and equid remains present (see e.g. Gibson 1972; Moorey 1978). Nevertheless, the elements are so similar to what is depicted with equids that the vehicles and harness parts buried are likely to be similar to those used with equids in the third millennium at least.

From the second millennium, we have seen that the true chariot has survived in Egyptian tombs, and even if exactly the same model was not in use in the Near East, we can assume that it was very similar, which is also supported by the finds of the yoke pommels and finials found in the Levant and Mesopotamia. The few extant metal bits provide the only identified bridle elements that have survived from the second millennium; only in the Neo-Assyrian period do we start to see blinkers and protective/decorative elements such as frontlets being made of for example ivory (see below for more on armour).

Wheeled vehicles in the textual record

The most common ancient terms for wheeled vehicles associated with equids are ^{giš}MAR (or ^{giš}MAR.GID$_2$.DA), Akkadian *ereqqum*, and ^{giš}GIGIR, Akkadian *narkabtum*. The former is usually translated as 'wagon', and the latter as 'chariot' (or sometimes 'war chariot', Vita 2008: 59). The terms are used quite broadly and do not easily map onto the typologies established by Littauer and Crouwel (1979, and papers in Littauer & Crouwel 2002) or Bollweg (1999). It does seem that the ^{giš}MAR / *ereqqum* was a heavy vehicle used mainly for transport of people and goods, while the ^{giš}GIGIR was used for a variety of purposes, including war and processions (see below). Both terms appear already in the late fourth millennium (Zarins 2014: 193–5), but are not directly associated with equids until the Early

Dynastic III period. The ^{giš}GIGIR can be qualified as both two-wheeled and four-wheeled (Sallaberger 1998), and a number of variations are found in the Ebla texts (Conti 1997), but most of the time the number of wheels is not specified.

At Old Babylonian Mari, we find the term *nūbalum*, which was apparently a vehicle reserved for the royal household and possibly a few high-status officials, pulled by horses or hybrid equids (*kudanum*) but not donkeys (van Koppen 2002). Mari also gives us *mayyaltum*, described by van Koppen as 'probably a large and comfortable vehicle for the king's family members in the royal train' (2002: 23, n. 26).[13] However, it seems to have been mostly pulled by cattle. *Narkabtum* may be qualified in a number of ways that provide small hints of their usage and ancient ways of categorization, for example, as belonging to the king or a deity (e.g. Šamaš, Ninlil, Enlil and Ninurta) or of a certain type or quality ('of war', 'of the steppe', light, heavy/big, 'good' and 'fully armed') (Richter 2004: 509; P277271). Unfortunately, these qualifications seem to be fairly rare and not standardized, so we are very much left wanting more information.

Wheeled vehicles are also found in cuneiform records indirectly through references to 'chariot' equids and equid 'teams' (ERIN$_2$, BIR$_3$/ṣamādu, ṣimdātum, ṣimittum). Teams of equids could both pull a wheeled vehicle and a plough, so for third millennium examples it must be determined in each case which is intended, while in the second millennium, ploughing is scarcely mentioned. From Middle Bronze Age Chagar Bazar, equids pulling wheeled vehicles are referred to in this manner, as teams, rather than with reference to the vehicle (Gadd 1940: 54–6).

From Volkswagen to Porsche

Pardee has called the chariot the Mercedes of the Bronze Age (2000: 223). It seems that wheeled vehicles, while never cheap due to the necessary raw materials and craftsmanship involved, did come in a variety of price classes. Although actual prices are scarce, this variety is likely due to the sometimes extreme adornment of equids, harness and vehicle. The 'war chariot' gifted to Ibbi-zikir of Ebla in the third millennium included a 'breastplate' of gold along with other harness elements and gold-decorated wheels (Archi & Biga 2003: 19–20; Dolce 2015: 129).[14] The wagon and harness parts found in the Ur Royal Tombs included expensive materials: copper, silver and electrum rein rings, copper and silver collars, and reins with silver and lapis lazuli beads. A 'lapis chariot' is mentioned in a composition from Girsu (P431881), and in an Old Babylonian hymn to a 'chariot' of Išme-Dagan and Enlil (pulled by donkeys) the vehicle is described as 'shining like lightning' (Civil 1968). From Mari, a letter refers to 'luxury chariots' with elements of alabaster, gold, silver, ivory and various types of wood (Durand 1983: 290–1, no. 253). Unsurprisingly, the extravagance of the Amarna letters provides us with the most elaborate description of the decoration of a team of horses, their chariot and harness. It is worth quoting selected sections of *EA 22* at some length (as translated in Moran 1992: 51–61):

> 4 beautiful horses that run (swiftly),
>   1 chariot, its *tulemnus*, its *thongs*, its covering, all of gold. It is 320 shekels of gold that have been used on it (the chariot)
>
>   ...
>
>   2 *maninnu*-necklaces, for horses; genuine *ḫulalu*-stone mounted on gold; 88 (stones) per string. It is 44 shekels that have been used on them.
>   1 set of bridles; their bl[ink]ers, of *gilamu*-ivory; their 'thorns', of go[ld; ...] ..., and ... [...o]f alabaster; [...] ... their *kuštappanni*; [...] ... [...] of *gilamu*-ivory; and their [...], of gold with a reddish tinge.
>
>   ...
>
>   1 (set of) reins; its base and straps, overlaid with silver; the *tašli*, of gold with a reddish tinge; its entire upper part is a gold figure [...] ...; the opening ... its surface ... [...]; it is studded with *dardaraḫ*-ornaments of gold; and the 'house' ... it is studded with *dardaraḫ*-ornaments, also of gold. 60 shekels (of gold) were used on it.
>
>   ...
>
>   1 leather halter; its 'flint-blade' of genuine *ḫulalu*-stone; its inlay, of genuine lapis lazuli; the *tašli*, (with) inlay of genuine lapis lazuli. Its centerpiece is set with *ḫiliba*-stone, and (this) centerpiece o[f ḫili]b[a-stone] is mounted on genuine lapis lazuli. 2 genuine *ḫulalu*-stones, mounted on gold, which are strung on its straps.
>
>   ...
>
>   1 cuirass set, of bronze, 1 helmet, of bronze, [f]or a man. 1 cuirass set, of leather. 1 helmet, [of br]onze, for the *sarku*-soldiers. 2 helmets, of bronze, f[or ho]rses.

This letter is also one of the few indications of an actual price – that of 320 shekels of gold (recall that horses at Ugarit are recorded at 35 to 200 shekels of silver, as discussed in Chapter 4). This of course is a high-end chariot. Another wheeled vehicle is noted in a Middle Babylonian record as costing 100 shekels of silver (*RLA*, 'Kampfwagen, A.').

5.3 Hunting

The practice of hunting with equids and wheeled vehicles is only known from artistic representations in the third and second millennia – in the later Neo-Assyrian period, this activity is also recorded in the royal inscriptions. It is most widely illustrated on objects from the Late Bronze Age, especially from the Levantine area. The best examples are perhaps two gold bowls from Ugarit in the 'international style' (Figure 5.10, A2). Figure 5.10 shows the typically Egyptian-inspired motif of a charioteer able to both drive the chariot with reins tied around his waist, and simultaneously shooting his bow. The chase occurs at a full gallop and with the aid of a dog. Seals and seal impressions also depict hunting scenes with chariots (Figure 5.9b,d,e). In some cases, the hunt and battle have been amalgamated into a single motif, as for example on a cylinder seal from Ugarit, where the charioteer is shooting at an attacking lion while the chariot team is trampling a body on the ground (Figure 5.9d).

A few earlier representations hint that the motif was already well established by the Late Bronze Age, but clearly picked up on and expanded to a much greater extent, possibly due to the new technologies that would have made the hunt more successful. For example, an Early Dynastic III-style cylinder seal depicts a four-wheeled wagon with a team of four donkeys in what looks to be a hunting scene, with the prey animals floating above (P502745 / CDLI Seals 012629). Seal impressions from Tell Chuera of a cylinder seal dated to the third millennium could also be a hunting scene (Figure 5.4b), albeit a very static one: in front of the equid(s) and wheeled vehicle are a dog, and what are probably a wild goat and an antelope – prey animals.[15]

These scenes are not those of common people hunting for subsistence. They are part of an expression of elite identity and activities considered appropriate especially for royalty (see also Feldman & Sauvage 2010; Dolce 2014; Weber 2008; 2017). The ability to go hunting with an expensive team of equids and a wheeled vehicle, accompanied by human and animal helpers, was a luxury afforded by few. It would also require a significant time investment to acquire the necessary skill-set involved. These images, in particular in the Late Bronze Age, are part of a style and ideology shared in the entire eastern Mediterranean. As such, they do not necessarily correspond to realities in the case of each ruler or elite individual. That is not to question the existence of the practice, but to emphasise the extent to which equids became intertwined with human identities, shared ideologies and political developments.

5.4 War

There can be no doubt that equids and their wheeled vehicles participated in battle beginning at least in the Early Dynastic III period, and probably also in Early Dynastic I-II. The seal impressions depicting straddle cars indicate a battle, with soldiers walking, fighting and/or getting trampled (Figure 5.2c-d). The plaques depict different moments in time, related to processions, but the weapons kept in the vehicle clearly hint at less peaceful activities, whether fighting or hunting (Figures 5.1; 5.2a). The 'battle wagons' of the third millennium, typically with their teams of four donkeys or kungas, are frequently depicted as actively engaging in violent clashes. The motif of equids and wheeled vehicle seemingly trampling a human body on the ground is a template that starts in Early Dynastic III but continues into the Late Bronze Age (Figures 5.4c,f and 5.5 for third-millennium examples). That the trampled persons are dead or injured enemy soldiers is most clearly illustrated on the Standard of Ur, where they are marked as such by being naked or semi-naked, in captivity (elbows tied behind their back and led by the victorious soldiers) and by their bleeding wounds. Active battle with dead bodies and one soldier hacking down another next to a four-wheeled wagon and team of equids is depicted on a seal impression from Tell Brak (Oates et al. 2001: fig. 313.1). The weapons used were axes and spears or javelins, the latter kept in a compartment at the front or to the side of the chariot box. Mostly the driver is focussed on communicating with the equids, but attempts at multi-tasking by also wielding a weapon are depicted (Figure 5.4d).

The motif of equids with a wheeled vehicle trampling enemies might be somewhat deceptive. In most situations, equids will attempt to avoid obstacles directly in front of them, although there are exceptions to this, for example if spooked or very determined to go in a specific direction, for whatever reason. Equids can also be trained to instead 'run down' an obstacle, or of course jump over it. The wheeled vehicle itself would run the risk of toppling over in the attempt to run over bodies on the ground, although the four wheels do make this type of vehicle more stable. However, it is not necessary for the vehicle to run over the bodies. The equids could easily knock a person over (and partly trample), and in doing so, the body would in most cases be knocked to the side rather than fall directly below the hooves of the animals. It is therefore possible that we should understand this motif as one containing a depth of field, where the human bodies are *next to* rather than *below* the equids; alternatively (or additionally), the motif is a shorthand for the chaos of the battlefield, and the harm caused by equids, wheeled vehicles and soldiers (cf. Littauer & Crouwel 1979: 32–3). In any case, the participation of equids and four-wheeled wagons in war is without question, even if we do not know exactly how they were employed or their strategic positions.

This is supported by textual evidence. An Early Dynastic IIIA text from Fara/ Shuruppak mentions 'chariots' (^{giš}GIGIR) in association with individuals going to or leaving battle (P010905; *RLA*, 'Kampfwagen, A.'). A dispute between Umma and Lagash lasting several generations ended in violent encounters, and the composite text *RIME* 1.09.05.01 (P431117) records that

> Enanatum, governor of Lagaš, in the field Ugiga, the field of Ningirsu, had (previously) fought with him, but Enmetena, the beloved son of Enanatum, defeated him. Urlumma fled into the middle of Umma and was killed. His donkeys, 60 teams, on the bank of the Lumma-girnunta canal were left behind, and their personnel's bones were all left out on the plain. Their tumuli in five places he heaped up.
>
> CDLI translation

The so-called Stele of Vultures concerns the same dispute and closely agrees with the above account (although the main protagonist may be Eannatum rather than his son) (Littauer & Crouwel 1973; Winter 1985). The king of Lagash is shown both leading a contingent of soldiers and driving a wheeled vehicle, but the entire stele is not preserved, so the type of vehicle and equids are lost. In another register, piles of enemy soldiers are being covered in soil and, next to this, there is a pile of dead quadrupeds, perhaps equids or cattle. Incidentally, this account helps explain the overall lack of equid skeletal remains, since these piles, located as they were in a field outside any settlement, are unlikely to be discovered archaeologically.

Slightly later in the third millennium, a conflict emerged between the two great cities of Mari and Ebla (detailed in Archi & Biga 2003). From the archival evidence from Ebla, we can infer that kungas and wheeled vehicles were part of the armed engagements through the mention of 'charioteers' (ugula sur$_x$-BAR. AN) accompanying Ibbi-zikir, a minister of the king, on an expedition. Such charioteers were clearly associated with the palace and king, and received gifts as reward for their participation – as reward or payment, Ibbi-zikir was gifted a new 'war chariot' (TM.74.G.102; Archi & Biga 2003: 19). For the third millennium, the equids involved in warfare were mostly donkeys and kungas. An Ur III text associates horses (ANŠE.ZI.ZI) with soldiers (P105830), while several other Akkadian and Ur III texts refer to kungas 'for soldiers' (Zarins

2014: 204, 214–15). Whether these equids ended up pulling vehicles, as mounts or as carrying supplies is not recorded.

Four-wheeled wagons continue into the first half of the second millennium, but are no longer clearly represented in battle contexts. This period in general suffers from meagre archaeological and iconographic evidence concerning equids, despite indications from numerous texts that they played an important role and were a standard part of official administration and economy. Archives from Mari, Chagar Bazar, Tell el-Rimah and Nippur have quite rich records associating wheeled vehicles and equids – donkeys, hybrids (probably mules or hinnies) and horses. As the previous and next chapters show, equids were part of warfare by providing transport and provisions, and as mounts. However, as noted by Moorey (1986), and reiterated in van Koppen's (2002) more recent study of the Mari and Chagar Bazar texts, none of them explicitly link these wheeled vehicles with warfare. This link is, however, made in Anatolian sources, where wheeled vehicles (gišGIGIR) are recorded as part of the armies of Hittite kings of the seventeenth century (Littauer & Crouwel 1979: 64-5), and one text mentions a 'chariot battle' near the city of Parsuhanda (Barjamovic 2011: 33).

The iconographic evidence is only slightly better. Depictions including wheeled vehicles almost all come from unprovenanced seals, dated based on their 'Old Syrian' or 'Cappadocian' style. One of these seals, in the Ashmolean Museum (Moorey 1986: pl. 2), clearly depicts a two-wheeled chariot pulled by two equids and followed by three walking figures, perhaps soldiers. The equids are trampling an enemy below their legs, continuing the motif from the third millennium; this is surely a battle scene. The action on other seals is more challenging to interpret, but could be either battle or hunting scenes. For example, another seal in the Ashmolean (Figure 5.9c) has a similar scene with a chariot, two equids (donkeys or hybrids) trampling an object below them (the seal is damaged in this part). Behind, three helmeted figures follow. In the field above, there are two antithetical antelopes, which could suggest hunting, but the composition is symbolic rather than indicative of prey animals.

In the Late Bronze Age, there seems to be a veritable boom in the role of horses and chariots in warfare – or, at the very least, in our textual evidence for it. This is surely related to some of the developments in the technologies related to equids as draught animals and the fast, two-wheeled chariot. These developments include the spoked wheel for a faster and lighter vehicle, horses as the primary chariot animals, the use of a bit and two reins instead of the lip ring with a single rein or rope, the use of bow and arrow from the chariot and a crew of two abreast (neatly summarized in Raulwing 2000: 43). Many of these features were not entirely new to the Late Bronze Age and they did not appear all at once: spoked, two-wheeled chariots appear in Figure 5.9a-c, all dated to the Middle Bronze Age; a bow is used by the driver in Figure 5.9b; and two equids and four reins are depicted on a number of other examples (e.g. Moorey 1986: plates 2, 5). The species on these is not identifiable, but we know from the Mari archives that horses pulled wheeled vehicles in the Old Babylonian period. Bits are not rendered in these or in later illustrations, but the metal bit found at Tel Haror (Figure 5.7e, dated to MB III, c. 1700/1650–1550 BCE, Bar-Oz et al. 2013) demonstrates that they were in use already in the first half of the second millennium. What is more, these changes are far from universal; they are not all or consistently applied in the Late Bronze Age.

Images of warfare do occur, but in the iconographic repertoire a hunting setting was preferred for the horses and chariot motif – which also means that we should perhaps not be surprised that these were not common in the earlier second millennium (cf. also Moortgat 1930). However, we can detect the continuation of the trampled-upon enemy below the legs of the horses (Figure 5.9d), sometimes accompanied by a row of armed figures walking behind. Interestingly, these do not usually depict two persons in the chariot, so it is uncertain how important this 'innovation' was.

The role of horses and chariots in war is better borne out by the written evidence. The desperate pleas for help recorded in the Amarna letters make it abundantly clear that a chariotry contingent was a prerequisite for survival against incoming attacks, as for example in *EA* 103, where the ruler of Byblos (Rib-Hadda) requests help from the king of Egypt (as translated in Rainey 2014: lines 32–57):

> Furthermore, may the king heed the words of his servant. Send garrison troops to the city of Ṣumur and to the city of ʿIrqata since all of the garrison troops have fled from the city of Ṣumur. And may it please the lord, the sun god of the lands and give me twenty pairs of horses and send an auxiliary force with all speed to the city of Ṣumur to protect it. All the garrison troops that remain are sick and few are the men who are in the city. If you do not send the regular army, then there is no city that will remain to you. But if the regular ar[my] will be (here), we will take all the lands for the king.

The famous Battle of Qadesh is the example par excellence of the prevalence of horses and chariots in the Late Bronze Age in the entire eastern Mediterranean. Named after the site in the Levant, the battle was a territorial dispute between the Egyptian king Ramses II and the Hittite king Muwattalli II in the thirteenth century. The outcome is thought to have been indecisive, with a peace treaty eventually being signed. What is astonishing in terms of horses is the numbers recorded (which, of course, we must remember, could be exaggerated) and some of the deceptive tactics employed. Horses and chariots were evidently in the thick of battle, and even the Egyptian king himself is described as storming forward in his chariot. The Hittite army is described as consisting of 2500–3500 chariots (Cline 2014: 81–2) – that is, a total of 5000–7000 horses! Although the chariots would only constitute a small part of a complete army (for the same Hittite army, 37,000 infantry are mentioned), the surrounding industry must have been extensive: breeding and training (or trading) of a large number of horses, training of expert personnel, soldiers and charioteers, chariotmakers requiring not only skill and developed technologies but also a steady supply of raw materials, weaponsmiths, armourers and so on.

Apart from the tassels depicted on equids in the third millennium, which may have had a protective and decorative function, protective armour for equids is not shown, and we may therefore be tempted to conclude that it was not used. However, a few Late Bronze Age records reveal that horses were in fact provided with protective armour for battle. This evidence comes from fourteenth-century Nuzi. Tablets from there list leather or leather and bronze scale 'cuirasses' and bronze 'helmets' for chariot horses in the military (Lacheman 1939: 540-1; Lion 2008; Maidman 2010: no. 21).[16] A lovely detail concerns the production of the armour, which included the use of goat skins and horsehair. Bronze 'helmets' for horses are also mentioned in the Amarna letter *EA* 22 (quoted above), and helmets and armour for horses are found in records from Ugarit (Loretz 2011: 72–5). For these, we may imagine something like the later Assyrian frontlets or similar plates placed on the side of the horse's head.

The *maryannu* and the origin of the 'true' chariot

There are iconographic examples of a spoked two-wheeled vehicle pulled by two equids (species not identifiable) as early as towards the beginning of the second millennium (Figure 5.9a). But it was not until the Late Bronze Age (the later part of the second millennium) that it became extremely popular, when it was part of the 'international' style and spirit (Feldman 2006) that is so characteristic of this period. The motif of horses-and-chariot was widespread across the eastern Mediterranean and widely recognized and understood (see e.g. Feldman & Sauvage 2010), and objects where traded across the entire region, as perhaps best exemplified by the famous Uluburun shipwreck (Pulak 1998). The motif of horses and chariot should be seen in this light; it is standardized to the extent that it is in some cases difficult to identify where it was made. Objects and styles from Egypt, the Levant, Cyprus and the Aegean moved and mixed freely: the gold bowls from Ugarit with a hunt from chariot exemplify this quite nicely (Figure 5.10, A2), as does an ivory gaming board found at Enkomi in Cyprus (Courtois et al. 1986: pl. XXIV.9).

There is an ongoing debate about the origin and spread of the true chariot, along with the horses that pulled them (Moorey 1986). The term *maryannu* is part of this debate. It is found in Late Bronze Age texts from Egypt, Bogazköy, Alalakh, Ugarit, Nuzi, and now also Qatna (Richter 2004); it appears to refer to a social group or status sometimes translated as 'chariot-warrior' (Albright 1930-31; see also Loretz 2011: 78–104). They often have a strong association with horses and chariots, as for example recorded in a Hittite treaty text:

> But Akit-Tešub fled from him (Šuttarna) in sooth, and entered the land of Babylonia; with him fled 200 chariots. But the king of the land of Babylonia seized the 200 chariots of Akit-Tešub and all their possessions, and took them for himself. Toward Akit-Tešub and his *maryannu* he acted in a hostile manner.
>
> Albright 1930–31: 218, quoting Weidner

The *maryannu* could thus be expert charioteers, but the designation does not seem to exclusively refer to this (von Dassow 2008: 300–14), and beside evidently taking part in battle – perhaps even as special units – we have little information about their relation to horses and chariots.

Linguistic analyses suggest that 'maryannu' has both Vedic and Hurrian components (Albright 1930–31; Reviv 1972; further references in Raulwing 2000: 117). This, along with linguistic analyses of a number of other terms tying them to Indo-European and Proto-Indo-European languages, has been used to argue for an origin of the true chariot and the horses-and-chariot combination outside the Near East itself. This outside origin may be the Eurasian steppes and in particular the so-called Sintashta culture, but the question of exactly where is itself tied to the question of the location of a Proto-Indo-European 'homeland'. The debate about this is expertly explained in the work of Raulwing (2000 with detailed bibliography; 2004 for shorter overview).

Throughout the Bronze Age, the Near Eastern world was one that was extensively connected with surrounding regions, and even further afield, with the Late Bronze Age being particularly intensive. Material culture moved, but so did people, animals and ideas, and it would thus be no surprise if the technology and knowledge of horses and chariots did the same. Having said that, the transformations in equids and wheeled vehicles can also be understood as occurring in the Near East itself (see also Littauer & Crouwel 1979: 68–71, contra Piggott 1979; 1983). The idea of equids and wheeled vehicle was present from at least the early third millennium, and none of the developments that occur in equids and types of vehicles and harness are so extreme or unfamiliar as to necessarily merit outside influence. In any case, as I have mentioned previously, the aim here is not to map directional arrows of influence in an origin-oriented manner, but to explore the equid–human relations. And the developments do have implications for these relations, in particular in terms of technology, knowledge of animals, and equid engagement in anthropogenic activities.

5.5 Transport and processions

Wheeled vehicles were used to transport goods, people and messages; they were also part of ceremonies and processions, typically those of royalty or divinity. As we will see in the next chapter, messengers would ride equids over both long and short distances to deliver their letters. They could also use wheeled vehicles. For example, a third-millennium tablet from Ebla mentions wheeled vehicles supplied to messengers by the king's 'charioteer' (ugula sur$_x$-BAR.AN) (Archi & Biga 2003: 15). Meier (1988) also notes that messengers in the Old Babylonian period used wheeled vehicles for transport and that, for the Late Bronze Age, a letter from Nuzi illustrates the use of 'fast chariots' by messengers:

> Now PN I hereby send (*altaparšu*), so give him a swift (*qalla*) chariot. And (when he returns) from that place to which he is travelling, give him (another) swift chariot to that he can come to me.
>
> Meier 1988: 86

The extensive caravan trade between Assur and Kanesh in the early second millennium discussed in the previous chapter also included the use of wagons (*ereqqum*), at least for shorter distances (Dercksen 1996: 64–7; Gökçek 2006). The wagons would usually be loaded with bulky goods such as straw, wood, textiles and copper. Loads of around 600 kg are recorded, equalling that of about eight donkeys. However, their speed of travel was slower, and they required roads and therefore such wagons may not have been possible on all journeys (Veenhof & Eidem 2008: 152; for roads and a list of selected texts mentioning wagons, see also Barjamovic 2011). In most instances, it is not mentioned how the wagons were pulled, but it seems both donkeys and cattle could perform this task. In a few instances, donkeys are implied, as for example in P297289: 'send me donkeys, bags, their harness and wagons' (lines 8–12, as translated in Dercksen 1996: 64).

Wheeled vehicles of various types featured in elite/royal and divine transport and processions. The luxurious materials decorating some wheeled vehicles and harness parts mentioned above ensure that the ensemble would have been quite the spectacle. Third millennium caravanserais such as those at Tell Brak or Tell Beydar were not only for caravan donkeys, but also supplied wheeled vehicles for transport and were associated with a high number of cartwrights (Sallaberger 1996a,b). The ruler of ancient Nagar (Tell Brak) is recorded as travelling by a 'chariot' pulled by kungas to Tell Beydar (Sallaberger 1998: 173). The occasions of processions are not always specified, but could certainly include festivals, important visits and celebrations of victories and/or peace treaties. The lavish 'chariot' with gold and gold-decorated parts given to the minister Ibbi-zikir of Ebla was for the 'ceremony of the oil offering of Mari' (Archi & Biga 2003: 20). For a 'triumph tour' at Old Babylonian Mari, the king would ride a *nūbalum* vehicle pulled by *kūdanum* equids; this type of vehicle seems to be specifically for official parades, and the *kūdanum* equids were required for the Akitum festival (van Koppen 2002: 25–6).

The wheeled vehicles qualified as belonging to deities were almost certainly also used in processions that were part of festivals and/or when the deity needed to visit a place outside their own temple. The second part of the hymn to a chariot of Išme-Dagan and Enlil has Enlil riding the chariot in a procession or festival (Civil 1968). In the *Epic of Gilgamesh*, an extravagant wheeled vehicle is described as made of gold, lapis lazuli and amber, apparently pulled by lions and hybrid equids (George 1999: Tablet VI, 6–21). While these are mythological narratives, we know that deities did physically travel to and from their temple abodes in the form of their statues, and we know that temples owned equids and wheeled vehicles, so there is no reason to doubt that such processions actually took place.

Processions and transport can be difficult to identify in the iconographic repertoire since there are limited characteristic features, but a few can be pointed out with some degree of confidence. The early plaques with straddle cars usually have three registers, with a procession progressing towards the banquet scene in the top register (Figure 5.2a-b). The importance of display is emphasised with the rows of humans, animals and goods, the slow pace and the driver walking next to or behind the vehicle. These are celebrations of some kind, but whether related to religious festivals, military victories, a mixture of the two or something else entirely remains an open question. Scenes with a religious or mythological component occur in seal impressions from Tell Beydar, where deities and/or divine boats are depicted (Figure 5.4e,g). The 'Peace' side and top row of the 'War' side of the Standard of Ur also depict processions and a celebration – in this case, related to a military victory (Figure 5.5). The second millennium presents us with few unambiguous examples, but the scene on an ivory furniture inlay from Megiddo is surely another procession related to the display and inventory of booty from a battle (Figure 5.9f). A parading of a chariot in front of the king is also recorded in a letter from Ugarit (Bordreuil 1991: no. 47).

An overview of equids and wheeled vehicles in the Bronze Age reveals the types of vehicles and communication systems used. These reflect experimentation, developing technologies and continuous negotiations between humans and equids. Some harness and bridle elements must have been more efficient than others, but each type corresponds to a negotiated relationship and experience of equine temperament and behaviour. While some elements may have been more suitable or efficient, each type worked in its own way. Donkeys, horses and hybrids all pulled wheeled vehicles at one time or another. In warfare, and to some extent hunting, equids and humans were at great risk and shared injuries, sickness and death (see also Chapter 8). Battle involved confrontation with enemies aiming to defeat equids and humans alike, but also included other dangers such as plagues (Potts 1999: 253) or dying from the cold while based in the field for months, as we hear in one Late Bronze Age letter from the frontline (Rainey 1972).

The equid-wheeled vehicle combination was strongly associated with elite levels of society that could afford and had the extensive administrative and organizational system in place to support it. Breeding, training and caring for these equids required a range of specialized personnel and resources only possible for those with great means; the resources, personnel and skill involved in the production of wheeled vehicles was an extensive parallel system.

Joint Journeys: Equids Carrying Humans

6.1 Equids as mounts

Equids and humans also shared the road in a physically closer manner. In short and long joint journeys, equids carried human riders on their backs.[1] In this interaction, there was more direct physical contact between equid and human, and a co-becoming through learning to navigate, balance and listening to physical and verbal cues. This co-becoming may be more or less intense, depending on the (type of) rider and equid and the tasks for which they were training. With the apparent exception of hemiones, all types of equids took part in this kind of interaction,[2] and there is evidence of riding being known from at least as early as the mid-third millennium. Riding was especially a domain of mounted messengers, and for ceremonial or processual occasions by elite individuals; riding purely for transport also occurred. Some deities are mentioned or depicted as mounted on an equid. Finally, riding is in a few instances associated with military and hunting activities.

Artistic representations provide some information about riding styles and the technologies developed. There is some overlap with the equipment used for transport and with wheeled vehicles but also distinct elements suitable for riding. Riding styles hint both at the purposes of riding, knowledge of equine behaviour and anatomy, and at how humans and equids interacted and communicated with each other.

Two- and three-dimensional representations of equids acting as mounts begin to appear in the mid-third millennium, with a concentration towards the end of the millennium, coinciding with the extensive Ur III archives recording equids. The first images showing equids with a rider are part of scenes on cylinder seals, preserved as sealings and seal impressions.[3] For example, two impressions from Kish dated to the Akkadian period depict a ridden equid (Figure 6.1a-b). Both are part of mythological scenes that include so-called 'contest scenes', battles between supernatural beings. The details are not well enough preserved or rendered to identify equid species or rider with certainty; in both cases, given the context of the scenes, it is possible that the riders are deities. The only clue to the species in Figure 6.1b is the long ears, which suggest a donkey. The riding style of both riders is reminiscent of what we see more clearly rendered on plaques from the early second millennium with the rider seated astride (see below). Only one front and one hind leg of the equids are depicted, and they are almost straight, with a slight angle forwards and backwards. Comparison with how animals and their movements are usually rendered in Near Eastern art provides a background for how to understand this posture (see Chapter 9). This is almost certainly intended to be equids in the canter or gallop, since all four legs are shown when walking, and the outwards angles suggest that they are not at a standstill. We are therefore looking at an event (regardless of the realm in which it takes place) which required speed, and where the gait of the animal is emphasised.

In contrast, a gold band from one of the Early Dynastic III tombs excavated by Woolley at Ur depicts an equid walking (Figure 6.1c). The animal is not immediately particularly equine-looking, but comparison with other animals (including the lack of horns), and the position of the ears characteristic of depictions of equids demonstrate that this is in fact an equid. The thin tail may indicate a donkey; based purely on the features on the image itself, this could also be a hemione or a kunga. The scene on the gold band consists of rows of other animals and humans, possibly booty, but in this case we appear to be in the realm of humans rather than deities.

Another set of seal impressions, this time from the Ur III period, is from the seal of Abbakala (Figure 6.1d). An equid-rider team is depicted, with the rider positioned similarly to those seen so far, carrying an object in his right, forward hand.[4] The impressions have been the focus of several discussions because the equid has been interpreted as a horse and would thus be the earliest known depiction of horse and rider (Owen 1991; Zarins 2014: 145). The tail is rendered fuller than that typically seen for donkeys, but unfortunately, the rendering is not detailed enough to make a completely secure identification. What it does demonstrate is that high officials were already associated with riding in the third millennium (whether or not the rider is Abbakala himself); the equid is again shown at a canter/gallop, indicating the importance of speed.

Two other types of artistic material are of interest here: terracotta plaques and figurines (see also Appendix I). Beginning with the figurines, we can note that in the second half of the third millennium, and continuing slightly into the second millennium, a significant number of equid examples appeared (Figure 6.2 for

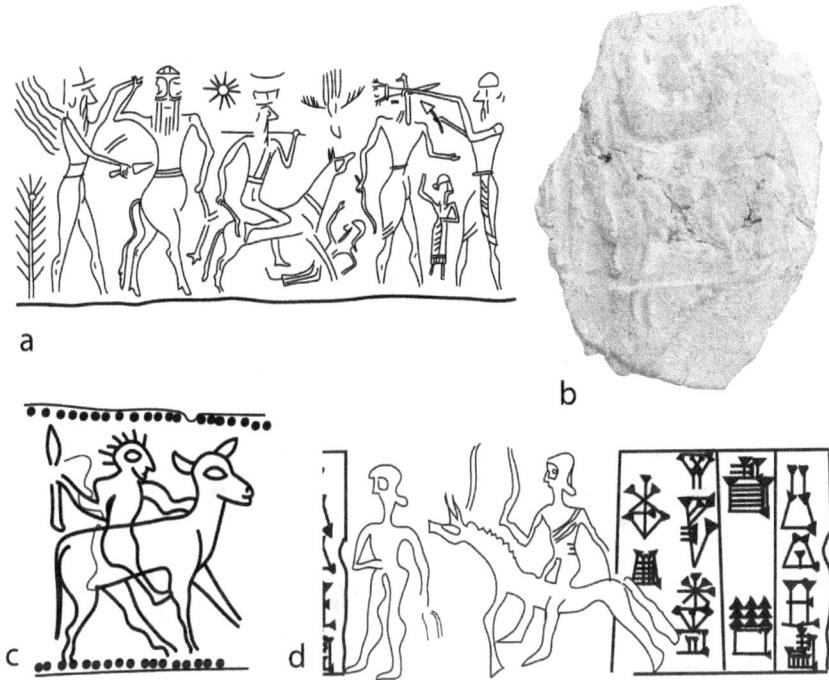

Figure 6.1 Early depictions of riding:

a. Serpentine cylinder seal, possibly from Kish. Louvre 22325, H. 3.9 cm, Akkadian, impression (drawn after Oates 2003: fig. 9.4).
b. Seal impression from Kish. Ashmolean Museum 1930.395, late Early Dynastic or early Akkadian (photo by the author). Courtesy of the Ashmolean Museum, University of Oxford.
c. Gold circlet band from Ur, Tomb PG 153. U. 8173, Early Dynastic III (drawing of part of band after Woolley 1934: pl. 139).
d. Impression of seal of Abbakala on clay tablet from Drehem. NBC 2200, Akkadian (after Tsouparopoulou 2015: fig. 5.2). Courtesy of Christina Tsouparopoulou.

selection). They are particularly prominent in northern Mesopotamia, at sites in the Khabur region. As discussed in Chapter 7, we know that at least Tell Brak, ancient Nagar, was famous for its breeding of equids, and the overall evidence from the entire region suggests that it was a hub for equid-related activities. The terracotta figurines are quite modest objects, almost all fragmentary and discovered in settlement contexts. They have been reported from Tell Mozan, Tell Brak, Selenkahiye, Tell Halawa, Tell Arbid, Chagar Bazar, Tuttul, Tell Chuera, Habuba Kabira, Tepe Gawra, Tell Beydar and Tell Afis. Similar figurines but generally in lower numbers have also been found at more southern and western

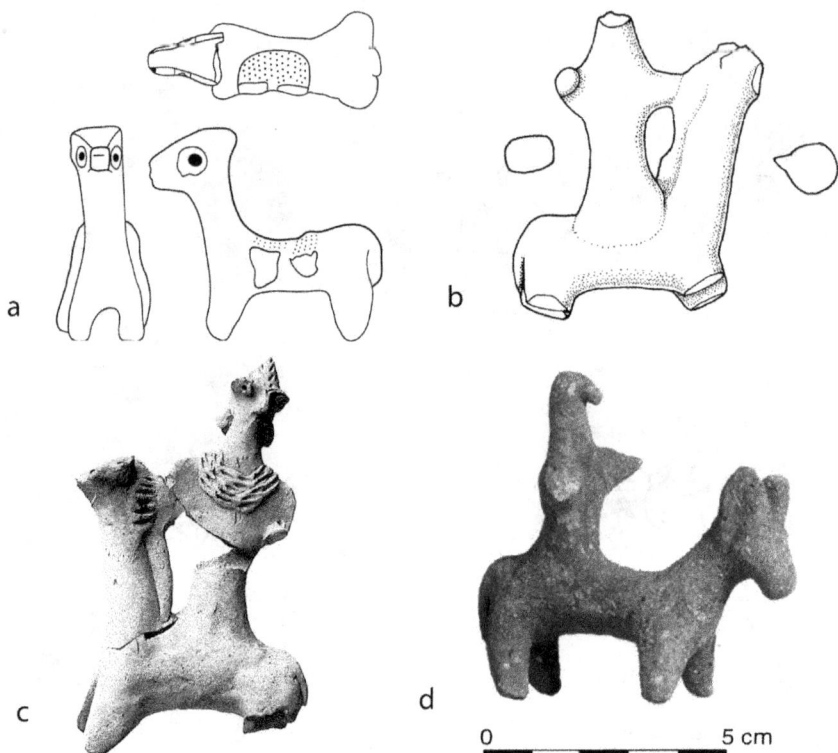

Figure 6.2 Terracotta equid and rider figurines:

a. Terracotta figurine from Tell Selenkahiye. SLK 67–206, H. 6.5 cm, Ur III (redrawn after Liebowitz 1988: pl. 30.3).

b. Terracotta figurine from Tell Halawa, Q5a:14 layer 2c Haus 2–44 Hof A. Reg. no. 85Q66 / Museum für Vor- und Frühgeschichte Saarbrücken, H. 8.8 cm, MB I, c. 2000–1800 BCE (after Meyer & Pruss 1994: fig. 39). Permission of Halawa Expedition.

c. Terracotta figurine from Tell Selenkahiye, Square X23 house. SLK 72.229, Ur III (after van Loon 1975: pl. VI:8).

d. Terracotta figurine from Hirbet ez-Zeraqon, House B1.3. EB III (after Al-Ajlouny et al. 2012: no. 5). Courtesy of Fardous Al-Ajlouny.

sites such as Mari, Abu Salabikh, Nippur and Tell Asmar (see Appendix G for a full list of sites and references).

The figurines tend to treat their subject matter in a cursory manner. Combined with their fragmentary preservation, this means that we are rarely able to determine the equid species with certainty.[5] Those carrying riders do not provide enough clues on this matter, but they do suggest that riding was a well-known and understood concept, and that a variety of styles existed. With these figurines, we most clearly encounter riders sitting side-saddle, along with information about equipment and equid–human interaction.

A small number of plaques made from moulds depict an equid and rider, with one mould surviving (Figure 6.3a; see also Appendix I). The motif is very similar on all the known examples (see Figure 6.3 for selection). The plaques have mainly been dated to the Old Babylonian period, but some may date back to Ur III (Frankfort et al. 1940: 212, fig. 126f⁶). They show a rider seated quite far back on the equid, usually with one hand in front of their body, holding either a rope or a neck strap, and the other behind the body, holding a long object that is probably a whip or goad. Whenever identifiable, the equids on these plaques are horses, as is clear by full tails and short ears, even if other features suggest that

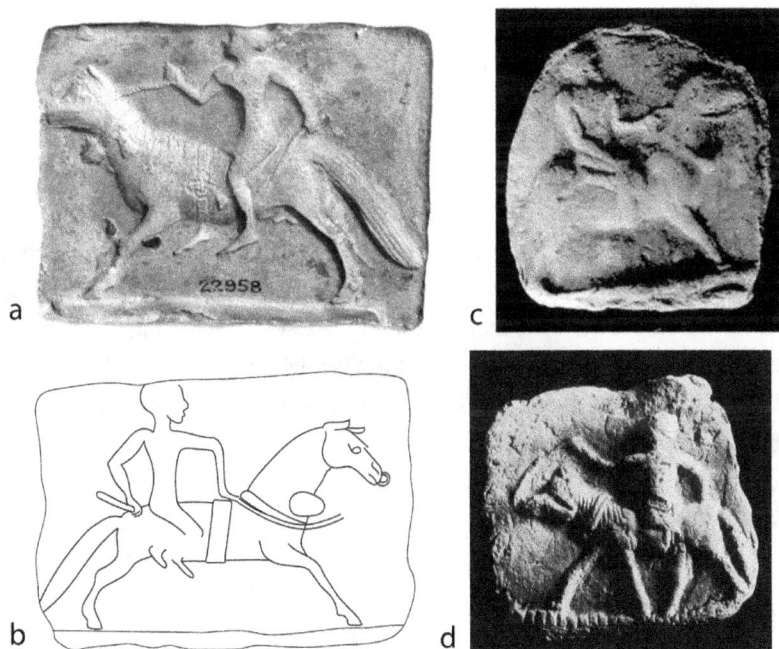

Figure 6.3 Terracotta plaques and mould with equid and rider:

a. Modern impression of terracotta mould. BM 22958, H. 7.3 cm. © The Trustees of the British Museum.
b. Terracotta plaque. Private collection, H. 6 cm (drawn after Moorey 1970: pl. XIIIa).
c. Terracotta plaque from Kish, Area C, Trench C10. Chicago Field Museum 158195, field no. K.1062, 8.7 × 8.5 cm, *c.* 2000–1750 BCE. © The Field Museum, Image No. A88030.
d. Terracotta plaque from Nippur. Fourth expedition, photograph no. 42, Old Babylonian (after Legrain 1930: pl. LII, no. 277). Courtesy of Penn Museum.

the craftsperson was not very familiar with the physique of equids.[7] In a few instances, the equids walk (e.g. Figure 6.3d), but mostly they are at full speed at a canter/gallop, apparently urged on with the use of the whip or goad.

Riding is recorded in cuneiform tablets, but coincides with other activities, especially those associated with messengers and individuals of high social status.[8] I will return to both of these in the sections below, but first I want to examine other ways in which equids are associated with riding. The ancient terms for riding (U_5/*rakābum*) have a broad meaning comparable to modern English – one could also ride a wheeled vehicle or even a boat. It is thus necessary to rely on context to determine the meaning and, unfortunately, this is sometimes ambiguous. There are few examples from the third millennium, and most suffer from difficulties of interpretation (Zarins 2014: 197–8, 204–5, 215). For example, equids from Ebla are qualified as 'to ride' (U_5, e.g. TM.75.G.2032; Archi 1998: 12; see also Conti 1997: 31–2), as are equids associated with the Bau Temple at Girsu in the Early Dynastic III period (Zarins 2014: 215), but these could also refer to wheeled vehicles.

The beginning of the second millennium sees many more references to riding in the texts. Tablets from Mari and Chagar Bazar use the term 'la-gu'. Van Koppen argues that this term designates an equid for riding (2002). In one tablet, we hear of a singer named Karanatum riding a *lagu* equid (P354566; Heimpel 2003: 180), and other Old Babylonian texts from Mari record *lagu* equids and equipment being used with them (P354719; P254333; van Koppen 2002: note 50). A proverb on joint journeys found in Old Babylonian tablets from Nippur and Ur (P231595) reveals some of the equid's discomfort, 'The horse, after he had thrown off his rider, (said): "If my burden is always to be this, I shall become weak"' (as translated in Gordon 1958: 19).[9]

We saw in Chapter 4 that equids transported goods both locally and long distance. They also transported humans, as for example recorded in an Old Babylonian letter from Tell al Rimah:

Speak to Iltani: thus Aqba-hammu. I have read your letter which you sent me. You wrote to me about your sister, saying: "There are no [donkeys] available to me (by which) I may send her to my lord." And you wrote to me also about the journeys to Ramātum. Now, I have sent the donkeys, and on donkeys you shall ride to Ramātum. When you arrive at Ramātum, let her ride and send her back to me. Also, about your provisions of which you wrote to me: I am assembling the silver, donkeys and donkey-drivers who will go to the king(?) and I shall send (them) to you following this letter.

P223904, translated in Dalley et al. 1976: text 66

It is also interesting to note here that women could equally be equid travelling companions. However, there is some vagueness concerning the manner of travel which illustrates some of the difficulties of interpretation mentioned earlier – was the sister meant to ride a donkey or a wheeled vehicle pulled by donkeys? The use of donkeys (in the plural) can mean either that she would change from one donkey to another when one tired (an entirely feasible scenario), or that a wheeled vehicle was used.

Equids providing means of transport are also hinted at in the Kanesh records, with strong indications that all but the very poorest could ride equids: 'There is no money for my expenses, not even a donkey for me to ride!' (P298482; Michel 2004: 193 and n. 33). Here, there is little doubt that the donkey was ridden, and the implication is that donkeys were very widely available as riding animals. Equids in general were thus not exclusively associated with high status, but this was at least partially predicated on species. Another version of transport by equid is represented by a terracotta figurine in the Ashmolean Museum (Museum no. 1913.452; Moorey 2001: pl. II), thought to date to the late third millennium. It depicts an equid with a canopy over its back, and a small anthropomorphic figure inside, sitting on the equid. This could be an abbreviated version of an equid with a wagon (the pierced muzzle would support this idea), but in any case suggests a manner of travelling that may be slow but more comfortable.

Donkeys carried riders from nearly all levels of society and were by far the most common equid. This does not appear to have stigmatized donkey–human relations in any significant manner: even rulers and deities rode donkeys, although it may be that rulers in at least some cases preferred hybrids. Horse–donkey hybrids in particular were closely associated with more elite persons as mounts. Horses were also mounts, but are less often recorded as such, and there is some suggestion (see below) that they were not considered suitable for royalty in the Old Babylonian period at least. There is little evidence of kungas as riding animals, nor do hemiones appear as such. If there was a preference for males or females this is not borne out in the cuneiform evidence, where the gender of the ridden equid is rarely specified. The terracotta figurines with riders also do not tend to render the either male or female genitals, but the plaques sometimes depict stallions (Figure 6.3a).

Battle and hunting

Equids and riders were also associated with the military. There is no indication that any kind of cavalry unit existed, but mounted riders (*râkib imêri*) occur in

relation to military personnel and the movement and provision of troops. We
see this again in letters from Mari, as for example:

> To my lord speak! Your servant Yatar-Addu (says), '4 thousand good troops, the
> generals Hammu-Rabi [and] Dada, [and] the diviner Kakka-Ruqqum, [3] riders
> of donkeys, are those in the lead of those troops. Three days ago (reckoned from)
> the day I sent this tablet of mine to my lord, we set out from Babylon. On the
> fourth day (from today) the troops will be close to Hanat. My lord must take his
> dispositions!'
>
> P354688; as translated in Heimpel 2003: 225–6

The link between rider and army is here unequivocal, with military personnel
leading the contingent (two generals and a diviner, who would have been an
integral part of the army as repeated divinations were standard procedure along
the way). A letter from Tell Leilan contains a similar account of a horse-general
team leading an army mounted (Eidem 1991: 131–4, L87-651). In other Mari
letters, a rider of donkeys dismisses troops (P355080) and riders of donkeys are
captured as hostages (P355123). None of the letters either prove or disprove that
mounted troops actively engaged in battle. Zimri-Lim is also recorded as leading
a battle mounted on an equid (the species is unclear, see Durand 1998: 487;
Guichard 2014: 15 col. ii.4, 43). Riding related to battle would appear to be
limited to generals or other leading figures. Otherwise, the role of equids as
mounts in association with the army seems primarily to be an extension of their
capacity as animals providing (fast) transport.

Contrary to images of equids pulling wheeled vehicles in battle, there are no
images of equids and riders directly engaged in warfare from the Bronze Age.[10]
The closest we have is perhaps the equid and rider on the gold band from Ur
(Figure 6.1c). No battle is depicted, but the rider holds a spear in one hand (and
wears a helmet?). This could be a general leading an army but hunting or even a
simple procession cannot be ruled out. The Akkadian-style scene on the
impression in Figure 6.1a is a contest scene, and the equid and rider trample a
body lying on the ground, just as we see wheeled vehicles do. In Figure 6.1b, the
equid-rider team is also part of a contest scene, and the rider brandishes a
weapon in one hand, held up high and in front. The scene on both of these is set
in the supernatural realm and the actors are deities and other supernatural
creatures, so we cannot directly infer from this that mounted riders engaged in
combat in the human realm. But it does reveal that the concept itself was known,
and such an idea does perhaps not come entirely from the imagination of a
craftsperson.

The texts do not often refer to hunting in any capacity, but a few images of equids with a rider could indicate that they took part in hunting.[11] One is an Akkadian-style seal (Frankfort 1939b: 118, 140, pl. XXIVa), where various wild animals are being hunted with bow and arrow, as well as tied up for transport home. The equid and rider are part of this scene, which takes place in a mountainous landscape, but there is no reason to suspect that it is outside the human realm. Sherds from an incised-decorated ceramic vessel found at Tell Munbaqa and dated to the late third millennium may also depict part of a hunting scene, although no prey is present (Machule et al. 1986: 95, 97, fig. 16.1). Two equids with their riders are shown (partially preserved); they are accompanied by a dog and a bird – animals which elsewhere are part of the multi-species ensemble of battle (Tsouparopoulou & Recht 2021).

6.2 Mounted messengers

Equids are fast, with a high level of endurance, which makes them excellent companions for the quick delivery of messages. Mounted messengers are found in the textual material, with examples in particular coming from the Old Babylonian period, in the archives of Mari and Chagar Bazar, along with references to riding in the Kanesh records. In the Old Assyrian letters recording the trade between Kanesh and Assur (see Chapter 4), beside the normal donkey caravans (*ellatum*), there were 'express' transports (*bātiqum*) (Dercksen 2004: 164–80, 255; Barjamovic 2011: 18). The letters make it clear that messages could be sent ahead of the caravans, for example as what is called 'notifying messages', where the merchant in Assur advises their collaborator in Kanesh (usually a family member) of the incoming arrival of certain goods (Veenhof & Eidem 2008: 74, 88). In other cases, warnings were sent of dangers along the road. Naturally, this means that a kind of transport faster than the usual caravans existed. These could consist of human 'runners', one option suggested by Barjamovic, but they could also be riders on equids, possibly even using a relay system to further improve speed (Barjamovic 2011: 18, n. 91).

Tablets from Mari clearly demonstrate donkeys and riders carrying messages:

> If messengers of the Kurdaite Hammu-Rabi, riders of donkeys (*râkib imêri*), have (already) arrived in Qaṭṭunan, the person bringing my tablet must move on to Ibal-Pi-El in Kurda together with the tablet that he carries.
>
> Heimpel 2003: 517, modified

and

> To [my] lord speak! [Your servant] Buqaqum (says), 'The district [is well]. Warad-[ ], Addu-Ešuh, Buratum, Ibalum, Ṣilli-Mamma, Iddin-Halab, [6] riders (*rakbu*) [of] my lord, (and) Lipit-Eštar (and) Mar-Erṣetim, 2 Babylonian riders (*rakbu*), moved on to my lord. They are carrying a message from Ibal-Pi-El'.
>
> P355041; as translated in Heimpel 2003: 385, modified

The Akkadian for (mounted) messenger is *rakbum*, and this in particular is found in Old Babylonian records. Lafont distinguishes between *rakbum* and the *râkib imêri* (lit. 'rider of donkeys') that we have already met, which actually refers to a specific group of dignitaries (Lafont 1997: 317; cf. Charpin et al. 1988: 72, n. h), and we have seen that they could serve in a number of capacities, including as army generals. As the two letters here demonstrate, they could both carry messages, although the *rakbum* were more specialised messengers. At least some of the mounted messengers were employed by palaces, as demonstrated in a document from Tell Harmal/Shaduppum (Lafont 1997: 328–9), which records a problem with messengers deserting by leaving for their home village but not returning back to service.

Mounted messengers and travellers associated with official institutions may not have owned the equid(s) they were riding. In Amarna letter *EA* 161, Aziru, the ruler of Amurru, writes to the king of Egypt concerning a man that he was hosting. Aziru remarks that the man was supplied with horses and donkeys for his journey (Rainey 2014: 798–9). Note again the plural, and the mixing of horses and donkeys, which suggests both that some were in reserve, and perhaps that some were used for carrying personal items.

Mounted messengers were also common in the Late Bronze Age, and in this period we have textual evidence that horses also engaged in this activity. For example, the ruler of Byblos complains to the king of Egypt in *EA* 88 that 'the envoy of the king of ʿAkkô was honored more than [my] ambassa[dor] because they supplied him with a horse, [but] they [too]k two horses [of m]y [man]. May he not come forth [empty hand]ed' (lines 45–51, as translated in Rainey 2014: 513). The line with the two horses can be interpreted in several ways (cf. Moran 1992: 160–2), but it is nevertheless clear that two horses are in some way associated with a messenger. This indicates that it would not have been unusual for a reserve equid to travel with messengers, implying both an acknowledgement of the limits of animal endurance (and a pushing of that limit), and an emphasis on speed. The quick delivery of messages would not only be convenient but also highly advantageous during times of crisis.

The political importance and extensive use of mounted messengers is further illustrated by a letter from the king of Hatti to the ruler of Ugarit (Louvre AO 21091), where rules are outlined concerning messengers: Hittite messengers may not take Egyptian horses, and Egyptian messengers may not take Hittite horses. The ruler of Ugarit, as a vassal to the Hittites, is expected to enforce this rule, since the messengers have to pass through his territory. This is supported by the generally hostile attitude to messengers and the dangers of their travels, with numerous accounts of attacks, messengers dying on the road, and commands to seize messengers (Meier 1988: 75–9). It is thus evident from the textual material that mounted messengers played an important role, and although this is not often expressed until the beginning of the second millennium, it is most likely that riding was also used for this purpose in the third millennium. The Sumerian equivalent of *rakbum* is RA$_2$.GABA, which occurs frequently in Ur III records, with a few examples from earlier periods (see ePSD2, 'ragaba'). However, its meaning and the type of mount are not entirely clear (Oates 2003: 117; Sallaberger 2004: 52 and n. 14; Michalowski 2006: 53). Equids are also sometimes associated with couriers (LU$_2$.KAS$_4$; Zarins 2014: 204).

The evidence for messengers so far has all relied on ancient texts. But can we also detect mounted messengers in the iconography? At first glance, the riders on the plaques discussed above appear to be naked or nearly naked (Moorey 1970: 43), but closer examination reveals that they do wear a short kilt, sometimes checkered and/or with a belt. A dagger sheath from Byblos (Figure 6.4) depicting a rider on a donkey probably belongs in the same category as those on the plaques. In this example, a band around the neck suggests that a top was also worn (although a necklace is also possible). The feet and lower legs are bare. Where the head is preserved, we can see that these riders wear a cap-like headdress and are clean-shaven. The consistency in this motif suggests that they depict a specific, specialized equid–rider combination. The speed present in many of them, the lack of a load for transport, and the lack of other figures that could indicate racing, support the idea that these images show equids and messengers. However, this identification must remain conjectural without further context – as a possible counterargument, Lafont's observations on the Byblos sheath may be noted. The sheath is made of gold, itself an expensive material, with an associated gold dagger, and Lafont suggests that the rider is a 'prince' (Lafont 2000: 214–15). We do not know who this rider is, but it is perhaps worth considering that the two scenarios need not be absolutely exclusive. The speed of the road and the owning of equids may have been considered an appropriate motif for persons of high status, whether or not they themselves were actually involved in delivering

Figure 6.4 Gold dagger sheath from Byblos, Temple of the Obelisk. Beirut Museum, 20th–19th centuries BCE (drawn after Amiet 1980: fig. 72).

messages. Certainly, such persons were associated with riding more broadly, as we shall see in the next section.

6.3　Ceremonial and elite riding

When riding as transport is mentioned in the texts, they most frequently concern individuals of high social status, including high officials, local lords or chiefs, rulers and even deities. The iconographic material supports the notion that depictions of riding were used in the ideology of high-status individuals. The official Abbakala, who we met previously, was a scribe in Drehem, and thought the equid and rider motif was suitable for his seal even in the Ur III period. The terracotta figurines from this period (some possibly earlier) with a rider in the side saddle position may also depict high status persons or even deities, as suggested by Magen (2001). These figurines are rare, but one such from Tell Selenkahiye has preserved details of the rider's outfit, which includes a neckband/necklace, piercings for earrings, and an unusual, pointy headdress (Figure 6.2c). A seal impression from Kanesh depicts the same position, also with an elaborately dressed rider, and as part of a religio-mythical scene (Özgüç 1965: pl. XXVI, no. 77). The side saddle position is a rather precarious one, and one not comfortable for high speed, which supports the idea that it was primarily used for activities that focussed on the display of equid and rider. The figurines do not allow for species identification beyond equid, but the equid on the Kanesh seal appears to be a donkey, or possibly a mule.

In fact, in the Kanesh records, beside the donkey being referred to as a common riding animal, an equid called a *perdum* is mentioned. Michel (2004) has convincingly argued that this is a hybrid equid, probably a mule or hinny. That this was the appropriate animal on which to arrive at an important event is recorded in a letter from a son to his father:

Give me that *perdum*. I have to go to *sikkatum*. I am your son, should I go on foot? Give it to me so that I can ride to *sikkatum* and so (uphold) your reputation ...Now the prince is offering me no less than two offices, that of *alahhinnum* and that of *šinahilum*, and I have promised the ruler a gift, a big one.

Michel 2004: 192; cf. Veenhof 1989: 518

Here, the manner of transport was obviously important for the public appearance of an ambitious young up-and-coming official. A comparable sentiment is expressed in an oft-quoted Old Babylonian tablet advising Zimri-Lim of Mari on the most appropriate means of transport for a king:

[Verily] you are the king of the Haneans, [but] secondly you are the king of the Akkadians! [My lord] should not ride a horse (ANŠE.KUR.RA). Let my [lord] ride in a chariot (*nubālum*) or on a mule (*kūdanum*) and he will thereby honor his royal head!

P339013; Malamat 1987: 33, modified

Evidently, the governor providing this advice did not consider horses fit for a king, which is perhaps an important clue in understanding why it took so long for horses to become prominent. The second part of the text has been translated as either meaning that the king should ride in a chariot or ride on a mule (the word translated as mule is *kūdanum*), or that the king should ride in a chariot drawn by mules (Way 2011: 82–5). It is thus unclear whether the governor thought riding itself was inappropriate, or if it was only riding on horses that was so, but certainly an association with a wheeled vehicle and/or *kūdānum* equids was acceptable.

Turning to the Late Bronze Age, several texts from Ugarit enumerate deities and lords/ladies riding equids. One has the goddess 'Aṭiratu order her servant Qudšu-Wa-'Amruru to tack up her donkey in order for her to travel to her husband 'Ilu:

And Lady 'Aṭiratu of the Sea responds:
Listen, O Qudšu-Wa-'Amruru,
O fisherman of Lady 'Aṭiratu of the Sea:
Tack up the donkey,
strap up the stallion,
put on the reins of silver,
the loops of yellow (gold),
prepare the reins of my jenny.
Qudšu-Wa-'Amruru listens:
He straps up the donkey,

straps up the stallion,
puts on the reins of silver,
the loops of yellow (gold),
prepares the reins of her jenny.
Qudšu-Wa-'Amruru grasps (her),
he puts 'Aṯiratu on the back of the donkey,
on the most beautiful part of the back of the stallion.
Qudšu begins like a torch,
'Amruru is like a star in front,
behind (follows) Adolescent 'Anatu.

translation after Way 2011: 50–1, modified

Notably, the mount here is still a donkey, and is even suitable for a goddess to ride. The tack used is more elaborate than what we see in other evidence, and made of expensive materials, as might be expected for a deity. What is also interesting here is the relationship between the goddess, her servant and the donkey(s). This passage makes it obvious that the servant would be responsible for the daily care of the animals, and very likely also responsible for training them. This, the description of the goddess needing help to mount, and the fact that others both lead and follow suggest that 'Aṯiratu was by no means a skilled equestrian. In another text from Ugarit with a very similar composition, the king or nobleman Dānī'ilu orders his daughter Pūġátu to tack up his donkey to prepare for a journey, again with equipment of fine materials (Way 2011: 52–3). There is in these a fascinating shift in gender roles, with the implication that women could also be responsible for the care of equids and could at the very least have the skill and knowledge to tack up.

6.4 Riding styles and equipment

Two main styles of riding can be detected in the iconographic evidence: astride and side-saddle. When the rider sits astride, they are nearly always shown in the 'donkey seat', which is quite far to the rear on the back of the equid (Moorey 1970: 42–3; Clutton-Brock 1992: 66). This position is somewhat suitable for donkeys, who have quite narrow shoulders and low withers compared to horses, leaving little support for a rider, and the feeling of falling forwards. The position is neatly rendered on a figurine from Hirbet ez-Zeraqon (Figure 6.2d) and is also quite clear on the terracotta plaques discussed above. However, this placement is not very suitable for riding on horses: it is the least stable part of the back, making it much harder to stay in place, and horses may react strongly to a human sitting on this weaker and often 'ticklish' part of the body. It is thus odd that the plaques, where horses can be clearly identified, depict the donkey seat. Along with our other combined evidence, it suggests that donkeys were the first riding equids in the ancient Near East, and that technologies and practices were directly adapted from experience with those equids.

The position far back on the back of the equid is in fact even hinted at in the texts. In the text from Ugarit with the goddess 'Aṯiratu riding a donkey, she is described as placed on a specific part of the back of the donkey – the translation quoted here has 'beautiful', but other scholars have used 'the croup' (Pardee 2000: 230), 'the easiest part of the back of the donkey' (Gibson 1978: 59), 'most comfortable' (Moor 1987: 52), or the 'blanket(-saddle) of the back' (Watson 2011: 158). It is known that the word used (with the root *ysm*) is a superlative, but not its exact meaning (Way 2011: 51, n. 125). Regardless, the placement on the back is emphasised, and it would make sense that what is here referred to is the 'donkey seat'.

The riders sitting astride have their legs slightly bent, awkwardly straight, or entirely bent.[12] The first is how legs would naturally hang when seated on an equid without the use of a saddle and stirrups, although it does require substantial thigh strength and skill to maintain the position in movement, and more so the higher the speed and level of side movement. The second is extremely awkward, and the most likely explanation is that the craftsperson had limited personal observation of a rider on an equid.[13] Bent knees are often combined with a girth or strap tied around the entire torso of the equid, with the knees tucked in under it. This must represent an attempt to stay seated and more comfortable on the back of the equid, perhaps especially for longer distances.

There are very few unambiguous examples of a rider sitting astride an equid in the position used by most equestrians today, placed directly behind the withers. This may be partly due to the fact that we have very few depictions of ridden equids from the Late Bronze Age, when we might expect horses to be more widespread and a new style of riding to develop. A few instances from the Late Bronze Age depict the rider rather on the middle of the back of the equid, certainly much closer to the withers (Calvet 2000: fig. 2), and with legs in a the more 'natural' slightly bent version.[14]

Side-saddle riders are mostly in the form of terracotta figurines (Figure 6.2a–c), along with a seal impression from Kanesh (Özgüç 1965: pl. XXVI, no. 77). Many of the terracotta figurines come from Tell Selenkahiye in modern Syria, but unfortunately are very fragmented, so many details are lost. As far as can be reconstructed, some riders are positioned roughly in the centre of the equid's back, while others cling to the neck and mane of the equid. As noted above, the side position is not suitable for long distances or travelling particularly fast due to the uneven balance that it entails (although a special saddle or 'stool' may make it a more comfortable ride). It also makes communication with the equid rather challenging, and riders side-saddle may have been accompanied by a person on foot.

Riding evidently required minimal equipment, but with slight variations depending on the task performed. When the riders sit astride, they often appear to use no aids at all, simply sitting bareback on the equid. This may indeed have been common practice, but some of the images may also have been so summarily rendered as to not provide such details. In many other examples, we can note the use of a whip or goad, and of a girth or strap around the torso of the equid, which the rider could use for support and to tuck their knees under for stability. The whip or goad could aid both in encouraging speed and in steering by tapping on the side of the equid. Whips (usan$_3$) made of wood and associated with equids are mentioned in Late Bronze Age texts from Emar and Ugarit (Arnaud 1985: 105–9; Bordreuil & Pardee 1989: 281); they are also found in Ugaritic texts, along with a range of other horse-related tack (Watson 2011). A saddle – or rather a kind of chair – is depicted in the seal impression from Kanesh. It might have consisted of a wooden frame, and a (wooden) 'saddle stool' (^{giš}gu-za) is included in an Old Babylonian long list of types of seats from Nippur that also includes a 'chariot seat' and a 'donkey saddle' (P229277). The Kanesh letters also refer to a backrest added to a seat, suggested by Dercksen as possibly being a side-saddle (2004: 274). A few examples of an object lying on the croup of equid terracotta figurines could be either a kind of saddle or a pack for transport (Figure 4.1h-l; see also Reade 1973: 172, pl. LXVIIIg). Stirrups were not yet in use, increasing the level of skill needed for riders to stay seated on the equid, especially at higher speeds.

A strap could also be tied around the neck of the equid, sometimes with a bell or knot at the front, and not dissimilar to those used as a chariot harness element. A rider on a bronze cup holds on to this neckstrap for balance (Muscarella 1981: 115–19, no. 67); on the sheath from Byblos, the rider instead holds on to the mane of the equid (Figure 6.4). Many other riders hold one hand in the same forward position, grabbing either the mane or a neckstrap; the same goes for riders in the side saddle position. Bridles were very rarely used by riders, but on some of the plaques and the seal impression from Kanesh, we see the use of the nose or lip ring with a single rope (e.g. Figure 6.3b, d). As with the wheeled vehicles, this rope is unlikely to have been a particularly efficient means of communication. The few examples of bridles come from terracotta figurines (e.g. from Tell Halawa, Meyer & Pruss 1994: 127, no. 119, fig. 38, pl. 17; from Tell Brak, Oates et al. 2001: 594, no. 61; from Habuba Kabira, Strommenger 2017: 91–2, plates 179.12, 182.5), and seem to consist of a simple noseband and headstall, probably without the use of a bit; this simple arrangement would be sufficient for steering and efficient communication between equid and rider. Most likely, the bridle and the use of two reins became common in the Late Bronze Age, when this arrangement was also more common with wheeled vehicles – the story of Lady ʾAṯiratu's tacking up refers to 'reins of silver' (probably beads strung) supports this; the other tack items in this are unfortunately not understood in enough detail to know exactly what elements they refer to.

Without the use of a bridle and two reins, communication between equid and rider may have occurred through the whip, bodily pressure and balance points of the rider, and verbal cues – or a combination thereof. For travel in groups, donkeys especially would simply follow in file, making bridles unnecessary. Individuals on foot accompanying an equid and rider could also help direct and step in in cases where an equid may feel uncomfortable or panic. Travelling at higher speeds, as might be expected of messengers, would require more extensive training of both equid and rider, but beyond a good level of endurance, would not be the most complex task carried out. On the other hand, any engagement in activities such as battle or hunting would demand rigorous training and a strong equid–human relationship (more about this in Chapter 7). In other words, the types of riding taking place during the third and second millennia mostly required medium-level skill sets from both equid and rider, with the texts suggesting a specialized system (i.e. the riders we meet do not appear to be the ones actually training with the equids in the first instance, nor are they their breeders or caretakers other than possibly when on the road). The equids mostly performed fairly simple but at times extremely strenuous tasks as riding animals. The styles and equipment developed were suitable for these tasks.

Management of Equids, or, How to Keep a Human

7.1 Fed, pastured, stabled

Fodder and pasture

Equids are grazers and primarily feed on pasture when on their own. When their freedom of movement has been limited due to interactions with humans, they may not be able or allowed to find enough pasture by themselves. Humans therefore need to provide fodder, in the form of forage and/or grain-based feed. Many of the textual records that mention equids are concerned with the provision of fodder for them, and there are probably more instances of this than anything else. In fact, some of the earliest documentation (from Early Dynastic III) relates to fodder allocated to equids. The nature of many of these records means that they do not directly reveal the information we might be looking for, so much has to be derived indirectly.

References to pasture and forage as a feeding strategy for equids are sparse. The majority come from records of their human handlers. Equid herders (anše sipa) occur regularly in third-millennium texts. They are sometimes associated with certain place names (for example, noted as 'stationed at', gub-ba-am$_3$), which probably means outlying towns and villages in the vicinity of which the equids may be pastured under the supervision of the equid herder. An Old Babylonian letter from Mari mentions difficulties with where to pasture cattle and donkeys in relation to the Khabur river (Heimpel 2003: Text 27 112), suggesting that pasture was a typical way for these groups of animals to be fed. Another letter refers to horses and donkeys belonging to an official called Sammetar grazing on land of a farmer (ARMT XXIV 5, van Koppen 2001: 494-5). Pasture is also implied in a Middle Assyrian tablet from Tell Chuera, where the horses of a certain individual 'should stay in Harbe and eat' (Kühne 1995: 213–14, 92.G.143). This probably means that pasture was better or more readily available, and that it would therefore be best to keep the horses in the city for the time being. Another tablet from the same series mentions visitors and their horses, with an instruction to provide the horses with barley and straw (Kühne 1995: 214, 92.G.155).

The vast majority of references to the provision of fodder for equids relates to grain-based feed. Nearly all of this is in the form of barley, although wheat, flour, vetch and emmer are also mentioned (Wiseman 1953: no. 240, 245, 250; Archi 1998: 9). Based on modern practices and knowledge of equids, this kind of feed should only be a supplement, especially for high-performance equids – for the diet of a normal donkey, The Donkey Sanctuary recommends straw and limited grazing, while grain-based supplements are only for very special circumstances (Evans & Crane 2018: 238–54, 262). The fact that such feed was used at all says much about equid–human relations, the integration of equids in a systematic way and the spatial limitations placed on them. It implies that equids were kept firmly within human-dominated spaces and that their freedom of movement was strictly managed. It also implies an elaborate administrative, managerial and specialised system in which equids as workers may in some sense be compared to human workers, receiving their daily rations of barley. In another sense, a whole set of procedures would have been in place to ensure the management and care of equids (as was the case for other animals, even if all procedures for each type of animal would not be the same).

Whether the physical space where equids were kept was an indoor/semi-indoor stable, a paddock or even a field, specialised personnel would be required at many levels (see also discussion below). The provision of barley is just one of these levels, but it belies many of the others, and demonstrates that equids were a well-known and integral part of the social and economic structures of the ancient Near East. The daily ration depends on a variety of factors, including species, size, age, required performance, state of health and access to other types of feed. A cautious estimated expectation for horses would be two to five litres of barley a day for a low- to high-performing equid. A lower amount of one litre could perhaps also be expected for rest periods or very young animals not yet working. Higher than five litres runs the risk of causing colic, a common affliction among modern equids, often related to feeding practices. Donkeys require less feed than horses and are able to live on diets of much lower nutritional value. Hybrids would likely require an amount in between these two, depending on activity levels.

Tablets might list an amount of fodder, a number of equids or a specified time frame (e.g. 'for the month of . . .'), but there are few instances of all these elements listed together, so it is difficult to establish exactly how much any individual equid might have been given on a daily basis. However, the few examples where a daily ration for one equid is either noted or can be deduced, as has been done by Zarins (2014: 229, Table 23), roughly correspond to the estimate. Thus, for the Early Dynastic III period, he identifies 1.5 to 4.5 daily litres of barley for kungas, and in the later third millennium, 2 to 5 litres for kungas and 5 to 6 litres for horses. There is little evidence for the amount fed to donkeys in the third millennium. One Ur III tablet from Girsu records a daily 8 litres of barley for a team of donkeys (BIR$_3$ ANŠE.LIBIR; P110508). If we assume the team consisted of four donkeys, they would thus receive 2 litres each per day (the number in the team is not specified, and could also be two, but in this period, four seems more likely).[1]

For the Old Babylonian period, adult donkeys at Chagar Bazar were fed 2 litres of barley a day, donkey foals were given 1 litre a day, hybrids 5 to 7.5, and horses are in one tablet given the large amount of 10 litres of barley a day (Zarins 2014: 229, Table 23). If the texts from Chagar Bazar are representative, equids belonging to the king received larger rations than those belonging to other individuals (van Koppen 2002: 24). As we saw in Chapter 4, it was also necessary to bring extra fodder for donkeys on their long caravan journeys from Assur to Kanesh, and to buy further provisions along the road. Here, barley again seems more common, but wagon loads of straw are also recorded.

Tablets from Late Bronze Age Ugarit list barley for horses and donkeys owned by the king, and horses owned by the queen, deities and individuals associated with 'houses' (Malbran-Labat & Roche 2008). The barley is measured in the unit GUR, which is thought to equal 50 litres (Malbran-Labat & Roche 2008: 251). The tablet RS 94.2356 thus lists

in the month of *rašu yêni*
194 GUR [9,700 litres] of barley for the horses of the king
12 GUR [600 litres] of barley for the horses of the queen
15 GUR [750 litres] of barley for the donkeys

If we assume that the horses were fed about 2 to 5 litres of barley a day, the king may have had about 65 to 160 horses, and the queen 4 to 10 horses; if their donkeys were fed about 1.5 to 3 litres of barley a day, this document would represent about 8 to 16 donkeys.

Fodder (and water) could also be deliberately withheld from equids. The Kikkuli text (see below) has a strict feeding regime with specified amounts of wheat, barley and hay for each meal (Kammenhuber 1961). Amounts vary, but one day (the first in Kammenhuber's reconstruction) the instruction is to feed them one handful of wheat, barley and hay, respectively, in the morning, two handfuls each of barley and wheat, and three of hay in the evening, and one handful of barley, one of wheat and four of hay at a later time. The ingredients were to be mixed. Sometimes a muzzle should be applied after the meal to prevent further consumption, and at other times, water or food is withheld entirely. The full programme suggested by Kikkuli seems very strict, but there is also an awareness of the needs of the horses as a result of strenuous activity. They are thus also given 'malt water' and salt water for replenishment – today's equivalent would be mash and electrolytes, commonly fed to horses after having performed in a demanding competition.

Stables

Very few stables have been recognized archaeologically in the Near East. Schaeffer identified a southeastern part of the tell at Ugarit as the royal stables, complete with troughs and an arena for 'dressage' and chariots (Schaeffer 1938: 317, pl. XXXV; 1954: 21–2). However, there is nothing from the published contexts to support this identification. Outside the main area discussed here, structures possibly representing stables have been recorded at Beycesultan in Anatolia and Amarna in Egypt (Pendlebury 1951: 132–3; Lloyd 1972). At Beycesultan, in western Anatolia, Lloyd reports a Late Bronze Age stable on the eastern summit of the tell (1972: 15–17, plates IXb, Xa). The evidence includes several tethering poles set into a wall, and a thick decayed layer of straw below which equid hoof prints could still be seen in the clay.

Part of the challenge in identifying stables archaeologically is that we are not entirely certain what they looked like in the third and second millennium. In fact, we should perhaps not rely too much on modern concepts of stables that typically consist of separate, easily detectable stalls, mangers and troughs, sometimes with associated facilities such as arenas, paddocks, pastures and so on. Departing from this concept, we can note that we do have fairly good evidence of spaces specifically for equids and equids present in the urban landscape. For example, the way stations or caravanserais at Tell Brak and Tell Beydar (Oates 2003) were resting places for equids and their fellow travellers. While the Tell Beydar way station has not been found archaeologically, the Tell Brak Area FS is a good candidate, with its remains of complete donkey skeletons, herbivore dung and facilities such as a trough, well and possibly tethering place (Oates & Oates 2001).

The 'inns' of the routes between Assur and Kanesh taken by the donkey caravans (see Chapter 4) also acted as interim resting places for both donkeys and humans. 'Houses' of equids are mentioned in the written records already in the Early Dynastic III period (e_2 anše, e.g. P010432; Biggs 1974: 96, no. 503), with further examples later in the third millennium (e.g. P431928, P129414), and continuing into the second millennium (e.g. P254251, P282850; Wiseman 1968: 182–3). Equids are listed as present in the stables of high officials at Mari in the Old Babylonian period, including that of a man named Asqudum (van Koppen 2002: 20). At Ugarit, stables with horses and storage of chariots may have been part of a unit of buildings related to equids (*trbṣ*, Loretz 2011: 104–7, 159). These houses may have been placed on the outskirts of the city, as implied by a text reporting an inspection of equids taking place at the 'House at the side of the city' (e$_2$-zag-uru-ka-ka, P220887, Zarins 2014: 264).

Equids also shared living spaces with humans more directly. At Mari, complete donkey skeletons were found within an inhabited space of the third millennium – not as deliberate depositions, but perhaps as succumbing to some kind of accident or natural disaster (Margueron 2004: 97, 101, pl. 24). An equid skeleton associated with sling missiles was found within the settled space at Tell Brak (HS3, Akkadian level 5, Matthews 2003: 197-8). Both of these suggest that equids were common within urban areas, and may even have physically been part of households. This is further supported by a Middle Assyrian collection of 'laws' that mentions the possibility of a donkey stabled in a man's house (Pritchard 1969: 187, no. 4).

The lived spaces of equids depended on their social status and function in relation to humans. For example, those working as pack animals naturally spent much time on the road, and those working in agriculture and local transport may have spent much time in paddocks or even pasture. Highly skilled equids or those in training may instead have spent more time in stalls – Kikkuli's horses certainly spent most of their time as such, although they are also occasionally turned out (Kammenhuber 1961). All these measures represent restrictions by one species on another. Humans dictated to varying degrees spaces where equids could stay, when, where and what to eat and drink, when to breed, and which companions to share their lives with. Push-backs against some of these restrictions may be detected in the form of pathologies suggesting crib-biting, which is a reaction to a confined space, representing boredom or stress (Wickens & Heleski 2010; Navas González et al. 2016: 81). Conversely, the need for muzzles is a response to equids eating when and what they please.

7.2 Ownership and personnel

Evidence of ownership of equids comes almost entirely from written records, but iconography provides supplementary information, and information about other personnel. Because the majority of the written records is from royal or official archives, we frequently hear of rulers and high officials owning or being in charge of equids. In palatial cities, the ruler would have owned equids (as is nicely exemplified at Ebla, see e.g. Archi et al. 1988: 266). For example, fodder ration lists include barley for the equids of the royalty of Tell Beydar (Ismail et al. 1996: 135), Abu Salabikh (P010423, Biggs 1974: 96, no. 494), Alalakh (Wiseman 1953: no. 240), Tell al Rimah (P224084, Dalley et al. 1976: text 314), Nuzi (Maidman 2010: 24–5, no. 3) and Ugarit (Pardee 2000), to mention just a few. The seals of the high official Abbakala from Drehem (Ur III) and Isharbeli from Tell Mozan (Akkadian) (Figures. 6.1d, 9.2a) illustrate how equids were part of the ideology and self-identity of high-status individuals. Similarly in the Amarna letters, the standard opening greeting includes enquiring after the king's horses and chariots in such a manner that makes it clear that they were an essential part of the household, and indeed of the king's identity as ruler.

Equids were also part of the household of deities and their temples. The Early Dynastic III Temple of Bau at Girsu owned equids, overseen by Baranamtarra (discussed further below). The equids of palaces and temples were typically in the charge of an 'overseer', a high official – Abbakala and Isharbeli may have had such duties. In these cases, it is sometimes difficult to disentangle who exactly owned the equids, and how actively engaged the overseer was in the daily routine related to the equids. An example from Mari may illustrate the matter: equids were kept in the stable of a diviner named Asqudum, but were among the assets of an official named Bunuma-Addu (Charpin 1985; van Koppen 2002: 20); these equids were for pulling wheeled vehicles. Another example comes from the so-called House of Urtenu at Ugarit, from whose archive we can glean overseeing of equids, including 'beautiful' horses of the king and royal household, negotiating chariot prices, and managing barley rations for equids (Malbran-Labat & Roche 2008: 254, 272). Evidently, equids formed part of the complex economic and social relations between rulers, high officials, administrators, merchants and other 'entrepreneurs' of the time.

The high price of equids, especially hybrids, and later horses, along with the specialist requirements associated with training for certain types of activities, made the ownership of equids prohibitive for large parts of the lower levels of society. The exception was the donkey, especially when helping with activities requiring more limited training, such as the carrying of goods or ploughing. There is good and fairly continuous evidence through the third and second millennia that donkeys could belong to 'workers'. A tablet from Girsu reads 'If to a šub-lugal worker a fine ass is born...' (Zarins 2014: 268, no. 20). The implication is that not only could a worker have a donkey, but that they could also breed donkeys. The Old Assyrian Kanesh letters show that the private merchants frequently owned donkeys, and suggest that only the very poorest did not have a donkey to ride (Michel 2004: 193), although this could refer to not being able to hire a donkey to ride, not necessarily to owning one. The donkey in this (hypothetical) scenario could be owned by a free man, a person neither at the bottom nor at the top of the social ladder, and is thus another example of equids associated with non-elite persons. These documents also testify to the much more local and lower-level interaction between equids and humans, and the importance of donkeys in local transport, as discussed at length by Goulder (2020, and see Chapter 4).

Looking beyond (elite) owners and administrators, who in fact may have had little physical contact with the animals, equids also encountered a great many other types of humans, with different social, economic and religious statuses, and with varying degrees of intensity. Several *chaînes opératoires* could be reconstructed based on overseers, farmers, herders, leatherworkers, cartwrights and chariotmakers, trainers, hunters and army personnel.[2] The humans that equids would have interacted with on a regular and more intense basis probably included herders, handlers and grooms, farmers, trainers, drivers/charioteers and perhaps riders. Some of these roles would have overlapped. In their first years of life and when on pasture, equids probably mostly encountered herders and handlers. The third-millennium archives often mention an equid 'herder' (sipa anše) or workers and ploughers associated with equids (e.g. at Early Dynastic III Tell Beydar, see Ismail et al. 1996: 145, 150, 157; also Zarins 2014: 200), the donkeys of the caravans between Assur and Kanesh were escorted by handlers (Larsen 2015: 186), and a list of workers from Kassite Nippur includes 'horse shepherds/carers' (*rē'i sīsî*) (Tenney 2011: 232).[3]

Grooms appear in an Old Babylonian tablet from Chagar Bazar (kar-tab-bi, Gadd 1940: 51), and in a pejorative manner in the Amarna letters in 'groom of your horses' (e.g. *EA* 299, 300), a phrase used to express submission. In the letter from Chagar Bazar, equids are in the charge of a trainer, and this may belie their daily work as caretakers of the everyday needs of the equids of where they were employed. They were most likely the individuals who spent more time in the presence of equids than anyone else, yet we know very little of their activities. If it were not for the text of Kikkuli, we would be in the same situation for the trainers. However, even without the text of Kikkuli, we can infer that the 'machine' of warfare (especially in the later part of the second millennium) and the wheeled vehicles of rulers would have required skilled human and equine experts.

Kikkuli and other trainers must have been employed by palaces and other institutions able to sponsor chariotry. Other military personnel that interacted with equids included generals, soldiers and of course charioteers (*rākib narkabti*). Charioteers or drivers need not have been part of the army, but the *maryannu* of the later second millennium were closely associated with (war) chariots, and appear to have been specialists in chariot warfare (see Chapter 5). If indeed professional charioteers, they may have at least partly trained their own horses, although the horses and chariots appear to have been supplied by the palace (von Dassow 2008: 300–14).

Women and deities

Equids did not exclusively appear in the domain of men. Women could own and gift equids and participate in their management and breeding programmes. Women could be transported by equids either riding or in a wheeled vehicle (e.g. P223904, P271037, Dalley et al. 1976: text no. 66; Moran 1992: 21–2, *EA* 11), work with equids, and equids were buried with both women and men (see Chapter 8). Equids were also associated with both female and male deities.

Through the third and second millennia, a few women stand out as having been particularly actively engaged with equids. For example, from Early Dynastic III Girsu, we have tablets referring to some of the activities of Baranamtarra, the spouse of Lugalanda, the governor of Lagash in the early twenty-fourth century. Baranamtarra was very engaged in temple management (in particular the temple of Bau) and an administrator of several estates (Stol 2016: 463). Hundreds of tablets record her transactions, and at least several dozen of these concern equids and equid 'herders' (anše sipa; e.g. P020413, P221702, P221449), with one noting 113 equids in the charge of Baranamtarra (P020171). Hybrids (anše kunga$_2$) and donkeys (anše šulgi) are mentioned most commonly, but hemiones also occur (anše edin-na, e.g. P020171). The equids are associated with ploughing (designated either as 'apin' or 'bir$_3$', e.g. P247596, P020103). Some would also have pulled wheeled vehicles, probably wagons (anše mar are recorded in P220892 and P220884).

Since Baranamtarra was a top-level manager, she is unlikely to have been directly involved in the rearing and training of equids, or indeed in their working lives except perhaps as transport. She did, however, oversee fodder allocations, and the tablets refer to both mares and 'foal bearing mares' (SAL-anše ama-ša-gan), young equids (amar) and equids of one to three years old (mu 1–3), suggesting that she was also involved in the breeding of equids at least at an administrative level. Baranamtarra was also involved at the other end of equid lives, as a tablet concerning equid skins (kuš) demonstrates (P221477). She bought (P220889) and received (P220890) equids. The gifting of equids between her and the wife of the governor of Adab (P221416) suggests that Baranamtarra was not the only woman in the Early Dynastic III period who managed equine-related activities, and the wife of another Lagash governor is also recorded as owning 28 equids (P220887).

From the early second millennium Kültepe/Kanesh archives, there are also instances of women being responsible for equids. A wife and husband are called equid 'chiefs' (P390672, Barjamovic 2011: 356), and a woman with an Anatolian name, Šišahšušar, married to an Assyrian, took care of their household in Kanesh, including tending their donkeys and cattle (Highcock 2018: 311).

At the third millennium material demonstrates, equids were part of the household of gods and goddesses from when they first occurred as domestic animals in the Near East, and (the images of) deities could be transported in wheeled vehicles. Occasionally, a more direct interaction can be detected. For example, some of the equid and rider figurines may depict a riding deity, as suggested by Magen (2001). Although quite worn, the Akkadian seal on Figure 6.1a seems to depict a deity riding an equid. In an Old Babylonian hymn, Inanna is referred to as loving horses, and described as sleeping with them (Civil 1966: 122; cf. Behrens 1998: 30).

At Late Bronze Age Ugarit, the queen owned her own horses (albeit in much lower numbers than the king), as recorded in texts listing fodder for equids (see e.g. the text RS 94.2356 quoted above; Malbran-Labat & Roche 2008; see also Caubet 2013 for discussion of a special association between women and horses at Ugarit). In another text from Ugarit, a female deity called 'Aṯiratu rides a donkey, saddled with fine trappings by her servant (Virolleaud 1932: 132; see also Chapter 6). This goddess may be related to Astarte, who is well-documented as riding horses in Egyptian material (Schmitt 2013) and a Hittite goddess associated with horses (Otten 1952).

7.3 Bred and branded

Some level of deliberate breeding of equids must have occurred already in the early third millennium, if not even in the late fourth millennium, when domestic donkeys first made their entry on the Near Eastern stage. Donkey mares and (their) foals are mentioned in an Early Dynastic III tablet from Girsu and on the later Gudea Statue F (Frayne 2008: 184-5).[4] Terms translated as pregnant donkey mare (eme$_5$ ša$_3$ (peš$_4$)), donkey mare that has given birth (eme$_5$ u$_3$-tu), donkey mare that has mated (eme₅ geš₃ zu-zu) are part of an Old Babylonian list of animals (from Nippur, P461397).

The mechanisms and choices of the breeding programmes are largely unknown to us. Donkeys may have been left largely to themselves to breed, but the new hybrid kungas, appearing perhaps sometime in the mid-third millennium, would have required much more active participation from humans. Hemiones would need to be caught alive and the two species persuaded to breed. This would have been a costly and time-consuming affair, presumably marked by trial and error before a good procedure and expertise were established.[5] The third-millennium records refer to a person called 'sipa-ama-GAN.ŠA' (herder of foal-bearing mares, as opposed to simply 'sipa anše', equid herder), who may have been responsible for the breeding of equids (Maekawa 1979a: 36).

Modern breeding of mules and hinnies demonstrates that this is more complicated than simple horse or donkey breeding, mainly because the different species are not always immediately inclined to want to interbreed (Travis 2004: 86–97). We are again lacking more specific, solid information about donkey–hemione hybrids due to the extinction of the Syrian onager, but the reports from Antonius on the attempts to breed various equid hybrids (including donkey–hemione) in the Schönbrunn Zoological Garden in the 1940s illustrate similar difficulties (1944). That is not to say that it was impossible or, as suggested by Maekawa (1979a: 37), only possible under very specific circumstances, but that additional effort had to be invested.[6]

One option, the one suggested by Maekawa, was to place hemione foals with donkeys so that they become familiar and comfortable with each other, and thus later more likely to breed (also recommended by modern breeders for some situations, Travis 2004: 96). This strategy is documented in the Shulgi B Hymn, specifically noting that captured young hemiones are placed with domestic donkeys. A number of terracotta figurines from Upper Mesopotamian sites (so far identified at Tell Mozan, Tell Arbid, Tell Brak, Tepe Gawra) depict equid stallions with a genital strap (Figure 9.1a; Speiser 1935: 69–70, pl. XXXIVc.5; Oates 2001; Hauser 2007; Bianchi & Wissing 2009; Makowski 2014; 2015).[7] I have not been able to find a satisfactory explanation for the function or need of these genital straps.[8] However, with their emphasis on the (uncastrated) male genitals, their date in the later part of the third millennium, when kungas were particularly popular as prestige animals, and their location in a region specializing in kunga breeding, it is tempting to speculate that they are related to that activity. Discussing the Tell Brak corpus, Oates has suggested that the genital straps are some sort of preventative measure (2001: 288), but given the cultural context and importance of equids, it could in fact be that they were a device intended to instead encourage breeding. It is perhaps unlikely to have been particularly successful, and the type of figurine, along with the preference for donkey-hemione hybrids, dies out in the beginning of the second millennium. Remarkably, Tell Mozan, Tell Brak and Tell Arbid have yielded a small number of terracotta equid figurines where the female genitalia are marked, and Hauser plausibly suggests these to depict mares *in oestrus* (Figure 9.1b; Hauser 2007: 373–374; Oates 2001: 272; Makowski 2016: pl. XXVIII). This would fit an overall emphasis on fertility and breeding.

One of the most exciting pieces of evidence for Near Eastern breeding programmes is that from Kassite Nippur. Here we find horses listed according to their coat colour, name and pedigree (Balkan 1954). The names in themselves are a marvellous detail which I will return to in Chapter 9. The pedigrees, however, tell us most clearly that the breeders and administrators kept careful track, and that, as today, it was mainly the male line that was traced.

The specific choices made in the breeding practices must have been based on the most desirable characteristics; some of these are lost to us or too obscure to understand, but others we can infer. Qualities such as size, colour, speed and endurance were likely part of the selection process. That there was deliberate selection for size at least in some circumstances is recorded in an Old Babylonian letter from Mari, which contains a request for ten donkey mares from the Sutu region in order to improve the size of the local population (P254333, Dercksen 2004: 258). Incidentally, this also reflects a recognition of the importance of the mare in breeding and passing on specific characteristics. Colour was part of the Nippur Kassite pedigrees, although this was perhaps also partly for identification purposes. In the Amarna letters, white horses were preferred, and this may go back at least to the Old Babylonian period, where letters from Mari express admiration for white horses (Oates 2003: 121).

In order for the effort put into breeding hybrids to be worth it, it must have resulted in equids with superior qualities. 'Hybrid vigour' can occur in cross-breeds, with qualities of both parents being exaggerated (for better or worse!). We know that mules often possess some of the most desirable (for humans) characteristics of horses and donkeys, for example in size, speed, endurance and temperament. We may surmise that a similar situation applied to kungas, who may have been fast like hemiones, willing to interact with humans like donkeys, and larger than either species.

Certain regions and sites were famous for their equids, and must have been specialized breeding or trading hubs. For example, in the third millennium, ancient Nagar (modern Tell Brak) appears to have specialized in the breeding of kungas (Oates 2001; 2003), and probably also donkeys. In the first half of the second millennium, the Sutu region was known for its large donkeys, Harsamna for red horses, and Qatna for white horses. The 'Land of Lullû' supplied horses to both Ebla and Nuzi (Tsukimoto 1997), but its exact location is unknown. In the Late Bronze Age, Babylonia was another specialized centre, as for example expressed in a letter from the Hittite king to the Babylonian king asking for horses which '[i]n the land of my brother are more plentiful than straw' (Beckman 1996: 136). Balkan suggests that they were bred in the neighbourhood of Dur-Kurigalzu (1954: 13, 42). Certain pastoral and agro-pastoral groups also appear to have had a close association with equids, and may have specialised in supplying equids (Zarins 2014: 200–1). These include the elusive Amorites, who were of course also strongly present in cities in northern Mesopotamia, and are thought to be responsible for the extensive leather production at Tell Umm el-Marra in the Middle Bronze Age (Nichols & Weber 2006; cf. also Zarins 2014: 207).

Branding

In the third millennium, equids belonging to temples or palaces were sometimes branded. Branding is recorded for various domestic animals, animal skins, and human slaves (ZA_3 $ŠU_2$ / is-im-da / *šimtu*: Foxvog 1995). Some of Baranamtarra's equids for ploughing are recorded as branded (P220889), and the same appears to be the case for foal-bearing mares, some returning from a caravan, gifted to her (P220864; P221970; P220890; Zarins 2014: 190). Another Girsu text, this time from the Ur III period, records a kunga being branded with the emblem of the donor city when added to a temple's herd of cattle for ploughing (P129907; Foxvog 1995: 5). A male donkey bearing the mark of the deity Ningishzidak is contested in yet another Girsu Ur III text (P211386; Maaijer 2001: 319, no. 7). What these few texts suggest is that branding was not necessarily directly or only related to ownership, but rather part of administrative procedures marking transactions. Equids could be branded when joining a herd or temple, but the mark may record origin, not the new ownership. Evidently, such marks were in any case no guarantee, as the last example of a donkey marked with a divine emblem illustrates.

Branding may have continued in the second millennium, as indicated by a tablet from Mari mentioning a price for marking the hind legs of a donkey (Foxvog 1995: 4, n. 13), and a Middle Assyrian law goes 'If anyone finds a stallion and removes the brand, (if) its owner traces it out ...' (Pritchard 1969: 192, no. 61). A couple of equid figurines from Tell Arbid in Syria, probably dated to the beginning of the second millennium, have marks of geometric shapes on their hind or front quarters (Makowski 2014: figs. 16, 18). These marks could represent branding, as suggested by Makowski (2014: 274). Such marks could be either permanent or temporary using a dye. Other means of marking equids that are unlikely to survive in our evidence could be use of dyes on various parts of the body, and braiding or special cuts of mane, tail or forelock – a specific type of hair-lock could be used for temporary slaves (Foxvog 1995: 3), and dyes are today commonly used on animals. These marks are also not always strictly linked to ownership, but also as various other identifiers, including female animals mounted by a male, animals who have been treated or need to be treated, and so on. At donkey festivals in India today, the donkeys are decorated with bright colours.

7.4 Veterinarians and equine health

Equids can suffer from a range of illnesses, some of which are more likely to occur due to their interaction with humans through, for example, restrictions in movement, changes in access to and type of food and water, and control of rest periods. Many of the afflictions can affect all the equid species discussed here, but today's veterinary medicine tells us that some species are more prone to certain diseases than others.

Written evidence refers to sick, injured, old and incapacitated equids, especially for the donkeys of the Assur–Kanesh trade (see Chapter 4); an Old Babylonian text from Nippur listing many animals also includes what has been translated as a 'she-donkey with arthritic hips' (eme$_5$ íb gig) and a 'she-donkey with diarrhea' (eme$_5$ ša$_3$ sur) (P461397). This is consistent with the conditions treated in the Ugarit manual and with the kinds of pathologies found on the bones. Few diseases or injuries have so far been detected on the faunal remains, but many diseases would not be visible on the bones. Periodontitis has been identified only on a donkey tooth from Kamid el-Loz (Bökönyi 1990: 122). The pathologies identified in a few instances are related to age and hard-working lives carrying heavy loads, traction and bit-wear. A donkey from Ashkelon had dental caries and 'wave mouth' (Horwitz et al. 2017). The 'wave mouth' can happen naturally, but the caries was likely due to the fodder provided by humans.

The existence of equine veterinarians (azu anše) illustrates that there was an awareness of equid illnesses/injuries and attempts to heal sick or injured equids. Kunga veterinarians appear already in the third millennium, travelling from Tell Brak/Nagar to Ebla (P241850; Biga 2006; 2009). Their origin in Nagar is consistent with that city specializing in the breeding of kungas, where it would be reasonable to expect staff knowledgeable in the treatment of these expensive animals. An 'azu anše' is also mentioned in an Early Dynastic III text from Fara/Shuruppak (P010663). Veterinarians are mentioned in Hammurabi's law code, for example in no. 224, 'If a veterinary physician operate on an ox or an ass for a severe wound and save its life, the owner of the ox or ass shall give to the physician, as his fee, one-sixth of a shekel of silver' (Harper 1904; see also no. 225).

Most exciting for this topic is the discovery of a treaty for the well-being of horses found at Ugarit (Gordon 1942; Cohen & Sivan 1983; Pardee 1985). These hippiatric texts provide a list of afflictions in horses, and the corresponding medicinal treatment and administration. Each item on the list is in a standard format: symptom; medicinal ingredients; how to make the potion; how to administer the potion. The instruction is always to pulverize the ingredients, and in one instance to also liquefy them; they are in every case to be poured through the nose of the horse. For example:

> Or if a horse discharges/d a putrid liquid, grain and bitter almond should be pulverized together, and it (the remedy) should (then) be poured into his nose.
>
> Lines 7–8, translation after Cohen & Sivan 1983

This, along with several other of the diseases, relates to what would appear to be stomach or intestinal problems, or some type of colic.[9] Colic is a general term referring to abdominal pain (Moore 2013), and is a fairly common problem with horses today. The causes of colic in horses and donkeys include a high grain-based diet, spoilt feed (e.g. mouldy), sand ingestion, lack of water, stress and dental problems (The Donkey Sanctuary 2018). All of these are more likely to occur when the animal's food and movements are controlled by humans. Horses may be more likely than donkeys to suffer from colic-like conditions, since their tolerance of grains like barley is lower than that of donkeys. However, donkeys tend not to express pain as dramatically as horses, and the disease is therefore often only detected at a very late stage when it might be too late.

The other symptoms mentioned in the Ugaritic texts are more difficult to understand, but seem to relate to various expressions of pain or discomfort. Most of the suggested remedies are also not well understood, and their efficacy therefore difficult to discern. Bitter almonds may have some beneficial medicinal qualities (Keser et al. 2014), but they also contain hydrocyanic acid, which is poisonous (Panter 2018). Today, equine medicine is more commonly given through the mouth or injected, but in some situations, the nose is used, as for example in the treatment of colic in checking reflux (The Donkey Sanctuary

2018) or administering oil or, if no other option is available, equids not able or willing to eat can be fed through a nasogastric tube (Geor 2001). Evidently, a range of types of equine suffering, both diseases and injuries, were observed, measures taken to alleviate them and specialized personnel trained to do so. How frequent and successful the treatments were in practice is not clear.

7.5 Mutual training

All interaction between equid and human involves some level of mutual learning. The more intense interactions in the Bronze Age Near East where there would have been a dynamic back-and-forth co-training of equid and human include ploughing, carrying of goods, carrying of people and pulling of wheeled vehicles. The intensity and time needed to become proficient varies for each of these, and depends on the final context in which it was to be carried out. Equids probably started their training around the age of three, although we do get examples of individuals as young as one year marked as 'giš' (yoked/draft equid).

Ploughing

The ancient records do not inform us about the training strategies employed when equids and humans worked together for ploughing and threshing activities. In this case, Goulder's ethnographic work in parts of Africa is very informative (2020: 79–81; 2021). She notes that, with enough people participating, donkeys can help with the ploughing with minimal training – this can often involve a certain amount of force, and at least one extra person for the turns. On the other hand, if a well-trained donkey and a single skilled human work together, they could do this without further aid and in a more efficient manner. Teams of donkeys, as we see them listed in third-millennium documents, would require further training, as would the humans working with them. The donkey's intelligence and long memory (compared to cattle) mean that they remember their training and do not usually need to re-learn each season if left on their own in between.

Carrying goods

Donkeys generally accept burdens placed on their back without much physical resistance. They also follow each other in file; a simple halter would therefore suffice to guide the donkey at the front, but it would also be possible to do without entirely. Navigation can be done by guiding of the first donkey, through voice commands and/or through herding. Donkeys can thus act as beasts of burden with extremely limited training of both human and donkey. However, especially for long journeys or for full days of work, the human companion would need knowledge of the physical needs of the donkey if it is to not suffer and be able to continue work. Donkeys can also learn to travel a specific route on their own; in modern times, smugglers have taken advantage of this ability and moved illegal goods across borders in this manner (Goulder 2020: 117), but there is no evidence that this was done in the ancient Near East.

Horses also do not require much training to carry goods; some resistance is likely in the first instance, but should also be manageable by non-experts. They do not however possess the same endurance as donkeys and are not able to go as far without water or feed; while they may follow in file, they are more likely to wander off on their own and would need stronger guidance to stick to the designated route. Donkeys are therefore much more suited for this kind of work, and were clearly the preferred caravan and land transport animal in the third and second millennia.[10]

Carrying people

For any type of riding, some level of training of both equid and human would have been a prerequisite, and risks would certainly have been lower if this was done by someone with experience. This applies to human and equid equally; the human would need to learn how to stay seated, balanced (even more so without the use of a saddle or stirrups), and, if not guided by an accompanying walking human or riding in a file of equids, how to communicate with the equid in order to move in the desired direction, and perhaps how to cope with long rides. The equid would similarly need to learn (and accept) to carry the weight on its back in a balanced manner, and to understand the communication with its rider. It is possible for two novices to 'learn by doing', but it makes much more sense that both human and equid learn from an expert when first starting.

However, riding for the purpose of covering a long or short distance in order to deliver a letter would require much less skill than hunting, fighting in battle or even participating in a public procession. The risks involved relate to the dangers of the road more than the skill of the equid and rider, and endurance would be more important than smooth communication. For transport purposes of this kind, as with the donkeys carrying goods, a simple bridle or halter would be enough, or it could be sidestepped entirely. Many equestrians today ride with a simple bitless bridle or even without bridle. In endurance riding (long-distance racing), the rider typically has very little contact with the mouth of the horse through the reins, as minute or immediate steering is not necessary. Today, we can also often see riders on working donkeys without the aid of a bridle or halter (Meutchieye et al. 2016). The iconography we encounter of equids and riders with rather minimal use of halters and bridles are thus perfectly in line with these kinds of activities.[11]

Engaging in hunting or battle from equid-back is a completely different beast. In order to avoid injury or death to rider or equid, the skills of both need to be at a very high level, and the communication between the two must be fine-tuned. This would take time, effort and expertise to achieve, both for human and equid. If the equid fails to quickly understand or respond to a request from its rider to move in a specific direction, it could result in either or both being, for example, hit by a spear or arrow, or at the end of a lion's launch. The same could happen if the rider fails to understand the signals of the equid concerning imminent dangers or its willingness to engage in a specific situation. The evidence for ridden equids being part of hunting or warfare in the third and second millennium suggests that it was a very rare occurrence and may not have involved being in the thick of the fighting (see Chapter 6). As such, there would not have been a fully developed programme to train equids and riders for it, in stark contrast to what we see for wheeled vehicles.

Finally, riding as part of public ceremonies or processions presents another scenario for which the equid needs some preparation. Many equids will experience large crowds, loud noises, fast movements and new smells as unsettling if not outright threatening. This may activate their instinct to fight or flee, with the possibility of damage or injury to nearby surroundings and to the rider. Any equid participating in such events may therefore have been exposed to some of these impressions beforehand in a controlled manner in order to prevent any major disasters.

The sources are silent on how equids and their human companions prepared for and gained experience in their roles in ploughing, movement of goods and riding, but with knowledge of human and equine temperament, behaviour and needs, along with some of the recorded personnel discussed above, we can infer some of the practices and mechanisms involved. For equids pulling wheeled vehicles, we have some wonderful details, thanks to the text of an actual horse-trainer, called Kikkuli.

Pulling wheeled vehicles

For the pulling of wheeled vehicles (or sledges), many of the same principles apply as for riding. Some training of both human and equid was necessary, but the intensity and skill level would depend on the context in which the ensemble acted. If taking part in public processions, hunting or battle, the same high level of skill and communication as for riding would be necessary. However, the skill set is not the same as for riding for neither equid nor human, so cannot simply be transferred from one activity to the other, although having learnt one will likely make learning the other smoother. Manoeuvring a wheeled vehicle requires careful balancing by the driver – even more so with two-wheeled vehicles – and ballast may also be necessary for balance and for turning and changing speed. The finesse of this would depend on size and type of vehicle, number and type of equids, terrain and speed, among other things.

Fortunately, a text on how to train chariot horses has survived, giving us an insight into the actual practicalities of training, the everyday life of expert horses and how they were treated by humans. This is the manual by Kikkuli the horse-trainer, from the land of the Mittani (Kammenhuber 1961; Raulwing 2000; 2005; 2009 and references therein). The manual is for an exercise and feeding routine, over 184 days long, for chariot horses. The horses were kept in stables and brought out for their exercise at different times of the day, often several times a day. The manual gives instructions on the distances they should go in each case, along with the speed. There is some uncertainty concerning the exact distances, since the terms used can be interpreted in a number of ways; calculations go up to 150 kilometres in one session, repeated on several consecutive days (Kammenhuber 1961, equating one unit of 'DANNA' with 10.7 kilometres). The speed is also a matter of some discussion. Walk, trot, canter/gallop, and even the tölt and flying changes in gallop have been suggested (Starke 1995; Raulwing 2009). Kammenhuber (1961), who provided the first complete translation of the text, uses walk, trot and canter/gallop to represent the incremental increase in speed instructed in the text, but as Raulwing notes, the text itself only describes an increase; it does not specify the pace according to modern concepts (2009: 12). In any case, the gradual increase fits with a modern exercise programme, where a slower pace is used in the warm up phase.

Beside the daily exercise (with some rest days), the text dictates fodder type and rations, watering, pasture and other measures such as use of muzzles, blankets and massages. Access to water and food is carefully controlled and monitored, and sometimes it is even specified that access to water should be withheld. These measures suggest that the horses were trained (and perhaps tested) for situations where water may not be available for some period of time. They also suggest intimate knowledge of equine needs and behaviour and a procedure designed to test them to their limit while ensuring that their bodies are kept in optimal physical condition. More than anything, it is reminiscent of the regimes of modern professional athletes or sportspersons.

Despite vigorous academic discussion and interpretations, the purpose of the training is not known (for a good overview of the history of research on the Kikkuli Text, and what we can and cannot conclude from it, see Raulwing 2009), although the general consensus seems to lean towards chariots and horses used in war. It is in any case clear that the daily exercise regime would have resulted in increased endurance and stamina that is in line with what we might expect of equids pulling wheeled vehicles taking part in hunting, battle or any kind of long-distance journey. Some equids had to travel very far before reaching the point of battle, as illustrated by Ramses II's expedition from Egypt to Qadesh to fight the Hittites in 1274 BCE. What the text does not tell us is how horses were trained or prepared for war or for pulling wheeled vehicles – there is nothing about balancing, means of communication, learning how to turn or dodge an arrow, or how to handle a charging enemy or wild beast. What we do know from it is that such carefully planned and long-term training strategies existed, and what they might have looked like. Of course, such strategies may well have had very different content in other places and at other times. That similar equine training and care programmes did exist elsewhere is demonstrated by Middle Assyrian fragmentary texts found at Assur, which also contain instructions on daily exercise, feeding and other care (Ebeling 1951).

The Kikkuli and Assur texts give a sense of a single organized programme for a substantial number of horses. This implies group training overseen by an expert (the horse trainer), rather than individual training with a specific charioteer tied to a specific team of horses, at least at this stage of the training. Charioteers may in this scenario have come in later. For equids and wheeled vehicles transporting high status individuals (or deities), a driver was usually in charge of the actual navigation, but a small amount of training would also allow the person themselves to carry out simple steering at a low and controlled pace. The vocabulary of texts from Ugarit reflects levels of training and an awareness of skill being connected with experience (Loretz 2011: 112–13).

8

Honourable and Dishonourable Deaths

The vast majority of equids from the ancient Near East are invisible to us in the archaeological record. Their representation in faunal assemblages is extremely low. Most of the time, we do not have information about how they died or what happened to their bodies after death. It is likely that most equids were simply chased or dragged out of urban or settled spaces when becoming too ill or too old to continue working, left to fend for themselves until dying in fairly open spaces (Buitenhuis 1991: 47). Such bodies would be consumed by scavengers and the bones likely scattered. However, another reason for the low visibility of equid remains is that we have very few identified examples of their daily lived spaces. A few possible stables and way stations were discussed in Chapter 7 and, at least at Tell Brak, we have faunal remains in such a space, but in general we lack the archaeological contexts of where equids spent their daily lives, eating, sleeping, training, mating and so on. This is partly because they may be challenging to identify archaeologically, but even more because such spaces are likely to primarily have been based outside settlements (including entirely on pasture). The information we do have concerning how equids died and what happened to their bodies relates to hunting, eating, skinning, fighting, sacrificing and burying, and I will here discuss each of these.

8.1 Eaten, skinned, hunted

Hemiones and possibly other wild equids (see Chapter 2) were present in the Near East in the millennia leading up to the Bronze Age, and continued to be so through to the first millennium, when Assyrian palace reliefs depict royal hunts of hemiones. Their numbers may have been much lower in the third to first millennia, but we have no firm evidence for their exact numbers and distribution. At fifth- and fourth-millennium sites, especially in Syria, Anatolia and the Levant, equids were certainly hunted for their meat (Grigson 2012), and could make up a more substantial part of the subsistence strategy. Their skins may also have been used, but this was not a primary reason for hunting. In the late fourth millennium, remains of wild equids have been identified at a number of sites (see Figure 3.2; Appendix K), and these may represent consumption and/or skinning.

Hemiones continued to be hunted in the third and second millennia. Our evidence for this comes partly from the faunal remains, and partly from written sources in a mostly indirect manner. Since hemiones were wild animals, the very presence of their remains within settlements must indicate hunting. Many of the faunal remains are found in contexts suggesting kitchen waste, with other consumed animals, and cutmarks on some of the bones indicate both meat extraction and skinning.[1] Animal hunts are a recurrent theme in Near Eastern art, often associated with and part of elite ideology, and perhaps most evocatively expressed in the hunts of Ashurbanipal (Watanabe 1998), which include hemiones. Equids, as we have seen, take part in these hunts, but in the third and second millennium their participation is mainly as pulling wheeled vehicles, almost never as prey. Prior to this we have rare images that may depict equids in the role of prey: one is a stamp seal impression probably dated to the mid-fourth millennium found at Tell Brak (Figure 3.5a). It shows two lions attacking an animal that may be an equid. The other is a Late Neolithic vessel from Anatolia, which shows a human hunter on foot with bow and arrow, shooting at an animal that has been interpreted as a wild equid (Bennett et al. 2017). The single example from the Bronze Age of an equid depicted as hunted is found on one of the Late Bronze Age gold bowls from Ugarit (Figure 5.10), where what is probably a hemione appears among the prey animals.

The written sources are also remarkably silent on the topic of equid hunting. This is perhaps surprising given their importance in the breeding programme of kungas. A rare exception is offered in the Shulgi B Hymn, which goes,

> For the hemione I do not lay out a net (snare), I do not dig a trap, I do not shoot (throw) any arrow (javelin) (at him). Like a worthy rival (I chase him) until his legs give out. Its young I place with the domestic ass.
>
> P469698, translated in Zarins 2014: 286, text no. 69

Here we have not only a list of possible means of hunting – and trapping – but also a hint at the character and status of hemiones. Even if in this instance, the animal would have been caught through exhaustion, the alternatives mentioned were probably used in other instances. Another text lists rope associated with hemiones, which could have been part of hunting practices (Zarins 2014: 274, no. 31). The capture of hemiones for their skins is mentioned in an Old Babylonian letter from Mari, where skins had specifically been requested (Heimpel 2003: 428, Text 27 51). This letter further suggests that certain men specialized in capturing hemiones. This must also have been the case in the third millennium, where we have indirect evidence for the capture of live hemiones in the form of the kunga hybrid. If we are correct in understanding this equid as a donkey–hemione hybrid, then live hemiones would have been necessary as part of the breeding programme. The combination is extremely unlikely to occur without human intervention, and even if so, would be very rare and produce a minuscule number of offspring, certainly not those we see in the archives of the third millennium. These records do not inform us whether one combination was preferred (female donkey × male hemione or female hemione × male donkey). Presumably capturing only a few male hemiones would be easier than many female ones, but the hybrid vigour may have been stronger with a hemione dame.

In any case, hemiones were hunted not only for their meat and skins, but also for reproductive purposes. Donkeys and horses were also a source of meat and skins. Cutmarks suggestive of both skinning and extraction of meat appear on equid bones throughout the Bronze Age (see Chapter 3 for sites and references). Faunal remains of equids continue to be represented in waste assemblages where the other animals present are thought have been eaten (e.g. Tell Brak, Weber 2001: 348). However, they make up only tiny percentages of the total assemblages. Contrary to what is often believed, equids *were* eaten, but it was far from common. In our extensive Ur III records, equids are qualified as 'šu-gid$_2$', perhaps to be understood as (slaughtered) 'for the kitchen', or as ba-ug$_7$ / ba-úš, translated as 'dead' or 'slaughtered' (Tsouparopoulou 2013: 153).

The Ur III records also provide us with evidence of equids being eaten by dogs and lions. Equids may be qualified in the texts as '(fodder) for dogs' or '(fodder) for lions'. A special set of dogs associated with the army received rations of meat through their general, and this meat included that of equids (Tsouparopoulou 2012; Tsouparopoulou & Recht 2021). These equids may have been injured, old or otherwise no longer able to continue their duties. They are primarily donkeys and kungas; apparently horses and hemiones were not considered appropriate for this, as there is only one instance of lions receiving horse meat as fodder (P106261). This may be because horses were relatively rare in this period, compared to the equids mostly having a prior association with the army. Hemiones were almost certainly not part of military activities (other than as booty), and if horses were, it would again have been very rare due to their scarcity. It is possible that lions received higher quality equids than dogs (this could also explain the rare horses being fed to them), as suggested by Owen (1979: 63); equids were shipped especially from Drehem/Puzriš-Dagan for the lions at Ur.

Beyond the written evidence (admittedly limited to a fairly short period in the third millennium), gnawing marks on equid bones consistent with dogs support the idea that dogs ate equids (e.g. Tell Brak, Weber 2001: 348, see also Chapter 3 for more examples). There is no way of linking such gnawing marks to a military regiment of dogs, and in fact, they represent mostly single bones of equids in habitation contexts, probably scavenged by dogs – which suggests that equid carcasses in some case would have been available. Abu Tbeirah may present us with an exception. In a pit below two graves, the deposit of animal bones included partially articulated remains of an equid (with a total of thirteen specimens). There were disarticulation cutmarks on the metatarsals, and nine of the bones exhibited gnawing marks (Alhaique 2019: 424–5). This would be consistent with the animal first being skinned and the remainder of the body fed to dogs and placed in the deposit before complete disarticulation.

Similarly, skins of donkeys and kungas were recorded along with those of hemiones in the Early Dynastic III and Ur III periods.[2] The skins are part of the accounting system, and a means of tracing dead animals and transfers between herders and administrators. They could ultimately have been used for a wide range of things, including as part of clothes, covers, containers, for leather objects and so on; the texts do not generally specify which, if any of these. Animal skins can be used to make glue, a substance whose uses would have been extremely wide ranging and necessary, but which is largely under-appreciated due to its invisibility and poor preservation. Glue would also act as a binder in paints. The possibility of equid skins being transformed into an adhesive appears in yet another Ur III text, where they are listed along with other animal skin glues (kuš anše še-gín; P416213). The hooves may have provided another source of glue, and the cutmarks indicative of skinning would probably be the same – in fact, the hooves may even have been kept attached to the skins at least temporarily.

As the example of glue illustrates, beyond meat and skin, animal bodies (dead and alive) can provide resources for a great number of things. Apart from woollen textiles, which usually involve live animals (although some of the dyes require dead ones, such as murex shells for purple), there was also an extensive leather industry (*RLA* 6, 'Leder(Industrie)'). This industry created many products used with equids, but generally we do not receive information about where or what animal the leather originated from. At Tell Umm el-Marra in the late third and early second millennium, analysis of the faunal remains has uncovered an extensive leather production with the use of hemione bodies (Nichols & Weber 2006). Hemiones make up an unusually large percentage of the faunal assemblage, and cutmarks and the selection of body parts suggest exploitation for skins. The industry already existed in the third millennium, but after a gap was greatly intensified in the Middle Bronze Age. Whether equid bodies in the ancient Near East were otherwise exploited for their tendons, sinews, blood, fat or other parts that required their death is not known at present.

The hairs of especially the tail (in particular the long ones on horses) are quite strong, and could have made good threads. This is also not mentioned in the written sources, and would not preserve in the archaeological record. Hair and other body parts may have been ingredients in medicinal potions or rituals, but this is not evidenced until the Neo-Assyrian period, where for example a 'medical therapeutic' text in the British Museum (perhaps from Assur) includes horse hair as part of the ritual (Heeßel 2018).[3]

The story of equids and their bodies continues most tangibly in their bones. These were manipulated and curated in a number of ways, as we will see below, but they, also, could be a resource. Many tools and even decorative objects in the ancient Near East were made of bone. Occasionally, we are even able to identify the animal they came from, and in just a few instances, we have examples of worked equid bone objects. One is a shaped and polished equid tibia from an Early Dynastic III/Akkadian burial at Nippur (Burial 21; McMahon 2006: 39, pl. 132.6), while a hollowed out and shaped equid metatarsus was found in Early Dynastic III Tell Asmar, perhaps used as a handle (Hilzheimer 1941: 14), and what may be an awl and a pin made from equid bones come from Tell Halawa (EBA and MB I; Meyer & Pruss 1994: 272, figs. 91–92, nos. 8–9). The leather industry at Tell Umm el-Marra also included the use of awls made from hemione bones (Nichols & Weber 2006: 48–9).

8.2 Buried, honoured and sacrificed

Clearly, not all equids were equal. In the third and second millennium, some equids were especially chosen to be buried or deposited as complete or nearly complete bodies within human-settled space (Recht 2018 with further references; also Way 2011). Some of these depositions are related to human burials, while others seem to have no such association. The former is typically interpreted as equids accompanying their 'human master', while the latter are usually understood as sacrifices, perhaps in some cases a type of foundation deposit, but the underlying practices are not always easy to understand. There is also another type of which there are so far only a few possible examples from the Near East in this time period, but which must nevertheless remain a very real possibility: non-ritual related finds of equid bodies, for example as victims of an accident or battle, or as trash or neglect, dumped or simply left to decompose. In each case, a range of different equid-human relations are implied with and within each of these categories, along with a variety of social statuses of individual equids (see also Appendices F and K).

Association of equid and human burials

While animal bones are not infrequently associated with human burials, the presence of complete animals is comparatively rare (Recht 2011). Far from all animals enjoy this privilege, and equids were a favourite – sometimes along with dogs (Wygnańska 2017; Tsouparopoulou & Recht 2021). The practice of burying equids with or near humans seems to first have become popular in the mid- to late-third millennium in southern and northern Mesopotamia.

The location of equid skeletons within mortuary contexts and in relation to human skeletons provides further hints to their relations. In a number of cases, we can see how equids were very much an integrated part of the whole funerary assemblage, but distinguished from humans by placement in a separate space. The equid skeletons would be placed for example in associated shafts and dromoi (Jericho Tomb B48, Tell el-'Ajjul Tomb 1417), in subsidiary spaces (Tell Mozan Chamber Tomb 37, Tell Arbid Grave G8/G9-S-37/55-2001), or in a higher layer than that of the humans, deposited after their burial (Tell Brak TC Oval Burial, Tell Ababra Grave 29, Tell el-'Ajjul Tomb 101) (see catalogue in Recht 2018). Other burials have equids in spaces that suggest equality with humans, or even primary focus. For example, in Tomb 5G at Madhhur, the two equids take up the main space of the large chamber, while the human skeleton has been delegated to a smaller niche in the northeastern wall (Roaf 1982: fig. 34). While the equids may be interpreted as part of the total assemblage of funerary offerings to the deceased, their spatial relation here is intriguing. Put differently: had the placements been reversed, we would likely assume the main burial was in the large chamber, the human surrounded by his offerings, including equids in a niche to the northeast.[4]

At Tell el-'Ajjul in the southern Levant, equid skeletons were associated with quite a few tombs (Petrie 1931; 1932; 1933; 1934; Wapnish 1997; see also assessment of these in Way 2010). While some were placed in what may be understood as secondary or subsidiary spaces, others tell a different story. Tomb

411 has a central circular chamber surrounded by three small niches. In the centre, an equid skeleton (apparently missing its hind legs) had been placed, while two of the niches contained the remains of at least five humans (Petrie 1931: 4–5, plates VIII.2–4, LV, LVII, LXI; Petrie 1933: plates XLVIII, L). A reversal of human and equid placements would again most likely have the main burial in the centre surrounded by offerings. Interpreting the human remains as offerings to the equid in this context is perhaps pushing a flat ontology too far, but it may be time we start to think more carefully about how we understand and privilege humans in relation to other animals. Whatever the sequence of events of the overall context, the one equid is spatially the absolute focus of this tomb. As such, we are here most likely looking at an *individual* with special social status (i.e. not a generic 'equid') where it was considered necessary or appropriate to bestow a certain honour by burying it in this manner, regardless of the cause of death.

The inclusion of equids in human burials can also be found in a few lists of funerary offerings from the third millennium. In *The Death of Ur-Nammu*, we hear that 'by his side, asses(?) [anše] were buried with him' (Kramer 1967). The offerings of a man named Bilalla and his wife Lalla include a team of donkeys (anše bir$_2$) and a wheeled vehicle, along with other luxury goods such as fine garments, wooden, copper, silver and lapis lazuli objects (Early Dynastic III, probably from Adab; see Foxvog 1980). Finally, an Ur III text from Girsu lists offerings for the burial of Ninenise, the wife of Urtarsirsira, where a team of kungas and a sledge are recorded:

1 woman's garment (of the wool from) barley-eating sheep,
1 long níg-lám-garment,
1 boxwood bed with thin legs,
1 chair, being open(-work?), of boxwood,
1 sledge (of threshing-sledge type) of boxwood,
1 team female kúnga-equids,
1 bronze hand-mirror,
1 ... of bronze,
1 Akkadian copper luxury(?) container,
1 copper ... luxury(?) item,
1 small bún-di-bowl

P220725, translation following Cohen 2005: 163–6

These examples, though rare, are consistent with the kinds of wealthy tombs that contain complete equid skeletons, with the exception of the sledges/wheeled vehicles, which have not so far been identified as accompanying equids.

A closer look at the contextual details of some of these burials reveal further variations and complexities in the equid–human relationship. First of all, we may note that there is no clear correlation between equids and men. Only in a few cases can equid skeletons be directly and exclusively associated with male human skeletons; in some cases, both male and female human skeletons are present, and in one case there was only a female skeleton (see Recht 2018: fig. 4). This may be rather surprising given that there is a tendency to assume that equids equal male-dominated activities such as hunting and warfare. However, our data here are extremely incomplete, and in most cases, there is either no information about the sex of the human skeletons (or it is based on offerings, a type of identification that is questionable), or multiple and secondary burials complicate the picture. The few textual references noted support the idea that equids were buried alongside both men and women.

Unfortunately, the same lack of information haunts the equid skeletons. Only in a fraction of the cases do we know the sex of the equid skeleton (based on the presence/absence of canines, which does come with a small degree of uncertainty but seems to be overall reliable). These present both male and female equid skeletons, possibly with a minor preference for male ones. The exception is Tell Umm el-Marra, where all the equid remains from the elite cemetery that could be sexed were male (Weber 2017). With the high number of equids in this context, it is very clear that there was a (probably exclusive) preference for male equids;[5] the same may be the case for the four male equids in a sounding dated to the mid third millennium at Tell Chuera (Vila 2005).

Perhaps the most exciting evidence to have come to light in recent decades comes from the excavations at Tell Umm el-Marra in Syria (Figure 8.1). At the centre of the acropolis was an Elite Mortuary Complex, in use *c.* 2550–2200 BCE (Schwartz et al. 2003; 2006). In this central and highly visible location 10 tombs (with human skeletons), 10 'installations' or features containing equid skeletons, and a range of additional structures probably related to rituals and ancestor veneration were excavated, in sequential phases (Schwartz 2013).[6] The number of equid skeletons found within the same space is extraordinary (with remains of at least 40 individuals, 25 complete), but their features and contexts make these equids very special. Jill Weber, the zooarchaeologist analysing the faunal remains from the site, has made a very good case for these equids to represent donkey–hemione hybrids – the famous kungas (Weber 2017). What is more, all identifiable individuals are male, but we see a range of ages.

The equid remains had been placed in separate structures labelled installations A–G by the excavators. The installations differ in structure from the human

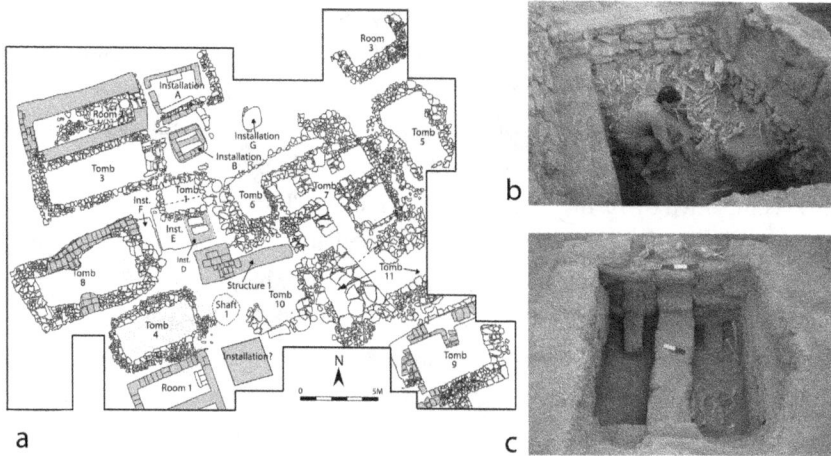

Figure 8.1 Tell Umm el-Marra Elite Mortuary Complex. Courtesy of Glenn M. Schwartz.

a. Plan of the cemetery (after Schwartz 2016: fig. 2).
b. Installation A.
c. Installation B.

tombs by being at least partially subterranean, made with mudbrick or stone, whereas the human tombs were partly or wholly above ground, with a limestone substructure. These structural differences, along with many more offerings deposited in the human tombs, suggest differences in social status, although against this should be noted that the installations are very centrally placed, with tombs and other features surrounding them. A complex set of activities, rituals and relations can be detected in the tombs, with evidence of ancestor veneration, memory creation and erasure, gender differences and possible human sacrifice (Porter 2012; Schwartz 2012; 2013). Some of the tombs contained disarticulated animal bones, including equid bones (Tombs 3, 4, 6, 7 and 9, perhaps not all deliberate deposits; Schwartz et al. 2006; 2012; Weber pers. comm.), but the vast majority of equid remains come from the installations. Complete and partial equid skeletons were interred in the installations, and they were sometimes accompanied by puppies, human infants and ceramic sherds.

Yet another complex set of relations and activities, many of which are difficult to disentangle, are reflected in the equid remains. Weber (forthcoming) has grouped the installations and individual burials into three types based on the equid depositions and the recently revised sequence for the cemetery.[7] Type I (Installations A, E, F, and G phase B) each has four young or prime aged equids

(4 to 14 years old). The manner of deposition varies for each installation, but the equids in each are of a similar age; these installations also contain additional equid remains that suggest depositions of skin and tail. Type II (Installations B and D) are semi-subterranean mudbrick structures with the main interments of two standing aged equids (up to about 20 years old) and infant deposits; these are accompanied by further equid and dog remains, human infants and ceramic sherds or vessels. Type III Installations (Installations C and G Phase C) are 'transitional', both in that they are thought to be chronologically between Type I and II, and in that they share depositional characters of both.

A compelling case is made by Weber to understand the young equids and those in their prime as deliberately killed (Type I and some of Type III). Significantly, she sees them as validation of authority within the sacred space of the cemetery, by virtue of the kunga's strong connection with royalty – to the extent that they may themselves be seen as royal (Weber 2012: 176–81; forthcoming). In contrast, the aged equids in Type II installations (and some of Type III) can be favourably compared to the human tombs, albeit in a 'scaled down' version. The equids' advanced age and general wear and tear of the body (arthritis, heavily worn teeth) have suggested to Weber that the equids in these installations died of natural causes, and their burials can be seen as analogous to the human burials. Examination of the construction type, body orientation (head to the west for both humans and equids), and presence of possible offerings further establishes this link.

Whether or not these particular equids died of natural causes or were ritually killed,[8] it is clear that they were highly valued animals, and must have required special care towards the end of their lives, as noted by Weber (2012: 167). What is also evident from the elite tomb complex as a whole is that only selected individuals were allowed burial within the space. This applied to equids as much as it did to humans. They were elite, and quite possibly royalty. For the humans, selection was likely predicated on familial relations, with other additional factors. For the equids, their close relation to the humans, their specific species and gender, probably along with skill, were necessary conditions. What is more, just as relations between humans within tombs can be postulated, the equids within an installation are likely to have known each other. They may even have been brothers (we cannot speak of fathers and sons, since kungas cannot produce offspring), but they may also have been working companions. Their interments in twos and fours could suggest that they were the teams of wheeled vehicles who had worked together in life and were placed together in death along the same lines.[9] It could also be the case that when one in an equid team died, the others of the team were killed and placed with it in the installation. While we know little about the behaviour of kungas, we do know that donkeys regularly form companion pairs (non-gender-based), and that the death of one can be devastating to the surviving animal (Evans & Crane 2018: 11, stress induced hyperlipaemia, sometimes even referred to as the remaining one dying of heartbreak). Especially for aged equids who were no longer able to work at full capacity and for whom it may be harder to form a new friendship, placing the pair together might make sense.

One instance of a single equid burial occurs in Installation G Phase A, and another possibly complete skeleton was found in Tomb 3 (Weber forthcoming). If we think in terms of relational clusters or teams of equids, these could be individuals who died or were killed out of turn due to an injury or disease that could not be cured. These could have been equids who were not part of a team, or in a team where a substitute could quickly be found; it is also possible that their importance derived from an equid–rider relationship. Beyond the complete and articulated equid skeletons in the installations, quite a few deposits of partial remains are reported, and it is worth taking a closer look at these in terms of the complexity and layering of mortuary rituals taking place in the cemetery.

At least some of these could represent deliberate curation of deceased equids. Human remains of this kind are typically interpreted as secondary burial, where the bones of previously deceased are moved, either to make space for new burials and/or as part of subsequent rituals that involve deliberate relocation of bones. At Tell Umm el-Marra, this occurred in Tomb 4, where a dense cluster of bones, perhaps in a container, was topped by a skull (Schwartz et al. 2006: 613). Sometimes only specific parts of the skeleton are selected in such activities – for humans, especially skull and long bones. The disarticulated equid bones may represent similar secondary burials surrounding the curation of previously deceased equids. Similarly for the skulls and toe bones found in Installations D and G, and the skin/tail deposits in Type I installations, but these could also represent skinning, tails and 'head-and-hoof' deposits, as suggested by Weber (2012: 167; forthcoming)[10].

At the Tell Umm el-Marra Elite Mortuary Complex, it thus seems that the distinction made was less one of animal vs human and more one based on social status. As mentioned above, only very specific selected individuals, equid and human, were allowed interment within the complex. Both were high status, potentially even royal, but variations in status can be seen within the human burials, between humans and equids, and within the equid burials. Exactly what the range depends on we must largely guess at; for humans, gender may have been one factor (Porter 2012), while for the equids, beside all being male, age may have been a factor, with elderly equids enjoying a higher status.

Currently nothing directly compares to the third millennium Tell Umm el-Marra Elite Mortuary Complex in terms of its equid interments. However, at Abu Tbeirah in southern Iraq, in the Early Dynastic III-Akkadian transition, equids were also found in an area with human burials. Some, usually partial remains, appear to be part of the human burials (e.g. Graves 5, 15, 24, and 100, Alhaique 2019: 422–4; Alhaique et al. 2021), but in one case, a donkey was found in its own separate pit (D'Agostino et al. 2015: 219; Alhaique et al. 2021). The other burials from the site are also pit burials, and do not always contain offerings, and as such, the equid fits this pattern neatly. It was a male domestic donkey (at least on the mother's side, as determined by mtDNA analysis), 5-5.5 years old. It was positioned with its legs folded tightly against the stomach, and its head twisted backwards. The latter could indicate cause of death, but in any case illustrates postmortem positioning of the body. As at Tell Umm el-Marra, a range of mortuary activities can be detected at Abu Tbeirah, including possible funerary banquets and secondary burials or relocation of osteological remains (Romano 2019: 72–5, 81–2). Associated with the equid was a small circular area containing burnt substances (Romano 2019: 75). This equid thus seems to have been treated along the same lines as some of the humans, perhaps again in what could be called a 'scaled down' version.

Roughly contemporary with the Tell Umm el-Marra and Abu Tbeirah burials is a grave from Abu Salabikh which also contained complete or nearly complete equid bodies. Grave 162 was found below the floor of a large administrative building (Figure 8.2). At least five equids (probably donkeys) were found in this space, four of which were placed in pairs of two (Postgate 1982; 1984: 95–7; Postgate & Moon 1982). Unfortunately, the grave was heavily disturbed; only a few offerings remained. The latter suggest human interment (no human burial was detected, likely due to the disturbance), but the relatively high number of equids could indicate that this was also not a simple case of equids as accessories to the deceased.[11]

Moving back north, mid-third-millennium Tell Chuera brings us four complete equid skeletons in three pits from a sounding (Vila 2005). All the equids were male, and two were aged, two mature (*c.* 10 years old). The equids were deliberately buried, as demonstrated by their positions and proximity to each other. They would appear to have been interred for their own sake. No human remains were associated with them. The nature of the excavation, as a sounding, could mean that human burials in the vicinity have not yet been

Figure 8.2 Plan of Abu Salabikh Grave 162. Early Dynastic III (after Postgate 1984: fig. 1). Courtesy of J. N. Postgate.

discovered, but the equid interments were in separate pits, dug specifically for these bodies. The age of two of the animals and the gender of all are reminiscent of the Tell Umm el-Marra animals, which may further support a case of these equids being honoured in their own right.

Extrapolating life from death, or living social relations from burial practices., comes with its own set of potential pitfalls, but in some of these cases (especially Tell Umm el-Marra, Abu Salabikh, Tell Madhhur, Tell el-Ajjul), it seems safe to say that the close association of humans and other animals suggests at least the representation of an intimate relationship in life. In other words, the equids are there because of their relationship to the deceased or to the group to which the deceased belonged. This is not a case of a generic human–animal relationship: it is one between a specific *individual* human and (a) specific *individual* equid(s). It is the individual, specific equid that mattered, although its importance and identity were also tied to its species, age and skills. The equid may represent wealth and refer to certain activities, and even be part of the negotiation of identity, before and/or after death. But it is never purely a symbol or symbolic; it is well-integrated into and sharing the space with humans, with its own set of associated rituals and placement of the body. In this, there is a recognition of the personhood and individuality of at least some equids.

These particular equids are likely to have been highly skilled or valuable favourites of the deceased human individual(s). Highly skilled equids required substantial investment in terms of time, financial input and mutual training. The skills could be related to wheeled vehicles or even riding, but probably not other types of load-bearing or ploughing, as there is nothing to suggest that these were particularly complex skills. Equids may have been valuable in other ways – for example as breeding mares and stallions, which would have been especially relevant for the breeding of hybrids with one 'wild' parent. Breeders of mules and hinnies in modern times are well acquainted with the possibility of decreased natural interest in coupling between the two species (Travis 2004: 97). Data for donkey–hemione hybrids are much harder to come by given the Syrian onager's extinction, but the limited observations made by Antonius point to similar challenges (1944). Mares or stallions with proven success are therefore likely to have been highly prized. Having said that, there is little in the archaeological evidence to suggest the value of buried equids related to breeding; rather it seems it was related to their role as draught and burden animals.

Ritual and other equid depositions

Equid skeletons without a clear association with human burials or indication that they were buried for their own sake have also been uncovered. The complete or nearly complete, and usually articulated skeletons, have been found placed under floors and walls, in pits or other apparently deliberate deposits. They are usually interpreted as ritual or structured deposits, referring to their intentional and symbolic nature, along with the sacrifice of the animal. Others may have no ritual connection; these will be discussed below.

None of the equid species have a history of being protective beings, as would often be found in foundation deposits. Nevertheless, depositions of equids below or within walls, in liminal spaces such as thresholds, or below sealed floors, may be interpreted as foundation (or building) deposits. The practice of placing deposits with various contents in such locations in ancient Mesopotamia is well-known and has been studied in detail by Ellis (1968), although he does not have examples of equids. The examples of equids are indeed quite far and wide in between and, as with other aspects, we must be careful not to assume that one interpretation fits all. Examples include a donkey within the walls of a house at Tell es-Sakan (EB III, Miroschedji et al. 2001: 97), two very young donkeys placed in a double-mirror pattern sealed below a house floor at Tell Azekah (EB III, Sapir-Hen et al. 2017), several donkeys below house floors in Area E of Tell es-Safi (EB III, Greenfield et al. 2012; Greenfield, Greenfield et al. 2018), a donkey beneath a wall at Tel 'Akko (MB II, Wapnish 1997: 352), an infant or prenatal equid in a wall foundation pit at Tell Jemmeh (MB IIB, Wapnish 1997: 337–43), a donkey skeleton in the blocking of a doorway to Acropolis East at Tell Umm el-Marra (MB II, Nichols & Weber 2006: 48),[12] and equids placed below the Place IV walls of Tell el-'Ajjul (LB IIB, Petrie 1932: 5, 14, pl. L).[13] The custom would appear to have been confined to the Levant and western Syria, and primarily in the late third and early second millennia.

The equid bodies integrated into structural elements, where identified by a specialist,[14] were all donkeys; the sex has only been identified in a few cases – four females from Tell es-Safi, all young adults (Greenfield, Greenfield et al. 2018), and one male from Tell es-Sakan, aged 6 to 9 (Miroschedji et al. 2001: 97). There is little data to go on, but it may be that there was a preference for younger animals, as no mature or aged individuals are recorded, and the equid from Tell Jemmeh was aged between prenatal and two weeks (Wapnish 1997: 337–43), while the two from Tell Azekah were 9 to 12 months old (Sapir-Hen et al. 2017).

The location within or below structural elements make it evident that these equids were deliberately placed; this is supported by the positioning of the bodies – for example with the mirror image created by the Tell Azekah donkeys, or the twisted-back head of a donkey from Tell es-Safi. The choice of equids is certainly not arbitrary. Since they are not obviously protective beings, this choice may be related to the identity of the humans making the deposit and/or the role of equids within the community. For Tell es-Safi, this has been discussed in several papers by Greenfield and colleagues (Greenfield, Greenfield et al. 2018; Greenfield, Shai et al. 2018; Greenfield et al. 2021), who argue that the complete donkey skeletons found below the floors (courtyards) of two buildings at the site are sacrificial deposits made by merchants. The symbolic importance of the donkeys thus derives from their role in the lives of the merchants who lived in these spaces. The Tell es-Safi donkeys provide one of the few hints at the method used to ritually kill equids. One donkey's cranium and upper neck was completely separated from the body and placed in an opposite position. The dismemberment probably occurred postmortem, but cutmarks on a cervical vertebra of another of the Tell es-Safi donkeys suggest that their throats were cut (Greenfield et al. 2021).

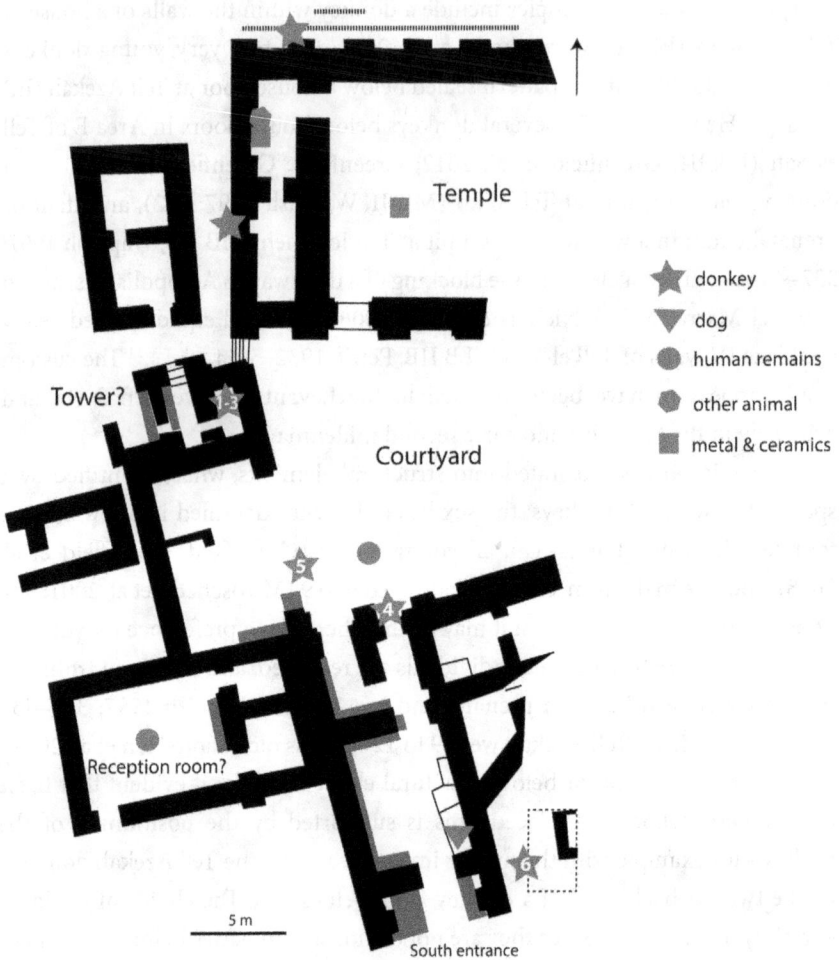

Figure 8.3 Plan of Tell Brak Area FS, Level 5. Find spots of equid and other remains marked. Akkadian (redrawn after Oates et al. 2001: fig. 42).

Equid bodies feature in a selection of other types of ritual deposits, each of which represents a unique context, but one that almost certainly involved the sacrifice of equids. The Akkadian (Level 5) monumental complex in Area FS of Tell Brak has been interpreted as a 'caravanserai' (Oates & Oates 2001; see also Chapters 4 and 7). The entire complex was 'ritually closed' with a number of deliberate deposits that consisted of objects and animal and human remains. At least eight donkeys, a dog, pig, gazelle and bird were part of these deposits (Figure 8.3; Clutton-Brock 2001).

The donkeys are probably the ones that (temporarily) lived in the caravanserai and whose daily lives consisted of carrying goods. This is supported by their variety and pathologies: Donkey 1 was an aged mare (probably over 20 years old); Donkey 2 was a young mare, aged 3 to 4; Donkey 3 was a 5-year-old male; Donkey 4 was an aged male (probably over 20 years old); Donkey 5 was an aged mare; and Donkey 6 was a 10-year-old mare (Clutton-Brock & Davies 1993; Clutton-Brock 2001).[15] Pathologies suggestive of a long working life (vertebrae damage and exostosis on hoof core) were identified on some of the individuals, and notching on incisors might suggest crib-biting – and hence stabling (Clutton-Brock & Davies 1993; Clutton-Brock 2003; cf. comments in Chapter 3 on crib-biting). The relationship between donkeys and building is thus neither random nor generic. The donkeys were part of the space, partly defined the space, and their importance is further emphasised by the finds of tablets from the complex recording equids and a substantial number of equid figurines from the site (Oates 2001). For the 'closing ritual', animals who had made it their home were chosen; the dog also fits neatly in this picture, acting perhaps as both guard and companion to both humans and equids.

A very different kind of ritual is represented by a large stone-built subterranean structure found at Tell Mozan, dated to about 2300–2100 BCE (Kelly-Buccellati 2002; 2005; Buccellati & Kelly-Buccellati 2004). This was located immediately outside the Royal Palace, and has been interpreted as a Hurrian *ābi*, a channel allowing communication with the underworld (Kelly-Buccellati 2002; Collins 2004). The structure is at least 6 metres deep (the bottom has not yet been reached in excavations) and has two main structural phases: an earlier, circular one, about 4 metres in diameter, and a later, keyhole-shaped one, over 7.5 metres at its greatest length. Access was through a narrow set of stone steps. Its contents suggest continued and regular ritual deposits over the period of use. These contents include an anthropomorphic vessel, a female figurine, a pig figurine, and seal impressions, along with a significant amount of animal bones (Kelly-Buccellati 2002; see also Recht 2014). The animal bones include a minimum number of individuals of 62 piglets, 20 puppies, 37 sheep/goat, and 10 donkeys, as well as fewer remains of other species (di Martino 2005). In this case, the animals were not complete or articulated skeletons, but it seems that very specific species were selected for the sacrificial rituals taking place at this deep pit. It would further appear that age was important, at least for the dogs and pigs, and this has been connected with their role in Hittite and Hurrian ritual (Kelly-Buccellati 2002). There are fewer donkey remains, but from a much larger animal. Their meaning in this ritual is difficult to gauge beyond their general importance at this time, along with the special relationship enjoyed between equids and dogs. In contrast to previous examples, there is nothing to suggest that specific individuals were chosen among any of the animals deposited in the *ābi*, but rather gain their value in a generic species sense.

Returning to Tell Umm el-Marra, but moving forward in time to the Middle Bronze Age, we find another deep shaft with animal deposits (Schwartz et al. 2012; Schwartz 2013). This shaft was dug into the third millennium Elite Mortuary Complex, but avoided disturbing any of the tombs. It is associated with a large circular monument or platform built in late MB I and covering the entire earlier cemetery.[16] Partly stone-built, and partly dug into the bedrock, the shaft was over 6 metres deep and 90–183 centimetres in diameter. It has its deep subterranean structure and sacrificial deposits in common with the Tell Mozan *ābi*, and combined with its location, may also suggest an attempt at some level of communication with the netherworld/ancestors. However, the deposits in this shaft are much more structured, and with a clear separation between the eleven layers of animal and human remains. The remains include partly and wholly articulated skeletons, with the most common animals being equids, dogs and sheep/goat, along with birds and one infant hare; human remains were found in the lowest layer (Schwartz 2013: 511). Most remarkably, and also in common with Tell Mozan, age was of great importance as many of the animals were infants or foetuses – including the equids. It may even have been the case that every layer contained bones of fetal animals (Schwartz et al. 2012: 187). That the shaft in some way creates a connection with the earlier cemetery – and the ancestors buried there –is demonstrated not only by its location, but also through the contents, with the predominance of equids and puppies referring back to the burials of those in previous times.[17] The many young animals indicate that this was an important criterion for inclusion, with less emphasis on individuality.

Yet another remarkable association of equid, puppies and birds come from Middle Bronze III Tel Haror. The Area K Sacred Precinct included a number of ritual deposits with animal skeletons: complete birds, puppies and a donkey, along with remains of sheep/goat, cattle, gazelle, deer and pig (Katz 2009: 29–119). The donkey was a four-year-old buried with a metal bit in its mouth and what appears to be remains of a saddle bag (Bar-Oz et al. 2013). The skull of an older donkey had been placed on top of its hind quarters, and both were covered by a layer of sediment, with further animal bones on top. The combination of saddle bag (indicating a beast of burden) and metal bit (indicating the pulling of a wheeled vehicle) is intriguing and a warning against simple interpretations that rely on a single role of equids. Here, it not only illustrates several meanings attached to a single animal; it may also be the case that some individual equids had a range of skills and would on separate occasions pull a wheeled vehicle, carry goods or humans, and perhaps even help plough fields.

In a number of other instances, finds of complete or nearly complete equid skeletons may represent ritual deposits, but the contexts are more ambiguous, and the possibility of rubbish dumps or even accidents should also be considered. Thus, complete or nearly complete equid skeletons in pits occur at Tell Jenin (Site 4, EB I, Al-Zawahra & Ezzughayyar 1998), Tell Lod (EB IB, Yannai 2008: 1914), Ashkelon (MB II, Horwitz et al. 2017), and Tell Nebi Mend/Kadesh (LB II, Grigson 2015). A small equid skeleton found in a corridor at Nippur may also have been buried in a shallow pit (Early Dynastic III/Akkadian, McMahon 2006: 23, pl. 28b). The donkey or donkey–hemione hybrid found in a temple rubbish dump at Abu Salabikh was probably dumped as part of the rubbish rather than as a ritual deposit (the so-called Ash-Tip – see Clutton-Brock & Burleigh 1978; Clutton-Brock 1986: 209, with corrections concerning species). Finally, two donkey skeletons and a human skeleton within a domestic house at Mari provide an unusual example of what may have been accidental deaths as a result of an earthquake *c.* 2700–2600 BCE (Margueron 2004: 97, 101, pl. 24). They also demonstrate that equids could be present in habitation contexts, albeit perhaps only temporarily.

Treaties

Besides being sacrificed as part of mortuary practices and foundation deposits, the written sources also inform us that equids were ritually killed as part of treaty-making and festival activities, particularly in the west, and perhaps with a special association with the Amorites. In letters from Old Babylonian Mari and Tell al-Rimah, donkeys, specifically donkey foals, were required as part of the rituals surrounding treaties (references collected in Dirbas 2014). The species was important at Mari at least; as noted by Malamat, a goat and a puppy were first brought forward, but were not considered adequate and a donkey foal was requested instead (Malamat 1995: 226). The sacrifice of a donkey in connection with treaties at Mari appears to have become such an integral part of the process that the phrase 'to kill a donkey' or versions thereof became synonymous with making a treaty. Thus, for example, in a letter from Zimri-Lim, the king of Mari:

> Speak to Hatnu-rapi, thus Zimri-Lim. I have read your letter which you sent to me. In the past you have often written that we should meet in Qattuna, saying: 'You there, bring (troops) upstream as far as Qattuna; and I here shall lead out

the kings my allies who enjoy good relations with me; let us kill donkey foals; let us put the "oath of the gods" between us.' You often wrote these words to me.

P223837, translation in Dalley et al. 1976: Text 1

A text from Late Bronze Age Ugarit lists offerings for a 'Ritual for national unity', in which a 'donkey of rectitude' is sacrificed (Pardee 2002: 77–83). Given its mention of a range of peoples from the surrounding areas, the importance of the donkey may be related to what we see for the peace treaties.

In some cities of the northwest, a festival called 'Sacrifice of the Donkey' (*hiyârum*) is recorded in the written sources in the second millennium (Dirbas 2014: 4–5). For example, two texts listing some of the offerings come from Alalakh (Durand 1988: 121–2), where they are associated with Ishtar. The festival is also recorded at Mari, Aleppo and Emar (Finet 1993; Magen 2001). Despite the name of the event, no donkeys are mentioned in these lists (in fact 'Festival of the Donkey' might be a better term for it). Magen has suggested a connection between this festival, figurines depicting a rider in the side saddle position, perhaps a deity, and a weather god (2001).

8.3 Killed in battle and other deaths

The dangers of the road were encountered in Chapter 4, where for example the long journey between Assur and Kanesh entailed the risks of succumbing to the weather, fatigue and attack from bandits. Similar risks, especially from attacks, are part of the Amarna correspondence, and could affect riders and caravans and their horses and donkeys.[18] In these cases, the equids were more likely collateral damage rather than specifically targeted, since they were valuable animals that could be part of the loot.

Another and much more immediate danger would be faced by equids engaging in battle, and to some extent in hunting (Lau 2017a,b; see also Recht forthcoming, b). Here, they would have been targeted directly in order to incapacitate an opponent. We know that equids fought alongside humans from around the middle of the third millennium, as most famously illustrated in the Standard of Ur (see Chapter 5 for more on equids and wheeled vehicles in war, and Chapter 4 for the possibility of equids with riders being part of battle). Recently, Porter and colleagues have suggested that co-burial of fragmentary remains of equids and humans at Tell Banat North (White Monument A) could be those of military equid and driver teams (Porter et al. 2021). The number of equids that were killed in this manner must have been quite high. In the aftermath of one of the battles of the border dispute between Lagash and Umma in the Early Dynastic III period, Enmetena, ruler of Lagash, abandoned 60 teams of the enemy's donkeys on the bank of the Luma-girnunta canal, along with their personnel (P222532, Frayne 2008: 197). A minimum of 120 donkeys were thus killed in a single battle, but the number is more likely 240, since teams of four seems to have been most common in this period. The dispute had been going on for some time, and a stele of Enmetena's predecessor, Eannatum, depicts him defeating Umma (including the use of wheeled vehicles), accompanied by an inscription (Barrelet 1970; Winter 1985; see Frayne 2008: 124–40 for the inscription).

Known as The Stele of the Vultures and only preserved in fragments, the third register on one side depicts a pile of human bodies. Immediately to the right of these is a human carrying a basket, presumably in the process of building the burial mound; to the right of this is a pile of six dead quadrupeds which may be equids (or sacrificial sheep or cattle). Their identification is uncertain because they have been decapitated, so we lack the features of the head. Beside this one possible example, dead or injured equids are not depicted in the iconography of the third and second millennia in the Near East. This changes in the palace relief of the Neo-Assyrians in the first millennium, where the horses of the enemies are shown tumbling about, and their dead bodies float in the river along with those of humans, as for example on Ashurbanipal's Til Tuba reliefs (BM 124801,b). Later texts do not record animal casualties in war, but we may surmise that a significant number of equids perished based on the size and frequency of battles – as for example in the Battle of Qadesh discussed earlier, where Ramses II mentions encountering 2500–3500 Hittite enemy chariots (Cline 2014: 81–2). This translates to a minimum of 5000 horses just on one side of the battle (assuming the numbers are reliable).

Just as caravan equids faced dangers on the roads, war equids are also reported as dying from plague during campaign (Potts 1999: 253). In a Late Bronze Age letter from a frontline, the sender complains about conditions where he has been stationed and exposed to the cold for five months: the horses are dead, the chariots broken and the army lost (Rainey 1972: 133). Equids surely also died of natural causes. Beyond the few examples mentioned above of certain individuals possibly dying of natural causes receiving special burial, their faunal remains largely escape us (as do those of other animals not killed by humans). The Ur III archives occasionally note the loss of equids and other animals by designating them as 'ri-ri-ga' (e.g. P315523), usually translated as 'dead (of natural causes, said of animals' (ePSD2, *degdega*), probably due to either illness, accident or age.

Equid–Human Relations and Equid Agency

9.1 Size, gender, age and colour (See also Appendix C)

Size

Even the largest equids of the ancient Near East were ponies by today's standards. Estimates of withers heights are not often provided in faunal reports, but can be at least partly reconstructed based on those that do exist, supplemented by calculations based on published measurements of selected skeletal elements. Published withers heights and estimates calculated based on published measurements are listed in Appendix E. Based on these, we obtain withers heights between *c.* 105 and 150 centimetres (the range of a small to medium/ large pony today, with just a few individuals reaching the height of a small horse).[1] Donkeys appear to lie in the lower range of these, with an average of about 114 centimetres – possibly with a slight decrease from the third to second millennium (from an average of *c.* 116 to 112 centimetres, but the sample size is limited). The very few examples of horses (five in total) indicate a larger animal at about 144 centimetres. Hemiones and hybrids lie between these. Only three specimens are identified as hemione, and one not well preserved. These provide withers heights between 127 and 132 centimetres. Possible hybrids in the form of hemione–donkey crosses only come from the one site of Tell Umm el-Marra, and these animals give an average withers height of 127 centimetres. There are no data for mules or hinnies.

Size mattered. For the Old Assyrian Assur-Kanesh trade, the desired quality of donkeys is that they should be tall of stature and small of teeth (Dercksen 2003: 52). Ishme-Dagan of Mari requests large donkey mares from Sutu to improve his own stock (P254333, Dercksen 2004: 258), and in a letter from the Hittite king Hattusili III to king Kadashman-Enlil II of Babylon, a request is made specifically for 'tall [horse] stallion foals' (Beckman 1996: 137). These sizes are of course relative, and tall in these cases may mean 120 centimetres withers height rather than 110 centimetres. For pulling wheeled vehicles, a match between the team members would also be important; the Old Assyrian letter mentioned above also requests mules which are similar to each other. Finally, equids may have been kept below a certain height in order to suit the chariots of the Late Bronze Age. Experiments carried out by Spruytte demonstrate that the type of chariot used could only accommodate horses of up to max. c. 125 centimetres (Spruytte 1983: 40). This is in fact significantly lower than the height indicated by the few available specimens of *E. caballus*, but these all come from third and early second millennium contexts, and it is possible that there was a decrease in size in the Late Bronze Age.[2]

Gender

It is sometimes assumed that stallions were preferred, especially for war and hunting. This slips into an assumption that male equids were more highly valued and associated with a greater level of prestige, with an underlying association of male/masculinity with power, strength and war and of female with foal-bearing, passivity, fragility and lower status. This slippage is problematic in a number of ways and suggests a possible gender bias in our approach, and it is therefore important to delve a bit deeper into 1) whether the evidence supports the idea of an ancient preference for male equids, and 2) whether there is evidence that male equids were more prestigious.

There can be behavioural differences between mares, stallions and geldings, but these are extremely dependent on species, breed and individual temperament. Each have their advantages and disadvantages for humans when engaging in various activities. Stallions may be less 'manageable' and prone to fight both each other and humans, which can make them quite a liability in critical situations (typically modern manuals on keeping donkeys recommend castrating as early as possible, see e.g. Svendsen 2009: 93, 102). On the other hand, these characteristics may also make stallions 'reckless' and more likely to plunge into danger. Geldings are usually much more likely to be willing to work with humans, with a greater focus on the task at hand but little of the recklessness of stallions. Mares can also be more willing to engage with humans, but often have a mind of their own and can sometimes be more 'stubborn' (sometimes amplified when in heat). Overall, mares, stallions and geldings of donkeys, horses and hybrids could all perform all the activities involving humans that we have come across in the ancient Near East. The nature of the interaction would depend as much on the individual equid as on their gender.

Both male and female equids have been identified in the faunal remains, but the majority of equid skeletal remains have not been or cannot be sexed. Sexing equids is usually based on the presence or absence of canines (a good but not 100 per cent secure indicator); the pelvis can also be used but is often too fragmentary. There is very little sexual dimorphism, and size is therefore not a reliable marker (Levine 1999: 13). It is not possible to securely identify geldings based on zooarchaeological analysis.[3] Based on the data we have, both male and female equids were buried as complete skeletons, sometimes associated with human burials (see Chapter 8). It is possible that male or female equids were required under certain circumstances. At the Elite Mortuary Complex of third-millennium Tell Umm el-Marra, there was a clear preference for male kungas, and this also appears to have been the case in soundings from Tell Chuera; conversely, female donkeys may have been preferred at Tell es-Safi.

Stallions are sometimes depicted in the iconographic material. The Standard of Ur has teams of four equid stallions (most likely – only the genitalia of the closest equid are actually rendered, see Figure 5.5). Stallions are shown in various other wheeled vehicle scenes, on several of the rider and equid plaques, and in terracotta figurines (Figures 3.5d, 5.10, 6.3a, 9.1a). In contrast, few mares are clearly depicted, and can in fact only be identified in a few terracotta figurines from Tell Mozan/Urkesh, Tell Brak and Tell Arbid (Figure 9.1b; Hauser 2007: 374, 389–94; Oates 2001: 272; Makowski 2016: pl. XXVIII). This could indicate that stallions were preferred, but two things prevent us from unreservedly drawing this conclusion (see also Recht 2018: 81–2). First, the female genitals would not be visible in two-dimensional profile renderings, other than possibly as an absence of male genitals. Second, 'neutral' or unsexed representations would look identical to female ones in two-dimensional media. The vast majority of our visual evidence does *not* depict genitalia; if an absence of genitals is a marker of female, then most depictions are of mares. However, a more likely explanation is that, in most cases, the gender of the equid was simply not important to the message of the specific depiction. Only the three-dimensional media more clearly reveal whether the animal was conceived as male, female or not gendered. A significant number of terracotta equid figurines are stallions: these primarily come from Khabur region sites and are dated to the late third millennium (see Appendix G). Many of them wear some sort of contraption tying the penis and/or testicles (Figure 9.1b; also found at the sites of Tell Brak, Tepe Gawra and Tell Arbid). The function of this is unknown, but almost certainly related to breeding programmes, and strongly associated with a region known for their breeding of equids in this period (see Chapter 7).

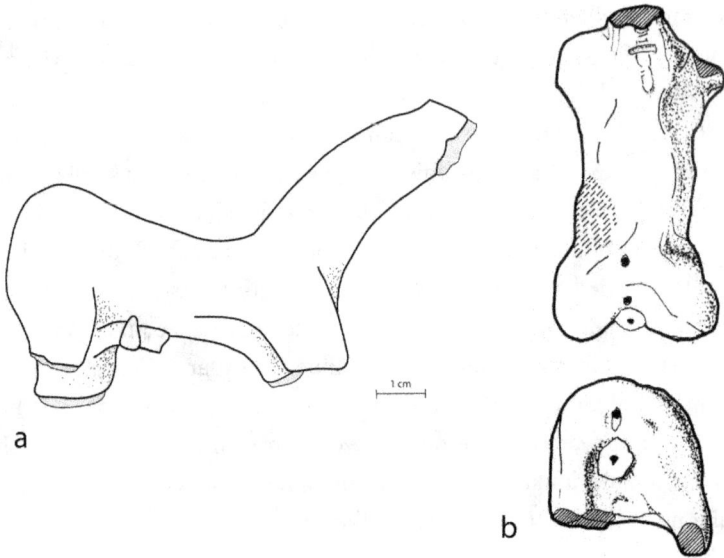

Figure 9.1 Terracotta equid figurines showing male and female genitals:

a. Terracotta figurine from Tell Brak, Area SS 224, Level 2/3, Phase M/N. Reg.
    no. 3070, Akkadian (drawn after Oates et al. 2001: fig. 311).
b. Terracotta figurine from Tell Mozan, Royal Palace Unit A7. Reg. no. A7.320,
    Akkadian (after Hauser 2007: 374, drawing by Claudia Wettstein). Courtesy of
    Rick Hauser.

The written records distinguish male and female equids by qualifying 'anše'
(see Appendix B).[4] These records do not indicate a strict division in the roles
played by mares and stallions; both can carry goods, act as riding animals,
plough and pull wheeled vehicles. It is possible that for some types of work,
mares or stallions may have been in the majority (for example at Lagash: see
Maekawa 1979a: 35–6). The donkey carrying a goddess in a text from Ugarit was
female, while the donkey with a rider who was perhaps a local chief was male
(see Chapter 6), and no gender is mentioned for the donkeys of Enlil in a hymn
to Išme-Dagan and Enlil's chariot (P463979, Civil 1968).

In instances where we might expect the gender of the equid to be noted if
stallions were considered more prestigious or appropriate for high-status
persons, none is recorded – as for example the letter to king Zimri-Lim of Mari
recommending that he should ride hybrid equids, not horses, as that would be
unsuitable for the king of the Haneans (P339013, Way 2011: 83). It would thus
appear that overall, any divisions in roles were based on availability and practical
matters related to breeding rather than a difference in the social status of mares

and stallions. However, specific contexts perhaps demanded or honoured either males or females (such as at Tell Umm el-Marra, Tell Chuera and Tell es-Safi).

Age

The written records classify equids based on life stages and likely corresponding to slightly different relations to humans. Thus, we find (suckling) foal (amar ga), young equid aged up to one (tur, amar), young equids aged one-three (mu + number), adult (gal), mature and milk-producing (mah_2) and old (libir, $šu$-gi_4). In the majority of cases, age is not specified, and we may assume that a healthy adult equid is intended. Typically, it seems that training did not start until around the age of three, or possibly in some cases a bit earlier. This is also consistent with modern equine practices. In one Middle Assyrian law, an equid is explicitly considered a stallion at the age of two (Pritchard 1969: 192, no. 58). Foals and

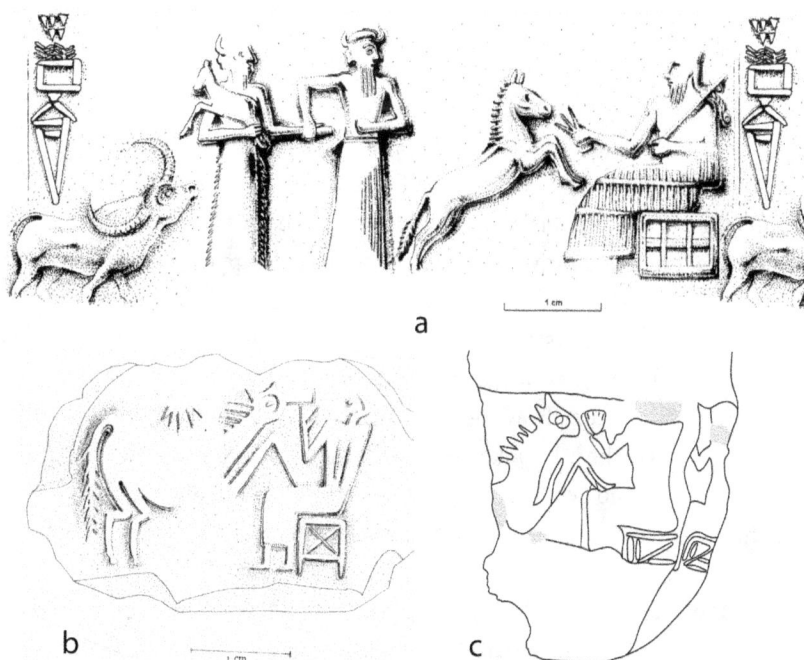

Figure 9.2 Sealings from Tell Mozan, Akkadian. Courtesy of The International Institute for Mesopotamian Area Studies. Motifs reconstructed from several sealings:

a. A13.28, seal of Isharbeli.
b. A9.27.
c. A14.26.

young equids were of little interest to artists and craftspersons, but the seal of Isharbeli found on seal impressions from Tell Mozan probably shows a mare followed by a person carrying her foal (Figure 9.2a), and impressions of a Late Chalcolithic stamp seal from Tell Brak may show a mare and her foal (Figure 3.5c). Foals or extremely young equids were sometimes part of ritual activities, as for example in a foundation deposit at Tell Jemmeh (Wapnish 1997: 337–43), a ritual deposit at Tell Azekah (Sapir-Hen et al. 2017), in tombs and the ritual deposit of the Monument 1 Shaft 1 at Tell Umm el-Marra (Weber 2012; 2017; Schwartz 2013), or indeed as part of sacrifices concluding a treaty (see Chapter 8). Once equids reach adulthood, the exact age no longer seems to have been important as it is not recorded. However, the faunal remains reveal that some equids could live quite long lives, even into their twenties. We find such older equids at Tell Madhhur, Tell Umm el-Marra and Tell Brak.

Colour

A range of coat colour is attested for horses and donkeys. The written sources especially mention black, red (probably both chestnut and bay) and white (babbar, 'silver', i.e. grey in modern terms). Black donkeys were especially prized in the Kültepe/Kanesh letters (Dercksen 2004: 258); the colour may in this case be associated with a specific 'breed' of larger donkeys or donkeys bred in a specific region. Presumably donkeys whose colour was not specified in these letters had a greyish or brownish coat. Horses instead appear to have been most popular as white. They are qualified as white already in the Ur III records (e.g. P104109), as are donkeys (e.g. P123433). Letters from Mari hint at the high regard of white horses, as one letter goes, 'About those white horses that are from Qatna, of which you are always hearing: those are really fine!' (Oates 2003: 121). Another goes, 'Further: I spoke (to Apla-Handa) about white horses, and he (said), "There are no white chariot-horses available. I shall write, and where white horses are available, they will bring them along. And for now I shall have red Harsamnean horses conducted to him (Zimri-Lim)." This he said to me. Now [ ] the red horses [n lines].' (Heimpel 2003: 406). White horses are also mentioned in the Amarna letters as part of the luxury gifts between rulers (e.g. *EA* 16). The Mari letters provide us with further hints concerning specialized breeding centres, and in addition to being visually impressive, the colour may also be related to overall desired qualities of horses coming from those regions. White horses in other periods had ritual and religious significance, an aspect that may also be relevant for the third and second millennia (Weidner 1952).

The Kassites, who appear to have been expert horse breeders, provide a broader range of coat colours and markings in the form of records found at Nippur (Balkan 1954). Unfortunately, beyond the addition of brown (probably bay), most of the terms used are not yet well enough understood to be translated. The much earlier third millennium archives also use the term 'sig$_7$', which Zarins understands as a reference to a type of coat colour (2014: 263); this could refer to a yellowish colour.[5] The visual evidence for equids in the third and second millennium is all in monochrome media, at least as preserved. If the wall paintings of the neighbouring regions of Egypt and the Aegean in the Late Bronze Age are anything to go by (and the extensive international spirit and popularity of the horses and chariot ensemble during this period suggest that they are) horses could be found in black, white, bay, chestnut, dappled and with various markings.

9.2 Tack and equipment

Various items of tack and harnesses have already been discussed throughout; this section contains further comments on some of these elements, along with new ones not yet encountered.

Bridles, reins, halters and tethers

Bridles, reins, halters and tethers are tied around the head or neck of an equid, and can be used to direct, lead, or tie an equid to a specific space (for the types of bridles used with wheeled vehicles, see Chapter 5; with riding, see Chapter 6). Terms designating these or related to them are found in the written record (see e.g. Na'aman 1977; Watson 2011), but tell us very little about the types employed. Texts from third millennium Ebla use terms which could refer to parts of bridles/ reins used with equids: ku$_3$-sal, nig$_2$-anše-ak and eš$_2$-kiri$_3$ (KA.ŠE$_3$) (Archi 1985; Conti 1997). They appear to come as part of a 'kit' with the wheeled vehicle and equids team, consisting of four ku$_3$-sal, two nig$_2$-anše-ak and one eš$_2$-kiri$_3$, but their exact function is not clear from the context. The ku$_3$-sal could be made of metal, and Archi suggests they could be decorative fittings for the bridle or something like bit guards (1985: 31). Decorative fittings are sometimes rendered on figurines, as for example on the frontlet of ones from Selenkahiye and Tell Halawa (Figure 5.8d, late third millennium, Liebowitz 1988: pl. 24.1; Meyer & Pruss 1994: 127, no. 110, fig. 37). The nig$_2$-anše-ak could be woollen, and may be either the bridle itself or a part thereof. Archi and Biga suggests 'bit' for eškiri (2003: 19–20), but this seems highly unlikely for the third millennium, and the term should probably rather be translated as 'rope' or 'tether' (ePSD2), presumably one of the other harness or bridle elements.

From late second millennium Emar, a tablet lists equid bridles (zib_2 tab anše), equid collar (gu_2-tab anše), equid blinkers (igi-tab anše), and equid reins (ul_3 tab anše), all made of leather (Arnaud 1985). All of these items were made of organic material (leather, wool, fibres) that has not been preserved in the archaeological record,[6] but there were also luxury versions which included elements of fine metals and semi-precious stones. We see this in the Amarna Letters (e.g *EA* 22; Rainey 2014) or in texts from Ugarit (e.g. Pardee 2000; 230; Way 2011: 49–50). In the Royal Tombs at Ur, remains of reins threaded with beads were found in Tomb PG 789, associated with cattle and a wheeled vehicle (Woolley 1934: pl. 34). An Old Babylonian text from Tell Asmar provides a rare hint of the care that would also have been needed to keep tack in good condition by the mention of lubricating oil for reins (*appatum*; *CAD* 1/2: 182).

Nose or lip rings; metal bits

The use of nose/lip rings and metal bits have already been discussed in some detail in Chapters 5 and 6 (examples in Figures 5.4, 5.5, 5.6, 6.3), including their functions and effect on equine responses (cf. also Littauer & Crouwel 2001). The earliest known metal bit to date comes from Tel Haror and is probably dated to the seventeenth or sixteenth century BCE (Bar-Oz et al. 2013). Bits may have been used earlier, but the evidence is still very tentative. Possible evidence of bit-wear has been suggested for donkeys found at Tell Brak in the Akkadian period (Clutton-Brock & Davies 1993; Clutton-Brock 2003), and at Tell es-Safi in EB IIIB (*c.* 2800–2600 BCE, Greenfield, Greenfield et al. 2018). In both cases, the wear is only minor and the age of the Tell Brak donkey, estimated to be over twenty, and the early date (before metal bits) calls for some caution, although it is possible that the wear could be caused by a bit made of organic material (e.g. bone, leather or even a rope – experiments suggest that these materials cause less wear; Brown & Anthony 1998).[7] A significant number of equid figurines are pierced through the muzzle (examples can be found in the assemblages of most of the sites listed in Appendix G). These may be for the use of a bit, as suggested by Littauer and Crouwel (2001), or for a lip/nose ring, but could also have been used as part of a pulling mechanism of the figurines. The bridles of applied clay never include elements that could indicate a bit. Until very recently, no indication of wear from a lip or nose ring had been identified on equid remains, but Jill Weber has now detected damage to incisors on the equids from Tell Umm el-Marra.[8] This damage could very well have been caused by a metal nose or lip ring. Both types of wear attest to equine pain and discomfort. Bit wear does not always occur with equids wearing bits. It is often caused by a bad fit in the mouth (the bit not placed correctly on the diastema or the wrong size for the equid's mouth), and/or the equid showing discomfort by biting on the metal bar with the upper and lower premolars. Bit wear is thus often a sign of active equine engagement with the bit.

Covers and rugs

A range of rugs, covers and (saddle) pads were associated with equids and are mentioned in the written records (e.g. Dercksen 2004: 270–7; Watson 2011). Pads might have been used below packs, the saddles used for side-saddle, and below the yoke for equids pulling wheeled vehicles. The Kikkuli horse training text (see Chapter 7) also has horses being covered in rugs as part of their care. In this case, we have an expression of knowledge of how to ensure the horses stayed healthy after strenuous exercise without too fast a cooling down period, or running the risk of disease by leaving a wet, sweating horse to turn cold. Another type of cover, perhaps specific to the Late Bronze Age, is depicted on a gold vessel from Ugarit (Figure A2). The horses wear a rug that covers their back, from the withers to near the tail; several tassels are attached along its lower lining. This type of rug was likely primarily for display, although it could also have provided some warmth to the horses during rest or slow walk. The gold vessel is the only clear depiction from the Near East of any kind of cover for equids in the Bronze Age, and only one of two existing examples of the attachment of plumes on the top of the horses' heads. Both of these elements are common on contemporary depictions of horses and chariots in Egypt.

9.3 Equid movement and gestures

Equids move in particular ways and have their own body language, with some aspects being specific to each species. Many of these movements and gestures provide information about the mood and intentions of an equid, and about the dynamics of the equid–human relationship. Let us then examine some of these as they can be found in the ancient Near Eastern material.

Gaits

Equids have three main gaits: walk, trot and canter/gallop (Figure 9.3; see also McGreevy 2012: 169–79).[9] The walk is a slow and steady four-beat gait in which at least one hoof is always touching the ground. The trot is a faster, two-beat gait interrupted by moments of suspension. It is usually much more difficult for a rider to sit on, especially on horses. The canter is a three-beat gait that turns into four beats in the gallop, which is even faster. The canter/gallop is asymmetrical, and can be either on the righthand or the lefthand rein. The equids of the ancient Near East are depicted standing, walking or at a canter/gallop, but not trotting; the gaits as rendered iconographically do not accurately reflect how equids actually move their legs. Instead, they follow artistic tradition of how all animals are shown when in movement. When walking, the left and right side respectively are depicted as moving in unison, in two beats, whereas in fact, the movement should be diagonal but asynchronous. The canter/gallop is depicted in a 'flying' or leaping movement, with the two front legs and the two hind legs respectively together. In reality, the four legs of the equid do not move at the same time, except in the canter, where one hind leg follows the opposite front leg. The depictions do not indicate a lack of ancient knowledge of equid gaits, but are simply conventions used for all animals to render different paces. The movements

Figure 9.3 The stages of the main gaits: walk, trot, canter and gallop (drawing by Inger Recht).

are used to convey speed and are appropriate to the overall message of a scene, with for example walking for processions and canter/gallop for engagement in battle.

This convention makes it the more surprising to find a few more faithful renderings of equid gaits. For example, seal impressions from Tell Beydar show the equid pulling a wheeled vehicle walking by moving its legs diagonally (Figure 5.4e; second stage of the walk in Figure 9.3). Although slightly damaged, a donkey on an inlay from Ur also seems to show the correct movement of the legs (Early Dynastic III, PG 800, Woolley 1934: 80, pl. 94). For the canter, a gold vessel from Ugarit shows this quite accurately in its three-beat version (Figure A2, between stage four and one of the canter in Figure 9.3), with the right hind leg and left front left moving simultaneously, and the other two legs following.

Ears

Equids have very good hearing (McGreevy 2012: 48–9). The importance of hearing is most clearly expressed in donkeys, whose large ears are perhaps a reflection of adaptation to the African homeland of *E. asinus*, aiding in communication and in heat dissipation (Burden & Thiemann 2015: 378). In any interaction with humans, hearing is a very important communication and recognition device. An equid will turn its ear or ears in the direction of the sound it wishes to pick up, and this movement may thus reveal where its attention is at any given moment. The positions of the ears can also express very complex sets of moods, such as discomfort/anger, careful attention and curiosity, and are part of conspecific communication (McGreevy 2012: figs. 6.1-6.7; Navas González et al. 2016: 121–3). Three main ear gestures can be recognized in the iconography, each corresponding to equid moods (Recht 2019). Both ears forward indicates eagerness and forward attention (e.g. Figure 5.2a, 5.9f, 6.3a-b). One ear forward and one backwards usually indicate that the equid is focussed; when this is combined with a rider or driver, the focus is on the communication to them (e.g. Figures 5.3, 5.4c, 5.6). Both ears backwards can indicate discomfort, distress, anger or protection of territory/other equids (e.g. Figure 5.4d,f, A1). These gestures are characteristically equine and reveal close observation of equine behaviour. They also provide an insight into the lives and feelings of equids, even if the depictions in some cases become rather standardized.[10]

Neck, head and mouth

A horse's neck is typically set higher than that of a donkey. Even so, we can see that all equids can be depicted as raising their head very high in an act that strains the neck (see examples in Figures 5.2, 5.4, 5.5, 5.6, 5.9, 5.10, A2). Occasionally, this even results in the neck slightly bulging in the front (Figures 5.4c, 5.6c, A1, A2). The raised neck and head occur with scenes of wheeled vehicles and is a reaction to the discomfort of a bit or lip ring. The head can either be pointed forward in an almost horizontal position (Figure 5.5), or squeezed backwards, almost touching the neck (Figures 5.10, A2). In a few instances, the equid even has an open mouth (e.g. Figures 5.2d, 5.4f, 5.6c, A2), probably another reaction to the bridle. All are attempts by the equid to avoid the pull of the reins, either by pushing against them or by pulling away from them. The highly held head may also have been encouraged by the driver, as it would help keep the yoke and yoke saddle in place and not slip over the head of the equids.

In other cases, an equid's head is turned slightly to one side. When single figurines are found with this gesture (Mallowan 1937: 130; Hauser 2007: 367, 416; also on a rein ring, Mallowan 1948), it gives the impression of a less static animal and perhaps a natural reaction to a nearby sound or movement. However, the gesture is more likely related to the pull of a rein, as it is exactly how an equid might initially react to a rein on one side being pulled by a driver or even rider (whereas for sound or visual input, the equid is more likely to move its entire body in the direction of the sensory input). This is most clearly illustrated in one of the few complete three-dimensional objects of equids with a wheeled vehicle, a copper model from Tell Agrab (Figure 5.3). The two inner or main equids turn their heads slightly inwards as a reaction against the two reins (one for each), while the two outriggers in turn react to the pull of the main equids. This closely corresponds to how equids might respond to the pull of a rein or rope; it also constitutes a small act of resistance, at least initially. Such a pull is usually intended as a command asking the equids to turn (or stop), but rather than immediately turning their whole body (and hence the direction), they merely turn their head. The development of two reins for each equid and harsher bit and bit guards can be understood as a human counter-action.

Tail

The tails of equids can also reveal their mood. Donkeys sometimes 'wag' their tail in excitement, and horses can hold theirs high as a response to excitement, when alarmed and/or at speed (for a detailed diagram of the various tail positions of horses and their meaning, see McGreevy 2012: 154, fig. 6.8). As we have seen, this is a useful indicator for distinguishing horses and other equids, but when the tail is lifted higher, it does also reveal something of the mood of the horses. Thus, we see in several seals and seal impressions that horses pulling chariots were either very excited and/or alarmed by the activities in which they were engaging, as for example in Figure 5.9b–d. Unsurprisingly, this more lifted tail usually accompanies a canter/gallop and fast action in hunting or battle.

Voice

The verbal communication of equids includes braying and whinnying. A shell inlay from Susa probably dated to Early Dynastic II-III wonderfully depicts an equid, probably a horse or hemione, whinnying/braying (Figure 9.4). The very wide mouth and head turned upwards in an almost horizontal position indicates that it is a rather stressful type of whinny, the equid perhaps calling after a companion that is out of sight or moving out of sight. An Akkadian period figurine from Tell Brak shows a similarly distressed equid (in this case, the species is not identifiable; Oates et al. 2001: 594, no. 62). A 'braying' donkey is mentioned in a composite text from Nippur (P461397), and in the text *Enmerkar and the Lord of Aratta* (P469674, Kramer 1952). *The Instructions of Shuruppak* advice against buying a donkey that brays (Biggs 1974: 60, no. 256, line 14). The reason is not clear in the text, but presumably is related to a distressed donkey not making a good working companion.

Figure 9.4 Shell inlay from Susa. Louvre Sb 5631, H. 3.2 cm, Early Dynastic II-III. Courtesy of Musée du Louvre (collections.louvre.fr/en/ark:/53355/cl010179457).

9.4 Agency, personhood and equid–human relations

As I have argued elsewhere (Recht 2019), much of the interaction noted here, along with the ancient observations of equine behaviour and the gear used, are a reflection of the agency of equids and the small and continuous negotiations between them and humans. Equids pushing against the reins and humans experimenting with means of communication is but one expression of the dynamics of the relationship. The employment of genital straps, whatever their exact purpose, is another, as are the elaborate training and care manuals. In fact, even though the relations were asymmetrical, we may see every encounter between equid and human as a kind of multispecies negotiation. Beyond the aspects explored so far, we find further hints of equids pushing back against humans, partly resisting the interaction, partly initiating it. For example, the caravan donkeys of the Assur–Kanesh trade are sometimes referred to as 'unruly' (Dercksen 2004: 265). An Old Babylonian proverb goes 'You should drive them like pack-asses into a death-stricken city' (Marzahn 2019: 74), implying not only that caravan donkeys might be reluctant participants, but also that some level of force was exerted to obtain their collaboration. Another proverb supports a similar reluctance of donkeys, 'The ass, after he had thrown off his packs, said: "The woes(?) of the past are (still) plentiful in my ears"' (P231595, Gordon 1958: 19, no. 5.39, slightly edited). Finally, donkeys fighting back is reflected in an analogy that refers to the risk of being kicked if standing behind one (George 1999: 145), and donkeys with a temper ('vicious') also occur in *The Instructions of Shuruppak* (Biggs 1974: 60, no. 256, lines 218–19).

Equid–human interaction was not always initiated or welcomed by humans. Equids could harass humans. We hear of this in a letter from Mari, where a camp must be guarded against hemiones (ARM 27, 4). It is not specified exactly how the hemiones were harassing the camp, but if we look back to accounts of recent centuries of onagers in India (Tegetmeier & Sutherland 1895), it may be that they were roaming through supplies and stealing food. In being interrupted, they may have defended themselves rather than have immediately fled.

More often, the reverse relationship occurred, with equids more or less voluntarily engaging in the interaction, and an obviously unequal power dynamic. Equids were killed by humans for a number of reasons (see Chapter 8) and must have endured many injuries and significant pain during battle and hunting, and were also frequently maltreated in other ways. The 'lowly' donkeys of caravan trades and those less visible in regular local transport were perhaps most prone to being neglected or treated badly. The donkeys of the Assur-

Kanesh trade are recorded as both dying and maltreated (Dercksen 2004: 268), and horses of the Ugarit army as starving (Bordreuil 1991: no. 6). Equids were also frequently taken as booty, as depicted on the 'Peace' side of the Standard of Ur and recorded in several texts (e.g. from Mari: Heimpel 2003: 360–1, 401–2). Since they were a valuable resource, some effort may have been taken to care for them, but they still suffered the same kind of uprooting of place and possibly companions as human prisoners.

Other kinds of violence that equids may have been subjected to by humans are more individualistic and apparently at the whim of human emotion. Two equid figurines from Tell Mozan have prompted Hauser to suggest that the nostrils of equids were sometimes slit (Hauser 2007: 402, 428). This practice is depicted in reliefs from fourteenth century Amarna (Clutton-Brock 1992: 77–8), and is thus not impossible to also have occurred in the Near East. In fact, the particularly marked and long nostrils on the Tell Agrab model (Figure 5.3) and on one of the horse and rider plaques (Figure 6.3b) support this idea. It is thought to have been a measure to aid breathing during exertion,[11] and Littauer thought the Egyptian examples might be a response to the low noseband that impedes breathing; supposedly, it also prevents whinnying (1969). Equally disturbing are mentions in Middle Assyrian law of the possibility of humans blinding horses or cattle (which does at least incur a fine), or having sex with a horse or a mule, which is not punishable (Pritchard 1969: 192, no. 77B; 197, no. 200A).

In rare instances, equids were given voice through proverbs and literary compositions, as in the example given above. In another example from Nippur, the horse complains about carrying a rider and after throwing one off, says, 'If my burden is always to be this, I shall become weak' (P231595, Gordon 1958: 19, no. 5.38; see more proverbs in Marzahn 2019). These are anthropomorphized versions of equids, but reveals at the very least something about their imagined pain and in turn some realization that equids were not always treated well. Equids are not common protagonists in myths and fables, but occasionally their anthropomorphization makes its way even into these realms. Thus, in a Late Bronze Age myth from Ugarit, a mare sends a message to the gods and asks for help extracting venom from a snake; one of the gods helps and later offers the mare wedding gifts (Pardee 2000: 232–3). Going back in time to the third millennium, a seal impression from Tell Asmar depicts an equid (perhaps donkey) and a lion in a typical banquet scene, seated on either side of a jar drinking through a straw (Frankfort 1955: no. 675, pl. 63). Another fable-like party is depicted on one of the lyres from the Royal Cemetery at Ur, with various animals carrying provisions, and an equid playing a lyre (U.10556, PG 789, Woolley 1934: pl. 105).

Certainly, *personhood* as well as agency was attributed to some equids, but the nature of our evidence means that this aspect tends to be invisible. Small hints are provided in references to individual equids kicking or being 'unruly', or in the intimate encounters between equids and humans depicted on the Tell Mozan sealings. Overall, depictions of equids are generic (and here the monochrome nature of most iconography does not help), but we must also acknowledge that features signalling specific individuals may escape us. For example, the horse figurine from Tell es-Sweyhat is so precise in its appearance as to approximate a portrait. The equids pulling wheeled vehicles for royalty may have been famous for their bravery and skill, but unlike the ancient Greeks, the artists of the ancient Near East did not see fit to supply names on their depictions. More substantial evidence comes from the archaeological record, where it is clear that some equids were highly valued and respected, either accompanying wealthy human tombs or given their own burials. Some may have been honoured teams of equids, while others were honoured as individuals. The Tell Umm el-Marra examples once again show that specific individual equids were so highly respected as to be taken care of well past their prime and optimal working life. These animals can be understood as having personhood, as also observed by Weber (2017).

More direct examples of equid persons come in the form of named equids. Naming constitutes some level of acknowledgement of individuals and of individual agency. The Kassite texts from Nippur listing horses, in their recording of pedigrees, also provide names of some of the horses (Balkan 1954: nos. 1–3). Thus, we meet Sambi, Armi, Pikandi, Šeris, Alzibadar, Ḫalsi, Šimriš, Burra-Minimzir and so on. The names often relate to their characteristic features, as with many pets today, including references to their colour or coat pattern. In the *Enuma Elish*, four teams pull Bel's chariot, each given a name, translated as: 'The Destroyer', 'The Merciless', 'The Trampler' and 'The Fleet' (Lambert 2013: 89). Although the animals pulling them may not be equids, this does give a sense that such teams could be perceived as particularly fierce. In Egypt, we find names of the pharaoh's horses recorded (Pritchard 1969: 250), giving further support to a similar practice possibly existing in the Near East.

That a high social status could be achieved by equids is illustrated by the Amarna letters and other Late Bronze Age royal correspondence (Pardee 2000: 225; Rainey 2014). The standard formal greeting in these letters was an enquiry after the well-being of the 'household' of the recipient – a household that typically included wives, sons, country, chariots and horses. Horses (in this case strongly linked with their chariots) were solid and integral members of the king's household. They were considered socially important, as was their health and well-being (at least formally; the practical implications are another matter). Human respect for equids as near-equal is also reflected in the Shulgi B Hymn, where a hemione is described as a 'worthy rival' in the chase or hunt (P469698, Zarins 2014: 286, no. 69).

A few seal impressions from late third millennium Tell Mozan have an unusual depiction of an equid–human encounter (Figure 9.2; Recht 2018: 82–3). The scene exists in at least three variations, with the best preserved also being of the highest artistic quality, with an inscription naming the scribe Isharbeli (Buccellati & Kelly-Buccellati 2000: 139; Hauser 2007: 52). The other two seals may have been attempts to emulate Isharbeli, as argued by Kelly-Buccellati (2015: 119–20); in neither case is an inscription preserved. The overall motif is that of a typical presentation scene. On Isharbeli's seal, a seated figure (king or god) is approached by a worshipper carrying a quadruped and presented by an interceding deity. Between these, and immediately before the seated king, who holds out a three-pointed object in his right hand (perhaps something edible), an equid greets him with both front legs raised, apparently reaching for the object. Judging by the tufted tail and relatively short ears, the equid may be a hemione, donkey or kunga, but if it is indeed the mother of the quadruped being carried by the worshipper, the latter can be ruled out. The encounter fits well within the artistic tradition of presentation scenes, but it is also one of the most delicate encounters depicted in ancient Near Eastern iconography. The posture of the equid is not natural for approaching another creature, but mimics that used for rendering equids pulling wheeled vehicles, and may therefore be a reference to the equid's expertise in that activity. In the two similar scenes, a seated figure is again approached by an equid (hemione, donkey or kunga), and the encounter is even more intimate, with the equid just touching the seated figure with its muzzle and hoof. These encounters are unusual because they are the only examples of face-to-face communication between equids and humans (or anthropomorphic figures). All other physical interaction revolves around carrying riders and other burdens, leading, training, and pulling ploughs and vehicles. It is thus a refreshing glimpse into non-violent one-to-one meetings between two species.

10

Conclusion

In many ways, the lives of equids in the ancient Near East were as varied as those of their contemporary human counterparts. Equids were present at almost all social levels, from aids and companion workers in the everyday activities of some of the poorest people to elite champions of chariots and steeds of deities. They carried water and grain for subsistence and fought in mighty battles still remembered today. Their bodies were left to decay in the steppe and honoured in elaborate tombs. They probably travelled further than any other nonhuman animal accompanying humans, traversing a space that covered thousands of kilometres from east to west and north to south. Equids were hunted, eaten, skinned, sacrificed and venerated. Although their names are largely lost to us, some equids became the equivalent of Hickstead, masters of their profession as war equids and akin to royalty, but the unsung heroes are the more anonymous masses of equids whose labour provided everyday help and companionship. For these, even their bones are mostly lost to us, but we can piece together at least part of their stories from a range of direct and indirect evidence.

Like humans, equids were social beings, living and working with other equids and other human and nonhuman animals. Just as not all humans were equal, so for equids, both individually and at species level. For example, the long journeys carrying merchandise were mostly undertaken by donkeys, as were those of local transport. They also took part in battle and pulled both wheeled vehicles and ploughs. Kungas did the same but appear to have been higher on the social scale, as evidenced by the price, the fodder they received, and the contexts in which they appear in texts and archaeological depositions. Horses and horse–donkey hybrids were similarly prestigious animals, with horses in particular strongly associated with the new, light chariot of the second millennium. Hemiones on the other hand appear to have mostly been part of breeding, hunting and skinning practices, rarely participating in the activities that the other equids were known for.

Equids made history in the ancient Near East. Without them, the world of the ancient Near East would have looked very different. As we have seen, equids had an enormous impact on human lives, including in aspects of economy, foreign relations and war, ideology and symbolism, craftsmanship and everyday activities. The story of the equids of the Bronze Age Near East is deeply entangled in the history of the area, to the extent that it becomes difficult, if not impossible, to determine causal relations. Equids were both part of and facilitated widespread societal transformations. These transformations mainly relate to equids – donkeys in particular – carrying goods and humans both over long and short distances, starting some time in the late fourth millennium BCE. The long-distance journeys, also occurring over water, allowed for greater intensification in trade and trade relations, with repercussions far afield in all cardinal directions. The second major transformation began in the third millennium when donkeys and kungas pulled wheeled vehicles as part of battle, but its main impact is only visible almost a millennium later, when horses and the fast, light chariot can be found at least as far west as Greece, and were a standard part of the armies of Mesopotamia, Anatolia, Egypt and the Levant.

One might wonder why it took so long for the change from donkeys or kungas and wagons to horses and light chariots to occur. The answer to this lies at least partly in the characteristics of each species, as we have seen throughout, and in their suitability for the social, economic and environmental conditions. For example, donkeys were likely better able to tolerate the kinds of fodder offered and a less regular supply of water, had higher endurance levels, were better able to navigate uneven terrain, had more comfortable gaits and a less 'nervous' temperament. In comparison, hemiones may have been much less willing to cooperate so closely with humans, and the advantage of the speed and flight mode of horses not outweighing the qualities of donkeys and kungas until the conditions of the mid-second millennium.

Shifting to a bottom-up perspective, this impact has even deeper and broader implications: humans needed to share both food and space with equids, which would involve an intensification in agricultural production and extension in appropriate pasture. Equids also required specialized personnel for daily care, management, breeding, training and so on, implying a highly organized system that could employ such personnel. The charioteers of the professional armies of the second millennium are but one such specialized group, but further down the line cartwrights and chariotmakers supplied such armies with wheeled vehicles; and even further back, supply lines of a range of raw materials (wood, metal, leather, stone) and craftspersons (smiths, woodworkers, leatherworkers, stone carvers). All of these were part of the world of the ancient Near East, and a very complex social and economic enterprise. Closer to the equids themselves, a whole host of breeders, farmers, herders, grooms and trainers surrounded and interacted with them at various stages of their lives. Many of these 'background' activities are largely hidden, but in fact comprise the most intimate and regular interaction with equids. These interaction involved recognition and negotiation of personhood and agency, both equid and human. These are the people who would have known equids better than anyone else – and vice versa. They would have recognized individual equids and each their specific 'quirks'; how to best interact with them in any given situation, to identify moods and when something was not well. The relations with these groups of people formed the foundation of all activities involving equids.

Engagement with humans also had a massive impact on equid lives. Space and movement, fodder, water, breeding and intra-equid companionship were all to some extent restricted or controlled by humans. The impact on individual equids depended on a number of characteristics, including species, age, gender, social and work status, and was further complicated by chronological and regional factors. Hemiones would have spent their lives on the steppes, with little contact with humans until they were hunted and either killed for their meat and skin or captured to act as breeding animals. Donkeys, horses and hybrids would be born into their herd and probably also spent their first few years on pasture, with their interaction with humans limited to the herder. Some equids might have begun training and work in their 'teenage' years, with the intensity and length of training corresponding to the tasks they were destined to perform. Other equids may have spent most of their lives on pasture, such as for example breeding mares, while yet others changed their habitat seasonally based on work in the fields and trade rhythms. Equids can be seen to push back or attempt to negotiate some of the human-imparted restrictions, and in turn we see some of the human responses to this resistance through, for example, experimentation with various types of equipment.

Mutual becomings of equids and humans through shared lives, space, movement and training were followed by mutual deaths and afterlives. Equids and humans died together on the road and in battle (and presumably hunting). In special circumstances, they were also buried together in contexts that hint at the high social status of both human and equid. Equids were also considered suitable for ritual depositions as well as for burial in their own right, although the vast majority probably died and were left outside areas of human habitation.

Throughout this book, we have followed the lives and deaths of equids in the Bronze Age Near East, and the many ways in which they interacted with humans. I hope in this to have conveyed some of the complexity of these interactions and their impact on human and animal alike. Equids were active, deliberate and charismatic participants in their relations to other beings, and I feel privileged to present a small part of their story, even if it remains patchy and with an inevitably incomplete human perspective and a distance in time of over 5000 years. Despite this chronological gap, human interaction with equids and other nonhuman animals are as important and pervasive as ever, yet their increasing invisibility and physical distance mean that they are more easily forgotten. The equids of the ancient Near East demonstrate some of the features of human-nonhuman relations and their importance, both in the past and today. The spirit, stoicism, vigour and swishing tails of the donkeys, hemiones, horses and hybrids were part of what shaped the ancient Near East as we have come to understand it, and their impact was felt in all levels of society.

Appendix A

Glossary of terms (modern)

Equid species

donkey   *E. asinus* (also sometimes 'ass')
hemione   *E. hemionus* (Syrian or Persian onager)
hinny   female donkey × male horse
kunga   donkey-hemione hybrid (word adapted from Sumerian)
mule   male donkey × female horse

> horse mule: male mule/hinny (also sometimes john mule or jack mule)
>
> mare mule/hinny: female mule/hinny (also sometimes molly mule or jennet)
>
> mule colt: young male mule
>
> mule filly: young female mule

Equid age, gender and pedigree

colt   young male equid, less than three years old
dame/sire   the equid mother/father
filly   young female equid, less than three years old
foal   young equid, usually up to one year old
gelding   castrated male equid
mare   female equid (donkey also jenny or jennet, mule/hinny also molly)
stallion   uncastrated male equid (donkey also jack, mule/hinny also john)

Harness, tack and elements related to wheeled vehicles

outrigger   equid attached next to a pole equid (also 'outspanner' or 'trace equid')
pole equid equid immediately next to the pole and attached to it
rein ring   element through which the reins are passed to avoid tangling (also 'terret')

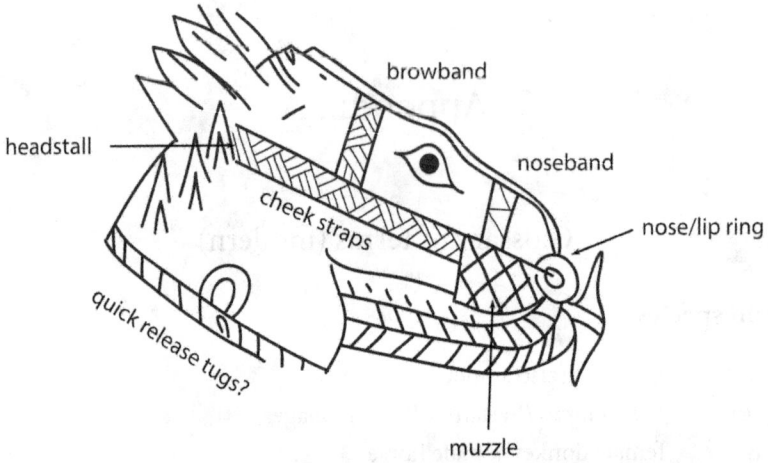

Figure A1 Diagram depicting tack elements typical of the third millennium BCE. Based on plaque inlay from Mari, Ninnizaza Temple. Reg. no. M 2468 / Damascus, Early Dynastic IIIA (drawn after Parrot 1967: pl. LXV no. 2468).

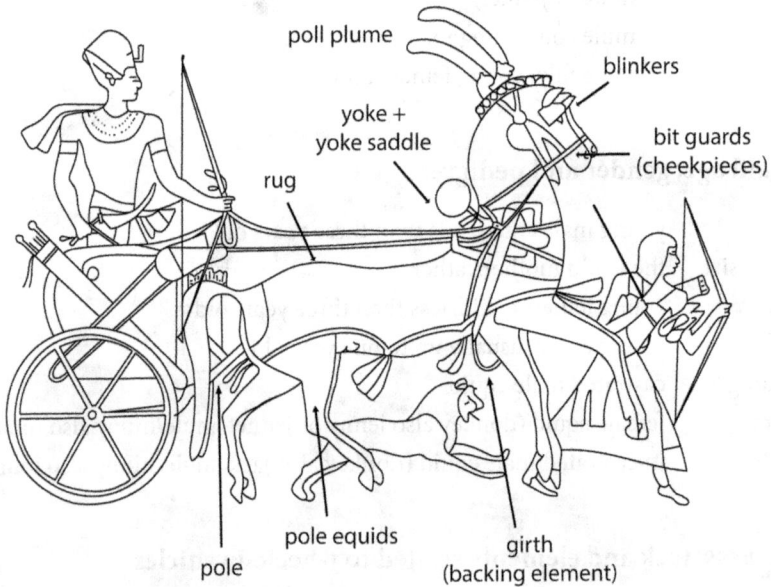

Figure A2 Diagram depicting tack elements typical of the late second millennium BCE. Based on gold bowl from Ugarit, near temenos wall of Temple of Baal. 14th – 13th centuries BCE (redrawn after Schaeffer 1949: 10).

Notes

1. Introduction

1 As translated in ETCSL, lines 16–18 (2.4.2.01).
2 As DeMello demonstrates, this line of argument, which involves 'othering' a specific group, closely mirrors that used to legitimize inequality between humans as well, based on for example gender, class or skin colour (2012: chapter 13).
3 For comparison with developments in Egypt and elsewhere, see Postgate et al. 1995.
4 With one important exception: since there is currently no word in English for the donkey-hemione hybrid, I have throughout decided to adopt the Sumerian for this, and will be calling this hybrid 'kunga' throughout (with kunga$_2$ being reserved for specifically referring to the phonetic value).
5 From here on, all dates, unless otherwise noted, are BCE.

2. Equid Species: Spirited Horses, Stoic Donkeys and Vigorous Hybrids

1 Earlier attempts to identify a broader range of *Equus* in general go further back – see e.g. references in McGrew (1944: 56).
2 Ducos considers the presence of *E. africanus* in the Near East to now be indisputable – primarily to be found in northern and eastern Syria (1975).
3 At Tell Mashnaqa, cutmarks were detected on a number of equid bones, possibly all from hemiones rather than donkeys (Vila 2006: 108). This could mean that donkeys had a different role, and that they were perhaps domestic.
4 Further subspecies occur or have occurred elsewhere in Asia and Africa (see Antonius 1932: 275; Mitchell 2018: 19), but are not thought to have been present in the Near East. Note that I prefer to use the term 'hemione' throughout, since this refers to *E. hemionus*, including both the Persian and Syrian variant, while 'onager' on its own strictly speaking does not include the Syrian variant.
5 Another wild species is *E.hydruntinus*. The exact status and definition of this extinct species remains a matter of some debate. It has proved difficult to pinpoint both morphologically and genetically (see e.g. Davis 1980; Orlando et al. 2009; Geigl & Grange 2012, cf. Bennett et al. 2017). Since it does not seem to have existed in the

Near East during the Bronze Age, it is not included here (Davis mentions no remains identified from after 10,000 BCE – Davis 1980: 308; but see now also Arbuckle & Öztan 2018).

6 If hemiones had been domesticated, we should be able to identify them in the genes of modern domestic species; offspring of hemiones/onagers and domestic donkeys should also be fertile, which they are not (Clutton-Brock 1992: 37).

7 A new study by Clavel et al. (2021) suggests that geometric morphometric analysis of the bony labyrinth shape (inner ear) could also be a useful indicator of equid species, including hybrids.

8 For a detailed description of the two early versions of this sign ('*gunû*-fied' and 'non-*gunû*-fied'), see Zarins 2014: 157–61.

9 For the reading dur$_9$-gir$_x$, suggested by Steinkeller (2005), see Appendix B.

10 I am grateful to Nicholas Postgate for this information, and for also pointing out that this absence does not mean that it was not actually in use.

11 Hurrian is another language present in the Near East, in particular in Syria and the Khabur region (the area known in Akkadian as 'Subartu'). There are indications that equids were an important part of Hurrian society, but the rather limited surviving Hurrian documents discovered so far shed limited light on this topic.

12 Indeed, this has been done with some success by Hauser (2007) in his study of terracotta animal figurines from third millennium Tell Mozan. With a set of precise measurements of the different parts of the body of the figurine, ratios were calculated and used to identify species, including differentiating equid species. This promising approach seems to have largely worked for the Mozan corpus, but has not yet been extensively tested on other assemblages.

13 Although this does not mean that they do not actually feel the same levels of pain as horses, but rather that they express it differently (Burden & Thiemann 2015: 379; Grint et al. 2015).

14 This appears to be mainly if the training methods are not adjusted according to which species of equid is on the other side of the interaction – i.e. if one attempts to train a donkey exactly as if it is a horse.

15 See also a good discussion and overview on Ontario Ministry of Agriculture, Food and Rural Affairs website: http://www.omafra.gov.on.ca/english/livestock/sheep/facts/donkey2.htm (accessed 31 October 2019).

16 Perhaps as little as 50–75 per cent of a horse/pony of the same size (Smith & Burden 2013; Burden & Thiemann 2015: 378; Meutchieye et al. 2016)

17 In contrast, Tegetmeier & Sutherland report both 'vicious' and very tame onagers in Morbi in India (1895: 27), but the animals they describe are of the Persian version.

18 As translated in Carleton L. Brownson. http://www.perseus.tufts.edu/hopper/text?doc=Xen.%20Anab.%201.5&lang=original (accessed 11 November 2019).

19 As the authors caution in both papers, the impact of some factors is difficult to evaluate. It is possible that certain types of tasks are more suited for some species (although there should not be a great gap between the equids), that previous training, and that the individual mood for learning or interaction of each animal have an influence. The results are nevertheless highly suggestive (cf. also McGreevy 2012: 84–5). As noted by Burden & Thiemann (2015: 377), it is also important to know that the quick learning ability applies to both wanted and unwanted behaviour (see also Svendsen 2009: 104).

3. Beginnings, History and Distribution

1 Establishing sex ratios may also be difficult because there is little sexual dimorphism in equids, and diagnostic elements such as the pelvis and canines are not often recovered from excavation.

2 Recent work by Taylor et al. (2015) on horse skulls from Bronze Age Mongolia discusses the possibility of osseous changes to the nasal portion of the skull as a result of exertion or heavy breathing. Such changes have not yet been noted for equids in the ancient Near East.

3 However, equid hoof prints have been found in a Late Bronze Age stable in western Anatolia, at Beycesultan (Lloyd 1972: 15, pl. IXb).

4 *E. hemionus* includes here both the Syrian and the Persian version, although most are believed to be Syrian onagers. The equids here could conceivably also belong to other wild equid species such as *E. africanus* or the elusive *E. hydruntinus* (see Chapter 2 for more on this). Noble (1969) also provides an account of the 'Mesopotamian onager', but unfortunately this is no longer up-to-date, as it is now clear that the onager was not domesticated.

5 Although there is an early variation of the sign ('non-*gunû*-fied'), which he believes may refer to hemiones (1978: 3–4; 2014: 154–61).

6 It has also been suggested that there was more than one more or less simultaneous domestication event; another contender being the Iberian peninsula (Uerpmann 1995).

7 However, see now the new results in Librado et al. (2021) suggesting an origin in the western Eurasian steppes.

8 *E. caballus* bones have been identified in mid-third millennium contexts at Tell Chuera, but radiocarbon dating has subsequently placed those bones in the second millennium (Vila 2006: 120; 2010). As the excavators do not seem to have had reason to suspect intrusion, this is an important cautionary tale.

9 For example, an unprovenanced stamp seal in the British Museum depicting a rider on a donkey (4000–3000 BCE, BM 135723), another stamp seal from the British

Museum with a donkey (*c.* 4500–3500 BCE, BM 113887), or incised bones from Susa depicting horses and riders (dated by the excavator to *c.* 3400 BCE; Mecquenem 1934: fig. 38.24–5), but with unclear circumstances of excavation (cf. Moorey 1970: 43).

10 I tentatively agree with this identification: the animal has a remarkably full tail, which does suggest horse. However, the overall rendering is very stylized and inaccurate in its details (e.g. the head and legs of the equid, the style of riding). I am most grateful to Christina Tsouparopoulou for sharing her personal photos of some of the tablets with the enrolled seal, and to David Owen for sharing his thoughts on this particular seal.

4. Equids Changing History I: Caravans and Transport of Goods

1 The choice of means of transport of course depends very much on the location of a site and the landscape in which it is placed – as Hammurabi said to the king of Mari, 'the means (of transportation) of your land is donkeys and carts; the means of this land is boats' (Heimpel 2003: Text 26 468).

2 This concept covers more than simply a group of donkeys carrying goods: it may have constituted a kind of partnership of merchants under the leadership of one or more individuals (see Dercksen 2004: 164–6). The terms *harrāhum* and *ālikum* are also used; the difference between the three is still not well understood (Dercksen 2004: 255). There were also 'express' transports (*bātiqum*) (see Barjamovic 2011: 41–2 for a list of examples; 18, note 91 for a discussion of the nature of these transport).

3 It seems the caravans usually travelled during the day, although there are examples of night journeys as well, as in a letter from Mari (Heimpel 2003: Text 26 524).

4 Or *gugamlum*; *nabrītum* is also used, and may indeed be closer to the meaning of paddock – Dercksen describes it as an 'enclosed field (communal) for keeping of donkeys' (2004: 267).

5 Note, however, that Salonen prefers to translate this as 'grey' in the context of the donkeys (1956: 45).

6 There were also human porters, primarily used for shorter journeys between trading posts. They carried loads of about 30 kilograms (Dercksen 1996: 61–3).

7 One letter (TTC 28) possibly mentions a horse (Veenhof 1972: 9; Barjamovic 2011: 364), but the reading of this has been questioned by Dercksen, who considers it a scribal error (1996: 68). In the Kanesh letters, horses otherwise only occur in the title of individuals known as the 'horse-master' (*rabi sisīē*) and his wife (Michel 2004: 192).

8 Despite Dercksen's claim to the contrary (2004: 259–60).

9 To date, very little is published on the faunal remains from Kültepe/Kanesh, and earlier excavations did not retain animal remains. For one report and the current

state of research, see Atici 2014, who records a total of fourteen *E. asinus* and twenty *Equus* fragments.

10 For comparison, The Donkey Sanctuary recommends a maximum burden of 50 kilograms for an average donkey, for intermittent 'entertainment' activities (https://www.thedonkeysanctuary.org.uk/what-we-do/knowledge-and-advice/working-donkeys).

11 Letters that mention the gifting of horses (usually with their chariots): *EA* 2, 3, 7, 9, 15, 16, 17, 19, 22 and 37.

12 Heltzer has a price of 10 shekels of silver, but notes that the tablet with this price is by an unreliable scribe (1978: 56, note 80). Pardee has a price of 30 shekels of silver for donkeys at Ugarit (2000: 223–4), and a letter from Kadesh to Ugarit has 2 talents (60 kg) of bronze for one donkey (Bell 2012: 182).

13 And in equids being present on Cyprus in the first place, since they are not indigenous to the island (see Recht *forthcoming,a*).

5. Equids Changing History II: Chariots and Traction

1 Maekawa notes that 'For plowing and seeding the níg-en-na fields in pre-Sargonic Lagash, the sag-pin [ploughman] employed only males among the ANŠE.DUN.GI-equids (anše-giš). Female ANŠE.BARxAN-equids were also frequently set to plowing as anše-giš, but the sag-pin employed few ANŠE.BARxAN males.' (1979a: 35–6).

2 For an Early Dynastic III seal depicting ploughing with cattle, see Crawford 2004: 56, fig. 3.3.

3 Other works include, but are by no means limited to Salonen 1950; Nagel 1966; Piggott 1979; 1983; papers in Fansa & Burmeister 2004; Raccidi 2012; Veldmeijer & Ikram 2013; Raulwing et al. 2019. See also references throughout this chapter.

4 With one exception: the 'sledge'. This type of vehicle is depicted in Late Uruk pictograms (Burmeister et al. 2019), and an extravagant example was found in the Ur Royal Tomb PG 800 of Queen Puabi (Woolley 1934: 74, plates 122–4). To date, there is just one possible association of equids with a sledge, found in the funerary offerings of Ninenise, wife of Urtarsirsira, a ruler of Lagash in the Early Dynastic III period (P220725, translated in Cohen 2005: 163–6).

5 Not all representations contain enough details to place them in one of these categories. Further types of wheeled vehicles are known, especially from terracotta models, but not yet directly associated with equids. The earliest depictions of wheeled vehicles in the Near East date to the Late Uruk period (see e.g. Bakker et al. 1999; Burmeister et al. 2019). For the function of the different types of harnesses, see Spruytte 1983, and more recently Brownrigg 2004; 2019.

6 Including Ugarit, Beth Shean, Megiddo, Hazor, Gezer, Tell el-Ajjul, Amman, Lachish, Ashkelon, Nuzi, Tell Brak and Nippur (Hilprecht 1893: pl. X; Petrie 1933: pl. XXVII.82–3; Starr 1937: pl. 121,K,Q,V,W; Woolley 1955: pl. LXXXII.27–9; Caubet 1991; Oates et al. 1997: 88, fig. 128, 245, fig. 222.72–3; Caubet & Yon 2001; Stager 2006: 173, figs. 3–4; Matoïan 2008).

7 Including Tel Haror (Bar-Oz et al. 2013), Tell el-Ajjul (Petrie 1933: 10, no. 221, plates XVII, XXV; Petrie et al. 1952: 15, no. 210, pl. VXII; Littauer & Crouwel 1979: fig. 48), Ugarit (Schaeffer 1938: 318, 319, fig. 46), Tell Haddad (Littauer & Crouwel 1988).

8 For a slightly different interpretation of their function, see Littauer & Crouwel 1985: 84.

9 The same concept can be applied in other regular interactions with particularly nervous horses that do not appreciate the farrier's trimming or the veterinarian's needle: shielding the hind view by simply placing a hand behind the eye may have a calming effect (see also McGreevy 2012: 312, fig. 14.4).

10 Such small metal parts may survive in the archaeological record without being recognized as having been part of a wheeled vehicle, since they could equally have served other functions. For example, bronze hasps found at Tell es-Sweyhat could have been part of a wheeled vehicle, as suggested by Holland (2001–02: 94–5, fig. 10.4–5), and Stager reports linchpins for chariots at Ashkelon (2006: 171–2, fig. 2).

11 Enough of the 'sledge' in PG 800 also survived for a suggested reconstruction to be made (Woolley 1934: plates 122–4).

12 These items have also been conveniently presented together as part of the Ur Online project: www.ur-online.org/term/4/.

13 Two types of ᵍⁱˢGIGIR are also found at Mari: ᵍⁱˢGIGIR and ᵍⁱˢGIGIR *ša ḫa-mu-ti-im*, translated as 'chariot' and 'fast chariot' respectively (ARM VII, 161).

14 Mention of a breastplate at this early period is surprising, and even if this was primarily made for display, it suggests the existence of equid armour.

15 Littauer and Crouwel have suggested that the presence of a dog in itself would indicate hunting (1979: 34), and Jans & Bretschneider (1998: 162) have also used it as one of the criteria for identifying hunting scenes. Dogs are especially associated with hunting, but they do also appear with equids and wheeled vehicles in battle scenes (Tsouparopoulou & Recht 2021).

16 A set of metal plates was also found at Nuzi, dated to the fourteenth century, which the excavator has suggested may be armour for chariot horses (Starr 1937: pl. 26L; 1939: 475); metal plates from Ugarit have been identified as possible armour for horses (Loretz 2011: 349, fig. 13).

6. Joint Journeys: Equids Carrying Humans

1 Early discussions of this topic include Potratz 1938: 22–7; 1966: 15–67; Legrain 1946; Salonen 1956; Downs 1961; Moorey 1970, but much has happened since then,

and more up-to-date treatments can be found in e.g. Owen 1991; Lafont 2000; Oates 2003; Zarins 2014.

2 Other animals may also have been ridden: there are plaques depicting a zebu and an elephant with human riders (Frankfort 1996: pl. 59c; Salonen 1956: pl. XVIII.1).

3 There are a few representations that may be earlier, but not included in the discussion here due to their uncertain provenance (stamp seal BM 135723), and due to questions of authenticity (engraved deer bones, Mecquenem 1934: fig. 38.24–5; cf. Zarins 2014: 104–5).

4 Oates (2003: 119) suggests that the rider might be sitting side-saddle, but there is nothing to suggest this as far as can be discerned on the preserved impressions, nor would the posture of the rider be any less awkward if that were the case.

5 For the Tell Mozan corpus, Hauser has applied a zoologically-based measuring system to animal figurines to determine species (Hauser 2007). This seems to have worked quite well for the equid figurines from the site but has not yet been systematically tested on assemblages from other sites.

6 Published as a camel, but this is an equid, probably a horse, judging from the full tail.

7 Moorey, apparently entirely ignoring the possibility of domestic donkeys, thought that those not depicting horses were 'onagers' (1970: 38); Downs seems to agree with this assessment (1961: 1195). This is extremely unlikely given the lack of evidence that wild equids performed such tasks.

8 Clear evidence for riding has not yet been identified on any of the osteological remains of equids, but as discussed in Chapter 3, such identifications are very difficult, and riding may leave no traces on the bones, especially on younger animals and/or if not very intensive. A human skeleton from Kish has been suggested to belong to a rider, based on the morphology of the femurs (Molleson & Blondiaux 1994).

9 Gordon further believes that the proverb is likely much older, since it was included in standard collections and found at several sites (1958: 19).

10 An Egyptian text mentions local rulers escaping battle on donkeys after the loss of their chariot horses (Littauer & Crouwel 1979: 96), and a 'scout' on horseback occurs in a tomb at Saqqara (Tomb of Horemheb, Delpeut 2021: fig. 3).

11 Oates takes it for granted that equids were ridden as part of hunting even in the third millennium (2003: 119).

12 There are also two examples which show the rider with one straight leg and one bent (Figure 6.1a; Frankfort 1939b: 118, 140, pl. XXIVa), for which I am not at present able to offer an explanation, but the posture is so characteristic that it likely had a specific meaning.

13 A rider may also attempt to gain stability on an equid at speed by leaning their torso back and legs almost straight forward, but this movement can only be successful in conjunction with the leaning back, which is not the case with these examples.

14 There are also rare examples of a third position, where the rider sits as far forward as possible and tightly clings on to the equid's neck (one from Hama, Fugmann 1958: 108, fig. 132; one unprovenanced, Moorey 2001: pl. I). It is not clear what they are intended to depict, but certainly this cannot be maintained as a riding position for any length of time. It may relate to some kind of game/acrobatic activity.

7. Management of Equids, or, How to Keep a Human

1 This tablet is included in Zarins' table as 'horse', but ANŠE.LIBIR is rather the donkey; see Appendix B for more details.
2 For example, for the large number of cartwrights at Tell Beydar, see Sallaberger 1998; for overseers (ugula) of equids at Ebla, see Archi et al. 1988: 266.
3 With a total of thirteen female and eighteen male workers, including some children; this list also includes leatherworkers.
4 AMA.GAN.ŠA also appear in this context; if Frayne's suggestion that these might be hemiones (see Appendix B, note 10) is accepted, then we might here have an early reference to donkey–hemione hybrids.
5 The practice is also known from other species: for example, wild goats (ibex) and domestic goats are recorded as cross-bred in Ur III documents (*RLA*, 'Ziege. A', 1.1).
6 Concerning mules and hinnies, fertility rates of the mare seem to be no lower than when mating with their own species (Allen et al. 2011: 2303).
7 Unfortunately, these equid figurines are not identifiable to specific species.
8 Consultations with horse and donkey veterinarians has not led to any solutions; all agree that the contraptions must have been painful, possibly causing harm to reproductive abilities, and with no obvious benefits.
9 As is also the case for later texts, where further details are provided – see Stol 2011.
10 Mules and hinnies could also have the temperament and endurance for it, but were rarely used as such in this period, probably because they were more expensive animals.
11 The side-saddle is a slightly different matter; it would require the equid to be trained, but perhaps less so the human – on the other hand, the position is unsuitable for long journeys and best with another human walking alongside the equid.

8. Honourable and Dishonourable Deaths

1 For a typology of cutmarks on animal bones, see Greenfield 2004.

2 Hemiones and skins may be associated in the written sources as early as Early Dynastic I-II (P005695; Postgate 1986: 199).

3 Donkeys and their bodies feature in traditional Chinese medicine (even today, see e.g. Mitchell 2018: 80).

4 Although the publication does not include a plan, the co-burial of a human and an equid from Early Dynastic III Al-Hiba/Lagash is perhaps another example of a seemingly equal relation between human and equid (Hansen 1973: 70).

5 This exclusivity did not last into the second millennium Shaft 1, where at least one of the equids were female (Weber, pers. comm.).

6 G. M. Schwartz has kindly informed me that the initial division into four phases (Schwartz 2013) has now been revised: Period VI: Tomb 5, 6, 8; Period V early: Tomb 3, Tomb 4 lower, Tomb 9, Tomb 10, Installation E, F, Area 2; Period V: Installation A, G, Area 1, Area 3; Period V later: Tomb 4 upper, Installation C; Period IV: Tomb 1 (early), 7, 11 (later), Installation B, D (to appear in forthcoming final report, pers. comm.).

7 Based on the revised scheme (previously four types – Weber 2012).

8 The main argument against all of them dying of natural causes is their apparent simultaneous burial. Weber remarks that there is evidence of the human tombs being reopened for further interments (2012: 179), and multiple deposits also occur in Installations B, C, D and G (Weber, pers. comm). Even if the time period between deposits cannot be established, this does mirror the human deposits.

9 It should be noted, however, that no actual evidence of wheeled vehicles have been reported from these contexts at Tell Umm el-Marra. Weber, however, leans towards considering the equid pairs in Type II installations as unrelated (forthcoming).

10 Head and hooves are also the main elements found in the Tell Banat North White Monument A equid-human deposits (Porter et al. 2021).

11 Another grave from Abu Salabikh, Grave 234, also held remains of two equids (only partly articulated and incomplete, probably due to ancient robbing activities), placed in separate parts of the tomb (Matthews & Postgate 1987: 96–7; Postgate forthcoming and pers. comm.).

12 Hemione bones were also found between the stone substructure and mudbrick superstructure of nearly every wall in the quarter with the leather industry (Nichols & Weber 2006; Weber pers. comm.).

13 From late fourth millennium Uruk, Boessneck et al. (1984) note equid remains associated with a temple, possibly a foundation deposit. At third millennium Tell Banat, an equid deposit is mentioned in relation to the foundations of Building B6 in Area C (Porter 2002a: 16, fig. 6; 2002b: 171, n.12), but this may a be fragmentary rather than a complete or partly articulated skeleton, and its exact relation to the building is not defined.

14 The equids from Tell el-'Ajjul are called horses by Petrie (1932: 5, 14), but do not appear to have been examined by a specialist, as would also not have been the custom at the time when they were excavated. It is probably no coincidence that these are the only Late Bronze Age examples, and from a site where horses would have travelled through in great numbers.

15 To date, osteological reports have been published for six of these (labelled Donkeys 1–6). The remaining two are mentioned as being in a pit cut into the western wall and adjoining fill of the temple cella wall, and on the terrace north of the antecella (Oates & Oates 2001: 42–3, 48). There were also 'numerous, more fragmentary [equid] bones' (Weber 2001: 348).

16 The pottery in the shaft itself is instead later MB II (G. M. Schwartz, pers. comm.).

17 With the caveat that one equid species was substituted for one or two others (donkeys and possibly horses for the earlier kungas), but this follows the general cultural development where kungas were no longer present in this period, but horses, donkeys and possibly mules had taken over; hemiones also remained important at Tell Umm el-Marra in this period.

18 To these we may add the risk of being attacked by prey animals. For example, a Middle Assyrian law lists the possibility of donkeys being eaten by wolves (Pritchard 1969: 192, no. 75), and one of the laws in Hammurabi's law code (number 244, Harper 1904) notes the possibility of donkeys being eaten by lions. That donkeys continued to face death on the road in the Late Bronze Age is also evidenced in a letter from Emar, although the exact cause of death is not recorded (Monroe 2009: 71).

9. Equid–Human Relations and Equid Agency

1 Calculations from Selenkahiye provide both lower and higher withers heights (Ijzereef 2001), but these are presented as a range based on bones from various individuals and using an older version of the tabulations, and have therefore not been included here or in the appendix.

2 However, comparative material from Egypt and the Aegean does not support such an idea. Withers heights of horses from Egypt have been measured at 136–151 centimetres (Chaix 2000), and from Greece at 131–133 centimetres (Boessneck & von den Driesch 1984).

3 In a skeleton from Egypt, the identification of it as a horse gelding has been suggested based on the morphology of the pelvis (Raulwing & Clutton-Brock 2009: 18), but there is at the moment no systematically tested method for identifying horse geldings (see also discussion in Nistelberger et al. 2019: 120).

4 There does not seem to be a qualifier for gelding associated with equids. Maekawa (1979b) has suggested that KUD, found with anše and other animals, means castrated. The term also occurs with female equids, and the argument is therefore not convincing (despite the suggestion that it then refers to sterilization of the mare).

5 The lexical Tablet Ḫḫ XIII, line 102 has sig₇.sig₇ as *arqu* (in a list of sheep, Landsberger 1960), which the *CAD* translates as 'yellow, green (as a natural color)'.

6 This is also reflected in Potratz' monograph (1966) on bridles in the ancient world, where the lists of finds of bridles or bridle elements for the Near East only include a few Late Bronze Age metal bits.

7 On the other hand, the donkeys at both sites are believed to be caravan donkeys, where the use of a bit would be unnecessary.

8 Pers. comm.

9 Ambling gaits such as the pace or the tölt are not applicable to the ancient Near East.

10 With a more speculative comment it may be noted that, while the one ear forward and one ear back certainly reflects mood, it is possible they were a visual signifier used to specify kungas. The animals depicted as such are from the period when kungas were prominent, in the mid- to late third millennium, and from objects such as the Standard of Ur, where we might expect such prestige animals to occur.

11 There is no evidence that it actually has this effect.

References

Al-Ajlouny, F., K. Douglas, B. Khrisat and A. Mayyas (2012), 'Laden Animal and Riding Figurines from Khirbet Ez-Zeraqōn and Their Implications for Trade in the Early Bronze Age', *Zeitschrift des Deutschen Palästina-Vereins*, 128 (2): 99–120.

Albright, W. F. (1930–31), 'Mitannian *Maryannu*, "Chariot-Warrior", and the Canaanite and Egyptian Equivalents', *Archiv für Orientforschung*, 6: 217–21.

Alhaique, F. (2008), 'Faunal Remains', in L. Nigro (ed.), *Khirbet Al-Batrawy II: The EB II City-Gate Fortifications, the EB II-III Temple*, 327–58, Rome: Università di Roma 'La Sapienza'.

Alhaique, F. (2019), 'Faunal Remains', in L. Romano and F. D'Agostino (eds), *Abu Tbeirah Excavations I: Area 1. Last Phase and Building A – Phase 1*, 419–38, Rome: Sapienza University Press.

Alhaique, F., L. Romano and F. D'Agostino (2021), 'Between Sacred and Profane: Human-Animal Relationships at Abu Tbeirah (Southern Iraq) in the Third Millennium BC', in L. Recht and C. Tsouparopoulou (eds), *Fierce Lions, Angry Mice and Fat-Tailed Sheep: Animal Encounters in the Ancient Near East*, 63–75, Cambridge: McDonald Institute for Archaeological Research.

Ali, A., K. Gutwein and C. Heleski (2017), 'Assessing the Influence of Upper Lip Twitching in Naïve Horses during an Aversive Husbandry Procedure (Ear Clipping)', *Journal of Veterinary Behavior: Clinical Applications and Research*, 21: 20–5.

Allen, W. R., J. H. Kydd, R. V. Short and D. F. Antczak (2011), 'Inter and Extraspecies Equine Pregnancies', in A. O. McKinnon, E. L. Squires, W. E. Vaala and D. D. Varner, *Equine Reproduction*, 2302–19, 2nd edn, Chichester: Wiley-Blackwell.

Al-Zawahra, M. and A. Ezzughayyar (1998), 'Equid Remains from the Bronze Age Periods at Site 4 of Tell Jenin (Palestine)', in H. Buitenhuis, L. Bartosiewicz and A. M. Choyke (eds), *Archaeozoology of the Near East III: Proceedings of the Third International Symposium on the Archaeozoology of Southwestern Asia and Adjacent Areas*, 130–4, Groningen: Centre for Archaeological Research and Consultancy.

Amiet, P. (1980), *Art of the Ancient Near East*, New York: H. N. Abrams.

Amiran, R. (1985), 'Canaanite Merchants in Tombs of the Early Bronze Age I at Azor', *'Atiqot*, 17: 190–2.

Anthony, D. W. (2007), *The Horse, the Wheel and Language: How Bronze Age Riders from the Eurasian Steppes Shaped the Modern World*, Princeton: Princeton University Press.

Anthony, D. W. and D. R. Brown (2003), 'Eneolithic Horse Rituals and Riding in the Steppes: New Evidence', in M. Levine, C. Renfrew and K. Boyle (eds), *Prehistoric*

Steppe Adaptation and the Horse, 55–68, Cambridge: McDonald Institute for
Archaeological Research.

Anthony, D. W., D. Y. Telegin and D. Brown (1991), 'The Origin of Horseback Riding',
Scientific American, 265 (6): 94–100.

Antonius, O. (1929), 'Beobachtungen an Einhufern in Schönbrunn, I: Der syrische
Halbesel (*Equus hemionus hemippus* J. Gehofft.)', *Der Zoologische Garten*, 1:
19–25.

Antonius, O. (1932), 'Beobachtungen an Einhufern in Schönbrunn, VII: Halbesel',
Der Zoologische Garten, 5: 261–75.

Antonius, O. (1944), 'Beobachtungen an Einhufern in Schönbrunn, XVII: Halbesel
Bastarde', *Der Zoologische Garten*, 16: 1–15.

Arbuckle, B. S. (2018), 'Early History of Animal Domestication in Southwest Asia',
in *Oxford Research Encyclopedia of Environmental Science* (http://oxfordre.com
/view/10.1093/acrefore/9780199389414.001.0001/acrefore-9780199389414-e-548,
accessed 18 June 2021).

Arbuckle, B. S. and S. A. McCarty, eds (2014), *Animals and Inequality in the Ancient
World*, Boulder: University Press of Colorado.

Arbuckle, B. S. and A. Öztan (2018), 'Horse and Hemione Hunting at Late Neolithic/
Chalcolithic Köşk Höyük, Central Turkey', in C. Çakırlar, J. Chahoud, R. Berthon and
S. Pilaar Birch (eds), *Archaeozoology of the Near East XII*, 41–58, Groningen:
Barkhuis Publishing & University of Groningen.

Archi, A. (1985), 'Circulation d'objets en métal précieux de poids standardisé à Ebla', in
J.-M. Durand and J.-R. Kupper (eds), *Miscellanea Babylonica: Mélanges offerts à
Maurice Birot*, 25–33, Paris: ERC.

Archi, A. (1998), 'The Regional State of Nagar According to the Texts of Ebla', in
M. LeBeau (ed.), *About Subartu. Studies Devoted to Upper Mesopotamia. Volume 2:
Culture, Society, Image*, 1–15, Turnhout: Brepols.

Archi, A. and M. G. Biga (2003), 'A Victory over Mari and the Fall of Ebla', *Journal of
Cuneiform Studies*, 55: 1–44.

Archi, A., M. G. Biga and L. Milano (1988), 'Studies in Eblaite Prosography', in A. Archi
(ed.), *Eblaite Personal Names and Semitic Name-Giving*, 205–306, Rome: Missione
Archeologica Italiana in Siria.

Argent, G. (2010), 'Do the Clothes Make the Horse? Relationality, Roles and Statuses in
Iron Age Inner Asia', *World Archaeology*, 42 (2): 157–74.

Argent, G. (2013), 'Inked: Human-Horse Apprenticeship, Tattoos, and Time in the
Pazyryk World', *Society & Animals*, 21 (2): 178–93.

Argent, G. (2016), 'Killing (Constructed) Horses – Interspecies Elders, Empathy and
Emotion, and the Pazyryk Horse Sacrifices', in L. G. Broderick (ed.), *People with
Animals: Perspectives & Studies in Ethnozooarchaeology*, 19–32, Oxford &
Philadelphia: Oxbow Books.

Armstrong Oma, K. (2010), 'Between Trust and Domination: Social Contracts between
Humans and Animals', *World Archaeology*, 42 (2): 175–87.

Armstrong Oma, K. (2017), *The Sheep People: The Ontology of Making Lives, Building Homes and Forging Herds in Early Bronze Age Norway*, Sheffield: Equinox.

Arnaud, D. (1985), *Emar 6: Textes sumériens et accadiens 1*, Paris: ERC.

Arnold, E. R., G. Hartman, H. J. Greenfield, I. Shai, L. E. Babcock and A. M. Maeir (2016), 'Isotopic Evidence for Early Trade in Animals between Old Kingdom Egypt and Canaan', *PLoS ONE*, 11 (6): e0157650.

Atici, L. (2014), 'Tracing Inequality from Assur to Kültepe/Kanesh: Merchants, Donkeys, and Clay Tablets', in B. S. Arbuckle and S. A. McCarty (eds), *Animals and Inequality in the Ancient World*, 231–50, Boulder: University Press of Colorado.

Bahn, P. G. (1980), 'Crib-Biting: Tethered Horses in the Palaeolithic?', *World Archaeology*, 12 (2): 212–17.

Bakker, J. A., J. Kruk, A. E. Lanting and S. Milisauskas (1999), 'The Earliest Evidence of Wheeled Vehicles in Europe and the Near East', *Antiquity*, 73 (282): 778–90.

Balkan, K. (1954), *Kassitenstudien I: Die Sprache der Kassiten*, New Haven: American Oriental Society.

Barjamovic, G. (2011), *A Historical Geography of Anatolia in the Old Assyrian Colony Period*, Copenhagen: Museum Tusculanum.

Barjamovic, G., T. Hertel and M. T. Larsen (2012), *Ups and Downs at Kanesh: Chronology, History and Society in the Old Assyrian Period*, Leiden: Nederlands Instituut voor het Nabije Oosten.

Bar-Oz, G., P. Nahshoni, H. Motro and E. D. Oren (2013), 'Symbolic Metal Bit and Saddlebag Fastenings in a Middle Bronze Age Donkey Burial', *PLoS ONE*, 8 (3): e58648.

Barrelet, M.-T. (1970), 'Peut-on remettre en question la "Restitution matérielle de la Stèle des Vautours"?', *Journal of Near Eastern Studies*, 29 (4): 233–58.

Bartosiewicz, L. (2008), 'Bone Structure and Function in Draft Cattle', in G. Grupe, G. McGlynn and J. Peters (eds), *Limping Together through the Ages: Joint Afflictions and Bone Infections*, 153–64, Rahden/Westf.: Marie Leidorf.

Beckman, G. (1996), *Hittite Diplomatic Texts*, Atlanta: Scholars Press.

Behrens, H. (1998), *Die Ninegalla-Hymne: Die Wohnungnahme Inannas in Nippur in altbabylonischer Zeit*, Stuttgart: Steiner.

Beja-Pereira, A., P. R. England, N. Ferrand, S. Jordan, A. O. Bakhiet, M. A. Abdalla, M. Mashkour, J. Jordana, P. Taberlet and G. Luikart (2004), 'African Origins of the Domestic Donkey', *Science*, 304 (5678): 1781.

Bell, C. (2012), 'The Merchants of Ugarit: Oligarchs of the Late Bronze Age Trade in Metals?', in V. Kassianidou and G. Papasavvas (eds), *Eastern Mediterranean Metallurgy and Metalwork in the Second Millennium BC*, 180–7, Oxford: Oxbow.

Bendrey, R. (2007a), 'New Methods for the Identification of Evidence for Bitting on Horse Remains from Archaeological Sites', *Journal of Archaeological Science*, 34 (7): 1036–50.

Bendrey, R. (2007b), 'Ossification of the Interosseous Ligaments between the Metapodials in Horses: A New Recording Methodology and Preliminary Study', *International Journal of Osteoarchaeology*, 17: 207–13.

Bennett, E, S. Champlot, J. Peters, B. Arbuckle, S. Guimaraes, M. Pruvost, S. Bar-David et al. (2017), 'Taming the Late Quaternary Phylogeography of the Eurasiatic Wild Ass through Ancient and Modern DNA', *PLoS ONE*, 12 (April): e0174216.

Bianchi, A. and A. Wissing (2009), *Ausgrabungen 1998–2001 in der zentralen Oberstadt von Tall Mozan/Urkeš: Die Kleinfunde*, Wiesbaden: Harrassowitz.

Biga, M. G. (2006), '(Foreign) Veterinarians at Ebla', *N.A.B.U.*, 2006 (4): 85.

Biga, M. G. (2009), 'On Equids, Other Animals and Veterinarians in the Texts of the Ebla Archives (Syria, 3th Millennium B.C., XXIV Cent. B.C.)', in D. Tabbaa and M. Al Hayek (eds), *The Proceedings of the Conference on Animals in Ancient Syrian Civilization*, 41–56, Hama: al-Baath University.

Biggs, R. D. (1974), *Inscriptions from Tell Abū Ṣalābīkh*, Chicago: University of Chicago Press.

Boessneck, J. and A. von den Driesch (1984), 'Die zoologische Dokumentation der Reste von vier Pferden und einem Hund aus einem mykenischen Schachtgrab in Kokla bei Argos (Peloponnes)', *Spixiana*, 7 (3): 327–33.

Boessneck, J., A. von den Driesch and U. Steger (1984), 'Tierknochenfunde der Ausgrabungen des Deutschen Archäologischen Instituts Baghdad in Uruk-Warka, Iraq', *Baghdader Mitteilungen*, 15: 149–90.

Bökönyi, S. (1986), 'The Equids of Umm-Dabaghiyah, Iraq', in R. H. Meadow and H.-P. Uerpmann (eds), *Equids in the Ancient World 1*, 302–18, Wiesbaden: Ludwig Reichert.

Bökönyi, S. (1990), *Kamid el-Loz 12. Tierhaltung und Jagd: Tierknochenfunde der Ausgrabungen 1964 bis 1981*, Bonn: Rudolf Habelt.

Bökönyi, S. (1991), 'Late Chalcolithic Horses in Anatolia', in R. H. Meadow and H.-P. Uerpmann (eds), *Equids in the Ancient World 2*, 123–31, Wiesbaden: Ludwig Reichert.

Bollweg, J. (1999), *Vorderasiatische Wagentypen im Spiegel der Terracottaplastik bis zur altbabylonischen Zeit*, Göttingen: Universitätsverlag Freiburg and Vandenhoeck & Ruprecht.

Bollweg, J. and W. Nagel (1992), 'Equiden Vorderasiens in sumerisch-akkadischen Schriftquellen und aus Ausgrabungen', *Acta praehistorica et archaeologica*, 24: 17–63.

Bordreuil, P. (1991), *Une bibliothèque au sud de la ville*, Paris: ERC.

Bordreuil, P. and D. Pardee (1989), *La trouvaille épigraphique de l'Ougarit 1: Correspondance*, Paris: ERC.

Boswell, J. (2015), 'Osteoarthritis of the Distal Tarsal Joints in Horses – Musculoskeletal System', Merck Veterinary Manual (www.merckvetmanual.com/musculoskeletal-system/lameness-in-horses/osteoarthritis-of-the-distal-tarsal-joints-in-horses, accessed 18 June 2021).

Boyd, B. (2017), 'Archaeology and Human–Animal Relations: Thinking through Anthropocentrism', *Annual Review of Anthropology*, 46 (1): 299–316.

Braun-Holzinger, E. A. (1984), *Figürliche Bronzen aus Mesopotamien*, Munich: C.H. Beck'sche.

Brokken, M. T. (2015), 'Bucked Shins in Horses – Musculoskeletal System', *Merck Veterinary Manual*, 2015 (www.merckvetmanual.com/musculoskeletal-system/ lameness-in-horses/bucked-shins-in-horses, accessed 18 June 2021).

Brown, D. and D. Anthony (1998), 'Bit Wear, Horseback Riding and the Botai Site in Kazakstan', *Journal of Archaeological Science*, 25 (4): 331–47.

Brownrigg, G. (2004), 'Schirrung und Zäumung des Streitwagenpferdes: Funktion und Rekonstruktion', in M. Fansa and S. Burmeister (eds), *Rad und Wagen. Der Ursprung einer Innovation: Wagen im Vorderen Orient und Europa*, 481–90, Mainz am Rhein: Philipp von Zabern.

Brownrigg, G. (2019), 'Harnessing the Chariot Horse', in P. Raulwing, K. M. Linduff and J. H. Crouwel, *Equids and Wheeled Vehicles in the Ancient World: Essays in Memory of Mary A. Littauer*, 85–96, Oxford: BAR.

Buccellati, G. and M. Kelly-Buccellati (2000), 'The Royal Palace of Urkesh. Report on the 12th Season at Tell Mozan/Urkesh: Excavations in Area AA, June-October 1999', *Mitteilungen der Deutschen Orient-Gesellschaft*, 132: 133–83.

Buccellati, G. and M. Kelly-Buccellati (2004), 'Der monumentale Palasthof von Tall Mozan/Urkeš und die stratigraphische Geschichte des *ābi*', *Mitteilungen der Deutschen Orient-Gesellschaft*, 136: 13–39.

Buitenhuis, H. (1991), 'Some Equid Remains from South Turkey, North Syria, and Jordan', in R. H. Meadow and H.-P. Uerpmann (eds), *Equids in the Ancient World 2*, 34–74, Wiesbaden: Ludwig Reichert.

Burden, F. and A. Thiemann (2015), 'Donkeys Are Different' *Journal of Equine Veterinary Science*, Proceedings of the 2015 Equine Science Society Symposium, 35 (5): 376–82.

Burden, F. and A. Trawford (2006), 'Equine Interspecies Aggression', *Veterinary Record*, 159 (25): 859–60.

Burmeister, S., T. J. H. Krispijn and P. Raulwing (2019), 'Some Notes on Pictograms Interpreted as Sledges and Wheeled Vehicles in the Archaic Texts from Uruk', in P. Raulwing, K. M. Linduff and J. H. Crouwel (eds), *Equids and Wheeled Vehicles in the Ancient World: Essays in Memory of Mary A. Littauer*, 49–70, Oxford: BAR.

Burrows, E. (1935), *Ur Excavations II: Archaic Texts*, London: British Museum.

Calvet, Y. (2000), 'Ougarit: Les animaux symboliques du répertoire figuré au Bronze Récent', *Topoi. Orient-Occident*, 2 (1): 447–65.

Caubet, A. (1991), 'Objets et instruments d'albâtre', in M. Yon (ed.), *Arts et industries de la pierre*, 265–72, Paris: ERC.

Caubet, A. (2013), 'Of Banquets, Horses, and Women in Late Bronze Age Ugarit', in J. Aruz, S. B. Graff and Y. Rakic (eds), *Cultures in Contact: From Mesopotamia to the Mediterranean in the Second Millennium B.C.*, 226–37, New York: The Metropolitan Museum of Art.

Caubet, A. and M. Yon (2001), 'Pommeaux de chars, du Levant à l'Élam', in C. Breniquet and C. Kepinski-Lecomte (eds), *Etudes mésopotamiennes: Recueil de textes offert à Jean-Louis Huot*, 69–78, Paris: ERC.

Chaix, L. (2000), 'An Hyksos Horse from Tell Heboua (Sinaï, Egypt)', in M. Mashkour, A. M. Choyke, H. Buitenhuis and F. Poplin (eds), *Archaeozoology of the Near East IV*, 177–86, Groningen: Archaeological Research and Consultancy.

Charpin, D. (1985), 'Les archives du devin Asqudum dans la residence du "Chantier A"', *MARI*, 4: 453–62.

Charpin, D., F. Joannès, S. Lackenbacher and B. Lafont (1988), *Archives épistolaires de Mari I/2*, Archives Royales de Mari 26, Paris: ERC.

Childe, V. G. (1958), *The Dawn of European Civilization*, 6th edn, New York: Alfred A. Knopf.

Chuang, R. and V. Bonhomme (2019), 'Rethinking the Dental Morphological Differences between Domestic Equids', *Journal of Archaeological Science*, 101: 140–8.

Civil, M. (1966), 'Notes on Sumerian Lexicography, I', *Journal of Cuneiform Studies*, 20 (3/4): 119–24.

Civil, M. (1968), 'Išme-Dagan and Enlil's Chariot', *Journal of the American Oriental Society*, 88 (1): 3–14.

Clavel, P., J. Dumoncel, C. Der Sarkissian, A. Seguin-Orlando, L. Calvière-Tonasso, S. Schiavinato, L. Chauvey et al. (2021), 'Assessing the Predictive Taxonomic Power of the Bony Labyrinth 3D Shape in Horses, Donkeys and Their F1-Hybrids', *Journal of Archaeological Science*, 131: 1-12 (online).

Cline, E. H. (2014), *1177 B.C.: The Year Civilization Collapsed*, Princeton & Oxford: Princeton University Press.

Clutton-Brock, J. (1986), 'Osteology of the Equids from Sumer', in R. H. Meadow and H.-P. Uerpmann (eds), *Equids in the Ancient World 1*, 207–29, Wiesbaden: Ludwig Reichert.

Clutton-Brock, J. (1992), *Horse Power: A History of the Horse and the Donkey in Human Societies*, Cambridge, MA: Harvard University Press.

Clutton-Brock, J. (2001), 'Ritual Burials of a Dog and Six Domestic Donkeys', in D. Oates, J. Oates and H. MacDonald (eds), *Excavations at Tell Brak 2: Nagar in the Third Millennium BC*, 327–38, London: British School of Archaeology in Iraq.

Clutton-Brock, J. (2003), 'Were the Donkeys at Tell Brak (Syria) Harnessed with a Bit?', in M. Levine, C. Renfrew and K. Boyle (eds), *Prehistoric Steppe Adaptation and the Horse*, 126–7, Cambridge: McDonald Institute for Archaeological Research.

Clutton-Brock, J. and R. Burleigh (1978), 'The Animal Remains from Abu Salabikh: Preliminary Report', *Iraq*, 40 (2): 89–100.

Clutton-Brock, J. and S. Davies (1993), 'More Donkeys from Tell Brak', *Iraq*, 55: 209–21.

Cohen, A. C. (2005), *Death Rituals, Ideology, and the Development of Early Mesopotamian Kingship: Toward a New Understanding of Iraq's Royal Cemetery of Ur*, Leiden: Brill.

Cohen, C. and D. Sivan (1983), *The Ugaritic Hippiatric Texts: A Critical Edition*, New Haven: American Oriental Society.

Cohen, S. (2016), 'The Beni Hasan Tomb Painting and Scholarship of the Southern Levant', *The Ancient Near East Today*, IV (7).

Collins, B. J. (2002), *A History of the Animal World in the Ancient Near East*, Leiden: Brill.

Collins, B. J. (2004), 'A Channel to the Underworld in Syria', *Near Eastern Archaeology*, 67 (1): 54–6.

Conti, G. (1997), 'Carri ed equipaggi nei testi di Ebla', in P. Fronzaroli (ed.), *Miscellanea eblaitica, 4*, 23–71, Firenze: Università di Firenze, Dipartimento di Linguistica.

Cook, W. R. (2002), 'Bit-Induced Asphyxia in the Horse', *Journal of Equine Veterinary Science*, 22 (1): 7–14.

Courtois, J.-C., J. Lagarce and E. Lagarce (1986), *Enkomi et le bronze récent à Chypre*, Nicosia: Zavallis Press.

Crawford, H. (2004), *Sumer and the Sumerians*, 2nd edn, Cambridge: Cambridge University Press.

Croft, P. (2004), 'The Osteological Remains (Mammalian and Avian)', in D. Ussishkin (ed.), *The Renewed Archaeological Excavations at Lachish (1973–1994), Vol. V*, 2254–348, Tel Aviv: Emery and Claire Yass Publications in Archaeology.

Crouwel, J. H. (1981), *Chariots and Other Means of Land Transport in Bronze Age Greece*, Amsterdam: Allard Pierson Museum.

Cupere, B. de, A. Lentacker, W. Van Neer, M. Waelkens and L. Verslype (2000), 'Osteological Evidence for the Draught Exploitation of Cattle: First Applications of a New Methodology', *International Journal of Osteoarchaeology*, 10: 254–67.

D'Agostino, F., L. Romano and K. Ali (2015), 'Abu Tbeirah, Nasiriyah (Southern Iraq): Preliminary Report on the 2013 Excavation Campaign', in M. G. Biga (ed.), *Omaggio a Mario Liverani, fondatore di una nuova scienza (II)*, 209–21, Madrid: Servicio de Publicaciones Universidad Autónoma de Madrid.

Dalley, S. (1977), 'Old Babylonian Trade in Textiles at Tell al Rimah', *Iraq*, 39 (2): 155–9.

Dalley, S., C. B. F. Walker and J. D. Hawkins (1976), *The Old Babylonian Tablets from Tell al Rimah*, London: British School of Archaeology in Iraq.

Davis, S. (1980), 'Late Pleistocene and Holocene Equid Remains from Israel', *Zoological Journal of the Linnean Society*, 70: 89–312.

del Olmo Lete, G. and J. Sanmartín (2003), *A Dictionary of the Ugaritic Language in the Alphabetic Tradition*, Leiden and Boston: Brill.

Delougaz, P. (1940), *The Temple Oval at Khafājah*, Chicago: University of Chicago Press.

Delpeut, L. (2021), 'The Role of the Horse in Ancient Egypt: In Society and Imagery', in L. Recht and K. Zeman-Wiśniewska (eds), *Animal Iconography in the Archaeological Record: New Approaches, New Dimensions*, 114-28, Sheffield: Equinox.

DeMello, M. (2012), *Animals and Society: An Introduction to Human-Animal Studies*, New York: Columbia University Press.

Dercksen, J. G. (1996), *The Old Assyrian Copper Trade in Anatolia*, Istanbul: Nederlands Historisch-Archaeologisch Instituut.

Dercksen, J. G. (2003), 'A New OA Text from Kültepe about Mules', *N.A.B.U.*, 2003 (2): 52.

Dercksen, J. G. (2004), *Old Assyrian Institutions*, Leiden: Nederlands Instituut voor het Nabije Oosten.

Dercksen, J. G. (2014), 'The Old Assyrian Trade and Its Participants', in H. D. Baker and M. Jursa (eds), *Documentary Sources in Ancient Near Eastern and Greco-Roman Economic History: Methodology and Practice*, 59–112, Oxford & Philadelphia: Oxbow.

Di Martino, S. (2005), 'Tell Mozan / Urkesh: Archeozoologia della struttura sotterranea in A12', *Studi Micenei ed Egeo-Anatolici*, XLVII: 67–80.

Dirbas, H. (2014), 'The Sacrifice of Riding Animals in Amorite and Arabic Traditions', *Subartu*, 8: 3–12.

Dobat, A. S., T. D. Price, J. Kveiborg, J. Ilkjær and P. Rowley-Conwy (2014), 'The Four Horses of an Iron Age Apocalypse: War-Horses from the Third-Century Weapon Sacrifice at Illerup Aadal (Denmark)', *Antiquity*, 88 (339): 191–204.

Dohner, J. V. (2007), *Livestock Guardians: Using Dogs, Donkeys, and Llamas to Protect Your Herd*, North Adams, MA: Storey Publishing.

Dolce, R. (2014), 'Equids as Luxury Gifts at the Centre of Interregional Economic Dynamics in the Archaic Urban Cultures of the Ancient Near East', *Syria*, 91: 55–75.

Dolce, R. (2015), 'Wooden Carvings of Ebla: Some Open Questions', in A. Archi (ed.), *Tradition and Innovation in the Ancient Near East: Proceedings of the 57th Rencontre Assyriologique Internationale at Rome 4–8 July 2011*, 121–34, Winona Lake, IN: Eisenbrauns.

Dornan, J. L. (2002), 'Agency and Archaeology: Past, Present, and Future Directions', *Journal of Archaeological Method and Theory*, 9 (4): 303–29.

Downs, J. F. (1961), 'The Origin and Spread of Riding in the Near East and Central Asia', *American Anthropologist*, 63: 1193–203.

Ducos, P. (1975), 'A New Find of an Equid Metatarsal Bone from Tell Mureibet in Syria and Its Relevance to the Identification of Equids from the Early Holocene of the Levant', *Journal of Archaeological Science*, 2 (1): 71–3.

Dudd, S. N., R. P. Evershed and M. Levine (2003), 'Organic Residue Analysis of Lipids in Potsherds from the Early Neolithic Settlement of Botai, Kazakhstan', in M. Levine, C. Renfrew and K. Boyle (eds), *Prehistoric Steppe Adaptation and the Horse*, 45–53, Cambridge: McDonald Institute for Archaeological Research.

Durand, J.-M. (1983), *Archives royales de Mari: Textes administratifs des salles 134 et 160 du Palais de Mari*, Paris: Paul Geuthner.

Durand, J.-M. (1988), *Archives épistolaires de Mari I/1*, Archives Royales de Mari 26, Paris: ERC.

Durand, J.-M. (1998), *Les documents épistolaires du palais de Mari II*, Paris: CERF.

Dyson Jr, R. H. (1960), 'A Note on Queen Shub-Ad's "Onagers"', *Iraq*, 22: 102–4.

Ebeling, E. (1951), *Bruchstücke einer mittelassyrischen Vorschriftensammlung für die Akklimatisierung und Trainierung von Wagenpferden*, Berlin: Akademie-Verlag.

Eidem, J. (1991), 'The Tell Leilan Archives 1987', *Revue d'Assyriologie et d'Archéologie Orientale*, 85 (2): 109–35.

Eitan, A. (1969), 'Excavations at the Foot of Tel Rosh Ha'ayin', *Atiqot*, 1969: 49–68.

Ellis, R. S. (1968), *Foundation Deposits in Ancient Mesopotamia*, New Haven: Yale University Press.

Emberling, G. and H. McDonald (2003), 'Excavations at Tell Brak 2001–2002: Preliminary Report', *Iraq*, 65: 1–75.

Engel Jr., M. and K. Jenni (2010), 'Examined Lives: Teaching Human–Animal Studies in Philosophy', in M. DeMello (ed.), *Teaching the Animal*, 60–102, Brooklyn: Lantern Books.

Evans, L. and M. Crane, eds (2018), *The Clinical Companion of the Donkey*, Sidmouth: The Donkey Sanctuary.

Fages, A., K. Hanghøj, N. Khan, C. Gaunitz, A. Seguin-Orlando, M. Leonardi, C. McCrory Constantz, et al. (2019), 'Tracking Five Millennia of Horse Management with Extensive Ancient Genome Time Series', *Cell*, 177 (6): 1419–35.e31.

Falkenstein, A. (1936), *Archaische Texte aus Uruk*, Leipzig: Harrassowitz.

Fansa, M. and S. Burmeister, eds (2004), *Rad und Wagen. Der Ursprung einer Innovation: Wagen im Vorderen Orient und Europa*, Mainz: Zabern.

Farrow, C. S. (2006), *Veterinary Diagnostic Imaging: The Horse*, Saint Louis: Mosby.

Feldman, M. H. (2006), *Diplomacy by Design: Luxury Arts and an 'International Style' in the Ancient Near East, 1400-1200 BCE*, Chicago: University of Chicago Press.

Feldman, M. H. and C. Sauvage (2010), 'Objects of Prestige? Chariots in the Late Bronze Age Eastern Mediterranean and Near East', *Egypt and the Levant*, XX: 67–182.

Finet, A. (1993), 'Le sacrifice de l'âne en Mésopotamie', in J. Quaegebeur (ed.), *Ritual and Sacrifice in the Ancient Near East*, 135–42, Leuven: Peeters.

Finkbeiner, U. (1995), 'Tell el-'Abd', *Damaszener Mitteilungen*, 8: 51–83.

Flynn, C. P., ed. (2008), *Social Creatures: A Human and Animal Studies Reader*, New York: Lantern Books.

Foxvog, D. A. (1980), 'Funerary Furnishings in an Early Sumerian Text from Adab', in B. Alster (ed.), *Death in Mesopotamia*, 67–75, Copenhagen: Akademisk Forlag.

Foxvog, D. A. (1995), 'Sumerian Brands and Branding-Irons', *Zeitschrift für Assyriologie*, 85: 1–7.

Frankfort, H. (1939a), *Sculpture of the Third Millennium B.C. from Tell Asmar and Khafajah*, Chicago: University of Chicago Press.

Frankfort, H. (1939b), *Cylinder Seals*, London: Macmillan.

Frankfort, H. (1943), *More Sculpture from the Diyala Region*, Chicago: University of Chicago Press.

Frankfort, H. (1955), *Stratified Cylinder Seals from the Diyala Region*, Chicago: University of Chicago Press.

Frankfort, H. (1996), *The Art and Architecture of the Ancient Orient*, 5th edn, New Haven: Yale University Press.

Frankfort, H., S. Lloyd and T. Jacobsen (1940), *The Gimilsin Temple and the Palace of the Rulers at Tell Asmar*, Chicago: University of Chicago Press.

Frayne, D. R. (2008), *Presargonic Period (2700–2350 BC)*, Toronto: University of Toronto Press.

Fugmann, E. (1958), *Hama. Fouilles et recherches de la Fondation Carlsberg 1931-1938, II/1, L'architecture des periodes pre-hellenistiques*, Copenhagen: Nationalmuseet.

Gadd, C. J. (1940), 'Tablets from Chagar Bazar and Tall Brak, 1937–38', *Iraq*, 7: 22–66.

Gaunitz, C., A. Fages, K. Hanghøj, A. Albrechtsen, N. Khan, M. Schubert, A. Seguin-Orlando, et al. (2018), 'Ancient Genomes Revisit the Ancestry of Domestic and Przewalski's Horses', *Science*, 360 (6384): 111–14.

Geigl, E.-M. and T. Grange (2012), 'Eurasian Wild Asses in Time and Space: Morphological versus Genetic Diversity', *Annals of Anatomy – Anatomischer Anzeiger*, 194 (1): 88–102.

Gelb, I. J. (1955), *Old Akkadian Inscriptions in Chicago Natural History Museum: Texts of Legal and Business Interest*, Chicago: Chicago Natural History Museum Press.

Geor, R. J. (2001), 'Nutrional Support of the Sick Adult Horse', in J. D. Fagan and R. J. Geor (eds), *Advances in Equine Nutrition II*, 403–17, Nottingham: Nottingham University Press.

George, A. (1999), *The Epic of Gilgamesh: The Babylonian Epic Poem and Other Texts in Akkadian and Sumerian*, London: Penguin.

Gibson, J. C. L. (1978), *Canaanite Myths and Legends*, 2nd edn, London and New York: T&T Clark Internattional.

Gibson, M. (1972), *The City and Area of Kish*, Miami: Field Research Projects.

Gilbert, A. S. (1991), 'Equid Remains from Godin Tepe, Western Iran: An Interim Summary and Interpretation, with Notes on the Introduction of the Horse into Southwest Asia', in R. H. Meadow and H.-P. Uerpmann (eds), *Equids in the Ancient World 2*, 75–122, Wiesbaden: Ludwig Reichert.

Gökçek, L. G. (2006), 'The Use of Wagons (*Eriqqum*) in Ancient Anatolia According to Texts from Kültepe', *Zeitschrift für Assyriologie und Vorderasiatische Archäologie*, 96 (2): 185–99.

Gordon, E. I. (1958), 'Sumerian Animal Proverbs and Fables: "Collection Five"', *Journal of Cuneiform Studies*, 12 (1): 1–21.

Gordon, M. B. (1942), 'The Hippiatric Texts from Ugarit', *Annals of Medical History*, 4: 406–8.

Goulder, J. (2020), *Working Donkeys in 4th–3rd Millennium BC Mesopotamia*, Abingdon & New York: Routledge.

Goulder, J. (2021), 'Face to Face with Working Donkeys in Mesopotamia: Insights from Modern Development Studies', in L. Recht and C. Tsouparopoulou (eds), *Fierce Lions, Angry Mice and Fat-Tailed Sheep: Animal Encounters in the Ancient Near East*, 249-61, Cambridge: McDonald Institute for Archaeological Research.

Gray, A. P. (1954), *Mammalian Hybrids: A Check-List with Bibliography*, Bucks: Commonwealth Agricultural Bureaux.

Greenberg, R. and N. Porat (1996), 'A Third Millennium Levantine Pottery Production Center: Typology, Petrography, and Provenance of the Metallic Ware of Northern

Israel and Adjacent Regions', *Bulletin of the American Schools of Oriental Research*, 301: 5–24.

Greenfield, H. J. (2004), 'The Butchered Animal Bone Remains from Ashqelon, Afridar – Area G', *Atiqot*, 45: 243–61.

Greenfield, H. J. (2010), 'The Secondary Products Revolution: The Past, the Present and the Future', *World Archaeology*, 42: 29–54.

Greenfield, H. J., ed. (2014), *Animal Secondary Products: Domestic Animal Exploitation in Prehistoric Europe, the Near East and the Far East*, Oxford: Oxbow Books.

Greenfield, H. J., T. L. Greenfield, I. Shai, S. Albaz and A. M. Maeir (2018), 'Household Rituals and Sacrificial Donkeys: Why Are There so Many Domestic Donkeys Buried in an Early Bronze Age Neighborhood at Tell eṣ-Ṣâfi/Gath?', *Near Eastern Archaeology*, 81 (3): 202–11.

Greenfield, H. J., J. Ross, T. L. Greenfield and A. M. Maeir (2021), 'Sacred and the Profane: Donkey Burial and Consumption at Early Tell eṣ-Ṣâfi/Gath', in L. Recht and C. Tsouparopoulou (eds), *Fierce Lions, Angry Mice and Fat-Tailed Sheep: Animal Encounters in the Ancient Near East*, 263–78, Cambridge: McDonald Institute for Archaeological Research.

Greenfield, H. J., I. Shai, T. L. Greenfield, E. R. Arnold, A. Brown, A. Eliyahu and A. M. Maeir (2018), 'Earliest Evidence for Equid Bit Wear in the Ancient Near East: The "Ass" from Early Bronze Age Tell eṣ-Ṣâfi/Gath, Israel', *PLoS ONE*, 13 (5): e0196335.

Greenfield, H. J., I. Shai and A. M. Maeir (2012), 'Being an "Ass": An Early Bronze Age Burial of a Donkey from Tell eṣ-Ṣâfi/Gath, Israel', *Bioarchaeology of the Near East*, 6: 21–52.

Grigson, C. (1993), 'The Earliest Domestic Horses in the Levant? New Finds from the Fourth Millennium of the Negev', *Journal of Archaeological Science*, 20: 645–55.

Grigson, C. (2012), 'Size Matters – Donkeys and Horses in the Prehistory of the Southern Levant', *Paléorient*, 38: 185–201.

Grigson, C. (2015), 'The Fauna of Tell Nebi Mend (Syria) in the Bronze and Iron Age – A Diachronic Overview. Part 1: Stability and Change – Animal Husbandry', *Levant*, 47 (1): 5–29.

Grint, N. J., C. B. Johnson, R. E. Clutton, H. R. Whay and J. C. Murrell (2015), 'Spontaneous Electroencephalographic Changes in a Castration Model as an Indicator of Nociception: A Comparison between Donkeys and Ponies', *Equine Veterinary Journal*, 47 (1): 36–42.

Groot, M. (2008), 'Understanding Past Human-Animal Relationships through the Analysis of Fractures: A Case Study from a Roman Site in the Netherlands', in Z. Miklíková and R. Thomas (eds), *Current Research in Animal Palaeopathology*, 40–50, Oxford: Archaeopress.

Grossman, K. and M. Hinman (2013), 'Rethinking Halaf and Ubaid Animal Economies: Hunting and Herding at Tell Zeidan (Syria)', *Paléorient*, 39 (2): 201–19.

Groves, C. P. and D. P. Willoughby (1981), 'Studies on the Taxonomy and Phylogeny of the Genus *Equus*. 1. Subgeneric Classification of the Recent Species', *Mammalia*, 45 (3): 321–54.

Guichard, M. (2014), *Florilegium marianum XIV: L'épopée de Zimri-Lîm*, Paris: SEPOA.

Hamilakis, Y. and N. J. Overton (2013), 'A Multi-Species Archaeology', *Archaeological Dialogues*, 20 (2): 159–73.

Hanot, P. and C. Bochaton (2018), 'New Osteological Criteria for the Identification of Domestic Horses, Donkeys and Their Hybrids in Archaeological Contexts', *Journal of Archaeological Science*, 94: 12–20.

Hansen, D. P. (1973), 'Al-Hiba, 1970-1971: A Preliminary Report', *Artibus Asiae*, 35 (1/2): 62–78.

Haraway, D. J. (2003), *The Companion Species Manifesto: Dogs, People, and Significant Otherness*, Chicago: Prickly Paradigm Press.

Haraway, D. J. (2008), *When Species Meet*, Minneapolis & London: University of Minnesota Press.

Harper, R. F. (1904), *The Code of Hammurabi*, Chicago: University of Chicago Press.

Harris, K. and Y. Hamilakis (2014), 'Beyond the Wild, the Feral, and the Domestic', in G. Marvin and S. McHugh (eds), *Routledge Handbook of Human-Animal Studies*, 93–8, Abingdon & New York: Routledge.

Hartung, K., B. Münzer and H. Keller (1983), 'Radiologic Evaluation of Spavin in Young Trotters', *Veterinary Radiology*, 24 (4): 153–5.

Hauser, R. (2007), *Reading Figurines: Animal Representations in Terra Cotta from Royal Building AK at Urkesh (Tell Mozan)*, Malibu: Undena.

Heeßel, N. P. (2018), 'A New Medical Therapeutic Text on Rectal Disease', in S. V. Panayotov and L. Vacín (eds), *Mesopotamian Medicine and Magic*, 310–42, Leiden and Boston: Brill.

Heimpel, W. (2003), *Letters to the King of Mari: A New Translation, with Historical Introduction, Notes, and Commentary*, Winona Lake, IN: Eisenbrauns.

Helmer, D. (2000), 'Étude de la faune mammalienne d'El Kowm 2', in D. Stordeur (ed.), *El Kowm 2. Une île dans le désert: La fin du Néolithique précéramique dans la steppe syrienne*, 233–64, Paris: CNRS Editions.

Heltzer, M. (1978), *Goods, Prices and Organisation of Trade in Ugarit*, Wiesbaden: Reichert.

Henson, F. M. D. (2018), *Equine Neck and Back Pathology: Diagnosis and Treatment*, 2nd edn, Hoboken, NJ: Wiley Blackwell.

Highcock, N. (2018), 'Community Across Distance: The Forging of Identity between Aššur and Anatolia', PhD dissertation, New York: New York University.

Hilprecht, H. V. (1893), *Old Babylonian Inscriptions Chiefly from Nippur*, Philadelphia: Anson Partridge.

Hilzheimer, M. (1941), *Animal Remains from Tell Asmar*, trans. A. A. Brux, Chicago: University of Chicago Press.

Hizmi, H. (2004), 'An Early Bronze Age Saddle Donkey Figurine from Khirbet El-Makhruq and the Emerging Appearance of Beast of Burden Figurines', in H. Hizmi and A. De-Groot (eds), *Burial Caves and Sites in Judea and Samaria from the Bronze and Iron Ages*, 309–24, Jerusalem: Old City Press.

Holland, T. A. (1992–3), 'Tell Es-Sweyhat Expedition to Syria', *Oriental Institute Annual Report*, 63–70.

Holland, T. A. (2001–2), 'Tell Es-Sweyhat: An Early Bronze Age Caravansary and Trading Post?', *Oriental Institute Annual Reports*, 85–96.

Horwitz, L. K., D. M. Master and H. Motro (2017), 'A Middle Bronze Age Equid from Ashkelon: A Case of Ritual Interment or a Refuse Deposit?', in J. S. E. Lev-Tov, P. Hesse and A. Gilbert (eds), *The Wide Lens in Archaeology: Honoring Brian Hesse's Contributions to Anthropological Archaeology*, 271–95, Atlanta: Lockwood Press.

Ijzereef, G. F. (2001), 'Animal Remains', in M. van Loon (ed.), *Selenkahiye: Final Report on the University of Chicago and University of Amsterdam Excavation in the Tabqa Reservoir, Northern Syria, 1967–1975*, 569–84, Istanbul: Nederlands Historisch-Archaeologisch Instituut Te Istanbul.

Ingold, T. (1994), *What Is an Animal?*, London & New York: Routledge.

Ismail, F., W. Sallaberger, P. Talon and K. van Lerberghe (1996), *Administrative Documents from Tell Beydar (Seasons 1993–1995)*, Turnhout: Brepols.

Jans, G. and J. Bretschneider (1998), 'Wagon and Chariot Representations in the Early Dynastic Glyptic: "They Came to Tell Beydar with Wagon and Equid"', in M. LeBeau (ed.), *About Subartu: Studies Devoted to Upper Mesopotamia*, 155–94, Turnhout: Brepols.

Johnstone, C. J. (2004), 'A Biometric Study of Equids in the Roman World', PhD dissertation, York: University of York.

Kammenhuber, A. (1961), *Hippologia hethitica*, Wiesbaden: Harrassowitz.

Kansa, S. W. (2004), 'Animal Exploitation at Early Bronze Age Ashqelon, Afridar: What the Bones Can Tell Us – Initial Analysis of the Animal Bones from Areas E, F and G', *'Atiqot*, 45: 279–97.

Kashkinbayev, K. (2013), *Berel Horses: Paleopathological Dimension Research*, Astana: Ministry of Education and Science of the Republic of Kazakhstan.

Katz, J. (2009), *The Archaeology of Cult in Middle Bronze Age Canaan: The Sacred Area at Tel Haror, Israel*, Piscataway, NJ: Gorgias Press.

Keel, O. (2010a), *Corpus der Stempelsiegel-Amulette aus Palästina/Israel von Anfängen bis zur Perserzeit. Katalog Band II: Von Bahan bis Tel Eton*, Fribourg and Göttingen: Academic Press.

Keel, O. (2010b), *Corpus der Stempelsiegel-Amulette aus Palästina/Israel von Anfängen bis zur Perserzeit. Katalog Band III: Von Tell el-Far'a bis Tell el-Fir*, Fribourg and Göttingen: Academic Press.

Kelly-Buccellati, M. (2002), 'Ein hurritischer Gang in die Unterwelt', *Mitteilungen der Deutschen Orient-Gesellschaft zu Berlin*, 134: 131–48.

Kelly-Buccellati, M. (2005), 'Introduction to the Archaeo-Zoology of the *Ābi*', *Studi Micenei ed Egeo-Anatolici*, 47: 61–6.

Kelly-Buccellati, M. (2015), 'Power and Identity Construction in Ancient Urkesh', in P. Ciafardoni and D. Giannessi (eds), *From the Treasures of Syria: Essays on Art and Archaeology in Honour of Stefania Mazzoni*, 111–30, Leiden: Nederlands Instituut voor het Nabije Oosten.

Keser, S., E. Demir and O. Yilmaz (2014), 'Some Bioactive Compounds and Antioxidant Activities of the Bitter Almond Kernel (*Prunus Dulcis* Var. *Amara*)', *Journal of the Chemical Society of Pakistan*, 36 (October): 922–30.

Kimura, B., F. B. Marshall, S. Chen, S. Rosenbom, P. D. Moehlman, N. Tuross, R. C. Sabin et al. (2011), 'Ancient DNA from Nubian and Somali Wild Ass Provides Insights into Donkey Ancestry and Domestication', *Proceedings of the Royal Society of London B: Biological Sciences*, 278 (1702): 50–7.

Kimura, B., F. Marshall, A. Beja-Pereira and C. Mulligan (2013), 'Donkey Domestication', *African Archaeological Review*, 30 (1): 83–95.

Kirksey, S. E. and S. Helmreich (2010), 'The Emergence of Multispecies Ethnography', *Cultural Anthropology*, 25 (4): 545–76.

Klingel, H. (1998), 'Observations on Social Organization and Behaviour of African and Asiatic Wild Asses (*Equus Africanus* and *Equus Hemionus*)', *Applied Animal Behaviour Science*, 60 (2): 103–13.

Kopnina, H. (2017), 'Beyond Multispecies Ethnography: Engaging with Violence and Animal Rights in Anthropology', *Critique of Anthropology*, 37 (3): 333–57.

Kosintzev, P. and Z. Samashev (2014), *Berel Horses: Morphological Research*, Astana: Ministry of Education and Science of the Republic of Kazakhstan.

Kramer, S. N. (1952), *Enmerkar and the Lord of Aratta: A Sumerian Epic Tale of Iraq and Iran*, Philadelphia: University of Pennsylvania Press.

Kramer, S. N. (1967), 'The Death of Ur-Nammu and His Descent to the Netherworld', *Journal of Cuneiform Studies*, 21: 104–22.

Kühne, C. (1995), 'Ein mittelassyriches Verwaltungsarchiv', in W. Orthmann, R. Hempelmann, H. Klein, C. Kühne, M. Novak, A. Pruss, E. Vila, H.-M. Weicken and A. Wener, *Ausgrabungen in Tell Chuera I: Vorbericht über die Grabungskampagne 1986 bis 1992*, 203–25, Saarbrücken: Saarbrücker Druckerei und Verlag.

Kveiborg, J. (2017), 'The Nordic Bronze Age Horse: Studies of Human-Horse Relationships in a Long-Term Perspective', PhD dissertation, Aarhus: Aarhus University.

Lacheman, E. R. (1939), 'Epigraphic Evidences of the Material Culture of the Nuzians', in R. F. S. Starr (ed.), *Nuzi: Report on the Excavations at Gorgan Tepa near Kirkuk, Iraq*, 528–44, Cambridge, MA: Harvard University Press.

Lafont, B. (1997), 'Le fonctionnement de la poste et le métier de facteur d'après les textes de Mari', in G. D. Young, M. W. Chavalas, R. E. Averbeck and K. L. Danti (eds), *Crossing Boundaries and Linking Horizons: Studies in Honor of Michael C. Astour on His 80th Birthday*, 315–34, Bethesda: CDL Press.

Lafont, B. (2000), 'Cheval, âne, onagre et mule dans la haute histoire mésopotamienne: Quelques données nouvelles', *Topoi. Orient-Occident*, 2 (1): 207–21.

Lambert, W. G. (2013), *Babylonian Creation Myths*, Winona Lake, IN: Eisenbrauns.

Landsberger, B. (1960), *The Fauna of Ancient Mesopotamia, First Part: Tablet XIII*, Rome: Pontificum Institutum Biblicum.

Larsen, M. T. (1967), *Old Assyrian Caravan Procedures*, Istanbul: Nederlands Historisch-Archaeologisch Instituut in het Nabije Oosten.

Larsen, M. T. (1976), *The Old Assyrian City-State and Its Colonies I*, Copenhagen: Akademisk Forlag.

Larsen, M. T. (2014), *Kültepe Tabletleri VI-c: The Archive of the Šalim-Aššur Family. Volume 3: Ali-Ahum*, AKT 6c, Ankara: Türk Tarih Kurumu.

Larsen, M. T. (2015), *Ancient Kanesh: A Merchant Colony in Bronze Age Anatolia*, New York: Cambridge University Press.

Lau, D. (2017a), 'Tiere im Krieg: Der mesopotamische Raum', in J. Ullrich and M. Roscher (eds), *Tiere und Krieg*, 21–33, Berlin: Neofelis.

Lau, D. (2017b), 'Zum kämpfen gezwungen: Tiere in den Kriegen der Antike', *Tierbefreiung*, 97 (December): 8–11.

Legrain, L. (1930), *Terra-Cottas from Nippur*, Philadelphia: University of Pennsylvania Press.

Legrain, L. (1946), 'Horseback Riding in Mesopotamia in the Third Millennium B.C.', *Bulletin University Museum (Philadelphia)*, 11: 27–32.

Lescureux, N. (2019), 'Beyond Wild and Domestic: Human Complex Relationships with Dogs, Wolves, and Wolf-Dog Hybrids', in C. Stepanoff and J.-D. Vigne (eds), *Hybrid Communities: Biosocial Approaches to Domestication and Other Trans-Species Relationships*, 83–98, London: Routledge.

Levine, M. (1999), 'The Origins of Horse Husbandry on the Eurasian Steppe', in M. Levine, Y. Rassamakin, A. Kislenko and N. Tatarintseva (eds), *Late Prehistoric Exploitation of the Eurasian Steppe*, 5–58, Cambridge: McDonald Institute for Archaeological Research.

Levine, M. (2012), 'Domestication of the Horse', in N. A. Silberman (ed.), *The Oxford Companion to Archaeology*, 2nd edn, 15–19 New York as place of publication, Oxford University Press.

Levine, M., Y. Rassamakin, A. Kislenko and N. Tatarintseva (1999), *Late Prehistoric Exploitation of the Eurasian Steppe*, Cambridge: McDonald Institute for Archaeological Research.

Levine, M., C. Renfrew and K. Boyle, eds (2003), *Prehistoric Steppe Adaptation and the Horse*, Cambridge: McDonald Institute for Archaeological Research.

Librado, P., N. Khan, A. Fages, M. A. Kusliy, T. Suchan, L. Tonasso-Calvière, S. Schiavinato, D. Alioglu et al. (2021), 'The Origins and Spread of Domestic Horses from the Western Eurasian Steppes', *Nature*, 598: 634–40.

Lieberman, S. J. (1968–69), 'An Ur III Text from Drēhem Recording "Booty from the Land of Mardu"', *Journal of Cuneiform Studies*, 22 (3/4): 53–62.

Liebowitz, H. (1988), *Terra-Cotta Figurines and Model Vehicles: The Oriental Institute Excavations at Selenkahiye, Syria*, Malibu: Undena.

Lindstrøm, T. C. (2012), '"I Am the Walrus": Animal Identities and Merging with Animals – Exceptional Experiences?', *Norwegian Archaeological Review*, 45 (2): 151–76.

Lion, B. (2008), 'L'armée à Nuzi', in P. Abrahami and L. Battini (eds), *Les armées du Proche-Orient ancien (IIIe-Ier mill. av. J. -C.)*, 71–81, Oxford: John and Erica Hedges.

Littauer, M. A. (1969), 'Slit Nostrils on Equids', *Zeitschrift für Säugetierkunde*, 34: 183–6.

Littauer, M. A. and J. H. Crouwel (1973), 'The Vulture Stela and an Early Type of Two-Wheeled Vehicle', *Journal of Near Eastern Studies*, 32 (3): 324–29.

Littauer, M. A. and J. H. Crouwel (1979), *Wheeled Vehicles and Ridden Animals in the Ancient Near East*, Leiden: Brill.

Littauer, M. A. and J. H. Crouwel (1985), *Chariots and Related Equipment from the Tomb of Tutankhamun*, Oxford: Griffith Institute.

Littauer, M. A. and J. H. Crouwel (1988), 'A Pair of Horse Bits of the Second Millennium B.C. from Iraq', *Iraq*, 50: 169–71.

Littauer, M. A. and J. H. Crouwel (2001), 'The Earliest Evidence for Metal Bridle Parts', *Oxford Journal of Archaeology*, 20 (4): 329–38.

Littauer, M. A. and J. H. Crouwel (2002), *Selected Writings on Chariots and Other Early Vehicles, Riding and Harness*, edited by P. Raulwing, Leiden: Brill.

Lloyd, S. (1972), *Beycesultan 3.1. Late Bronze Age Architecture*, London: British Institute at Ankara.

Loretz, O. (2011), *Hippologia Ugaritica: Das Pferd in Kultur, Wirtschaft, Kriegführung und Hippiatrie Ugarits: Pferd, Esel und Kamel in biblischen Texten*, Münster: Ugarit-Verlag.

Losey, R. J., V. I. Bazaliiskii, S. Garvie-Lok, M. Germonpré, J. A. Leonard, A. L. Allen, M. Anne Katzenberg and M. V. Sablin (2011), 'Canids as Persons: Early Neolithic Dog and Wolf Burials, Cis-Baikal, Siberia', *Journal of Anthropological Archaeology*, 30 (2): 174–89.

Loud, G. (1939), *The Megiddo Ivories*, Chicago: University of Chicago Press.

Maaijer, R. de (2001), 'Late Third Millennium Identifying Marks', in W. H. Soldt (ed.), *Veenhof Anniversary Volume: Studies Presented to Klaas R. Veenhof on the Occasion of His Sixty-Fifth Birthday*, 301–24, Leiden: Nederlands Instituut voor het Nabije Oosten.

Machule, D., K. Karstens, H.-H. Klaproth, G. Mozer, W. Pape, P. Werner, W. Mayer, R. Mayer-Opificius and M. Mackensen (1986), 'Ausgrabungen in Tall Munbāqa 1984', *Mitteilungen der Deutschen Orient-Gesellschaft*, 118: 67–145.

Maekawa, K. (1979a), 'The Ass and the Onager in Sumer in the Late Third Millennium B.C.', *Acta Sumerologica*, 1: 35–62.

Maekawa, K. (1979b), 'Animal and Human Castration in Sumer. Part 1: Cattle (gu4) and Equids (ANŠE.DUN.GI, ANŠE. BARxAN) in Pre-Sargonic Lagash', *Zinbun*, 95–137.

Maekawa, K. (2006), 'The Donkey and the Persian Onager in Late Third Millennium B.C. Mesopotamia and Syria: A Rethinking', *Journal of West Asian Archaeology*, 7: 1–9.

Maekawa, K. (2018), 'On the Sumerian Terms for Donkey', *N.A.B.U.*, 2018 (1): 4–9.

Magen, U. (2001), 'Der Wettergott als Eselsreiter? Gedanken zur Volksfrömmigkeit am mittleren Euphrat (Gebiet des Assad-Stausees) am Ende des 3. und zu Beginn des 2.

Jts. v. Chr.', in J.-W. Meyer, M. Novak and A. Pruss (eds), *Beiträge zur vorderasiatischen Archäeologie Winfried Orthmann gewidmet*, 246–59, Frankfurt: Johann Wolfgang Goethe-Universität, Archäologisches Institut.

Maidman, M. P. (2010), *Nuzi Texts and Their Uses as Historical Evidence*, edited by A. K. Guinan, Atlanta: Society of Biblical Literature.

Makowski, M. (2014), 'Terracotta Equid Figurines from Tell Arbid: New Evidence on Equids, Their Equipment and Exploration in North Mesopotamia during Third and First Half of Second Millennium BC', *Études et Travaux*, 27: 257–78.

Makowski, M. (2015), 'Of Men and Equids: Piecing the Clay Images from Tell Arbid Back Together', *Études et Travaux*, 28: 121–40.

Makowski, M. (2016), *Tell Arbid I: Clay Figurines*, Warsaw: Insitute of Mediterranean and Oriental Cultures, Polish Academy of Sciences.

Malamat, A. (1987), 'A Forerunner of Biblical Prophecy: The Mari Documents', in P. D. Miller, P. D. Hanson and S. D. McBride (eds), *Ancient Israelite Religion*, 33–52, Minneapolis: Fortress Press.

Malamat, A. (1995), 'A Note on the Ritual of Treaty Making in Mari and the Bible', *Israel Exploration Journal*, 45 (4): 226–9.

Malbran-Labat, F. and C. Roche (2008), 'Bordereaux de la "Maison d'Ourtenou (Urtēnu)", à propos de la gestion des équidés et de la place de cette maison dans l'économie palatiale', *MOM Éditions*, 47 (1): 243–75.

Mallowan, M. E. L. (1937), 'The Excavations at Tall Chagar Bazar and an Archaeological Survey of the Habur Region. Second Campaign, 1936', *Iraq*, 4 (2): 91–177.

Mallowan, M. E. L. (1948), 'A Copper Rein-Ring from Southern Iraq', *Iraq*, 10 (1): 51–5.

Manning, A. and J. Serpell, eds (1994), *Animals and Human Society: Changing Perspectives*, London & New York: Routledge.

Margueron, J. (2004), *Mari, métropole de l'Euphrate au IIIe et au début du IIe millénaire av. J.-C.*, Paris: Picard.

Marzahn, J. (2019), 'Equids in Mesopotamia – A Short Ride through Selected Textual Sources', in P. Raulwing, K. M. Linduff and J. H. Crouwel (eds), *Equids and Wheeled Vehicles in the Ancient World: Essays in Memory of Mary A. Littauer*, 71–83, Oxford: BAR.

Matoïan, V. (2008), 'Des roches précieuses dans le Palais royal d'Ougarit: Les calcédoines rubanées (agates)', in V. Matoïan (ed.), *Le mobilier du Palais Royal d'Ougarit*, Lyon: Maison de l'Orient et de la Méditerranée.

Matthews, R., ed. (2003), *Excavations at Tell Brak 4: Exploring an Upper Mesopotamian Regional Centre, 1994–1996*, London: British School of Archaeology in Iraq.

Matthews, R. and J. N. Postgate (1987), 'Excavations at Abu Salabikh, 1985–86', *Iraq*, 49: 91–119.

Mattila, R., S. Ito and S. Fink, eds (2019), *Animals and Their Relation to Gods, Humans and Things in the Ancient World*, Wiesbaden: Springer.

McGreevy, P. (2012), *Equine Behavior: A Guide for Veterinarians and Equine Scientists*, 2nd edn, Edinburgh: Elsevier.

McGrew, P. O. (1944), *An Early Pleistocene (Blancan) Fauna from Nebraska*, Chicago: Field Museum of Natural History.

McMahon, A. (2006), *Nippur V. The Early Dynastic to Akkadian Transition: The Area WF Sounding at Nippur*, Chicago: Oriental Institute of the University of Chicago.

McMahon, A., J. Oates, S. Al-Quntar, M. Charles, C. Colantoni, M. M. Hald, P. Karsgaard, L. Khalidi, A. Sołtysiak, A. Stone and J. Weber (2007), 'Excavations at Tell Brak 2006–2007', *Iraq*, 69: 145–71.

Mecquenem, R. de (1934), 'Fouilles de Suse, 1929–1933', *Mémoires de la mission archéologique de Perse*, 25: 177–237.

Mecquenem, R. de (1943), 'Fouilles de Suse, 1933–1939', *Mémoires de La Mission Archéologique de Perse*, 29: 3–161.

Meier, S. A. (1988), *The Messenger in the Ancient Semitic World*, Atlanta: Scholars Press.

Meutchieye, F., N. N. Kwalar and A. F. Nyock (2016), 'Donkey Husbandry and Production Systems', in F. J. Navas González, J. V. Delgado Bermejo and J. C. Vargas Burgos (eds), *Current Donkey Production & Functionality*, 725–63, Córdoba: UCO Press.

Meyer, J.-W. and A. Pruss (1994), *Ausgrabungen in Halawa 2: Die Kleinfunde von Tell Halawa, A.* Saarbrücken: Saarbrücker Druckerei und Verlag.

Michalowski, P. (2006), 'Love or Death? Observations on the Role of the Gala in Ur III Ceremonial Life', *Journal of Cuneiform Studies*, 58: 49–61.

Michel, C. (1996), 'Le commerce dans les textes de Mari', In. J.-M. Durand (ed.), *Mari, Ébla et les hourrites: Dix ans de travaux*, 385–426, Paris: ERC.

Michel, C. (2004), 'The *Perdum*-Mule: A Mount for Distinguished Persons in Mesopotamia during the First Half of the Second Millennium BC', in B. S. Frizell (ed.), *PECUS: Man and Animal in Antiquity*, 190–200, Rome: Swedish Institute.

Milevski, I. (2009), 'Local Exchange in the Southern Levant during the Early Bronze Age: A Political Economy Viewpoint', *Antiguo Oriente*, 7: 126–60.

Milevski, I. (2011), *Early Bronze Age Goods Exchange in the Southern Levant: A Marxist Perspective*, London: Equinox.

Milevski, I. and L. K. Horwitz (2019), 'Domestication of the Donkey (*Equus Asinus*) in the Southern Levant: Archaeozoology, Iconography and Economy', in R. Kowner, G. Bar-Oz, M. Biran, M. Shahar and G. Shelach-Lavi (eds), *Animals and Human Society in Asia: Historical, Cultural and Ethical Perspectives*, 93–148, Cham: Palgrave Macmillan.

Minero, M., E. D. Costa, F. Dai, L. A. M. Murray, E. Canali and F. Wemelsfelder (2016), 'Use of Qualitative Behaviour Assessment as an Indicator of Welfare in Donkeys', *Applied Animal Behaviour Science*, 174 (January): 147–53.

Minniti, C. (2008), 'The Middle Bronze Age Animal Remains from Area P at Tell Tuqan', in F. Baffi (ed.), *Tell Tuqan Excavations 2006–2007*, 231–9, Galatina: Congedo Editore.

Miroschedji, P. de, N. Sadek, D. Faltings, V. Boulez, L. Naggiar-Moliner, N. Sykes and M. Tengberg (2001), 'Les fouilles de Tell es-Sakan (Gaza): Nouvelles données sur les contacts égypto-cananéens aux IVe-IIIe millénaires', *Paléorient*, 27: 75–104.

Mitchell, P. (2018), *The Donkey in Human History: An Archaeological Perspective*, Oxford: Oxford University Press.

Molina, M. (2016), 'Archives and Bookkeeping in Southern Mesopotamia during the Ur III Period', *Comptabilités*, 8: 1–19.

Molleson, T. and J. Blondiaux (1994), 'Riders' Bones from Kish, Iraq', *Cambridge Archaeological Journal*, 4 (2): 312–6.

Monroe, C. M. (2009), *Scales of Fate: Trade, Tradition, and Transformation in the Eastern Mediterranean ca. 1350–1175 BCE*, Münster: Ugarit-Verlag.

Moor, J. C. de (1987), *An Anthology of Religious Texts from Ugarit*, Leiden: Brill.

Moore, J. N. (2013), 'Overview of Colic in Horses – Digestive System" Veterinary Manual (www.msdvetmanual.com/digestive-system/colic-in-horses/overview-of-colic-in-horses, accessed 18 June 2021).

Moorey, P. R. S. (1970), 'Pictorial Evidence for the History of Horse-Riding in Iraq before the Kassite Period', *Iraq*, 32 (1): 36–50.

Moorey, P. R. S. (1978), *Kish Excavations, 1923–1933*, Oxford: Clarendon Press.

Moorey, P. R. S. (1986), 'The Emergence of the Light, Horse-Drawn Chariot in the Near-East c. 2000–1500 B.C.', *World Archaeology*, 18 (2): 196–215.

Moorey, P. R. S. (2001), 'Clay Models and Overland Mobility in Syria, *c.* 2350–1800 B.C.', in J.-W. Meyer, M. Novak and A. Pruss (eds), *Beiträge zur vorderasiatischen Archäologie Winfried Orthmann gewidmet*, 344–51, Frankfurt: Johann Wolfgang Goethe-Universität, Archäologisches Institut.

Moortgat, A. (1930), 'Der Kampf zu Wagen in der Kunst des alten Orients. Zur Herkunft eines Bildgedankens', *Orientalistische Literaturzeitung*, 33 (11): 842–54.

Moortgat, A. (1962), *Tell Chuēra in Nordost-Syrien: Vorläufiger Bericht über die dritte Grabungskampagne 1960*, Köln and Opladen: Westdeutscher Verlag.

Moortgat-Correns, U. (1988), *Tell Chuera in Nordost-Syrien: Vorläufiger Bericht über die neunte und zehnte Grabungskampagne 1982 und 1983*, Berlin: Gebr. Mann.

Moran, W. L. (1992), *The Amarna Letters*, Baltimore: Johns Hopkins University Press.

Morris, B. (2000), *The Power of Animals: An Ethnography*, Oxford and New York: Berg.

Mourad, A.-L. (2020), 'Foreigners at Beni Hasan: Evidence from the Tomb of Khnumhotep I (No. 14)', *Bulletin of the American School of Oriental Research*, 384: 105–32.

Murray, L. M. A., K. Byrne and R. B. D'Eath (2013), 'Pair-Bonding and Companion Recognition in Domestic Donkeys, *Equus Asinus*', *Applied Animal Behaviour Science*, 143 (1): 67–74.

Muscarella, O. W. (1981), *Archäologie zur Bibel: Kunstschätze aus den biblischen Ländern*, Mainz: Zabern.

Na'aman, N. (1977), 'Ašītu (sg.) and Ašâtu (pl.): Strap and Reins', *Journal of Cuneiform Studies* 29, (4): 237–39.

Nagel, W. (1966), *Die mesopotamische Streitwagen und seine Entwicklung im ostmediterranean Bereich*, Berlin: Hessling.

Navas González, F. J, J. Jordana Vidal, J. M. León Jurado, A. Arando Arbulu, A. K. McLean and J. V. Delgado Bermejo (2018), 'Genetic Parameter and Breeding Value Estimation of Donkeys' Problem-Focused Coping Styles', *Behavioural Processes*, 153: 66–76.

Navas González, F. J., M. Miró Arlas and A. F. Nyock (2016), 'Temperament, Behaviour, Movements and Body Language', in F. J. Navas González, J. V. Delgado Bermejo and J. C. Vargas Burgos (eds), *Current Donkey Production & Functionality*, 72–160, Córdoba: UCO Press.

Newberry, G. W. F. P. E. (1893), *Beni Hasan, Part I*, London: Paul, Trench, Trübner & Co.

Nichols, J. (2019), 'Guardian Donkeys Protecting the Herd', *ABC Rural*, 23 April 2019 (www.abc.net.au/news/rural/2019-04-23/donkey-guardians-protect-herd-from-wild-dogs/11018666, accessed 18 June 2021).

Nichols, J. J. and J. A. Weber (2006), 'Amorites, Onagers, and Social Reorganization in Middle Bronze Age Syria', in G. M. Schwartz and J. J. Nichols (eds), *After Collapse: The Regeneration of Complex Societies*, 38–57, Tucson: University of Arizona Press.

Nir, S. M. (2011), 'Star Show-Jumping Horse Dies During Competition', *The New York Times*, 6 Nov. 2011 (www.nytimes.com/2011/11/07/sports/hickstead-star-show-jumping-horse-dies-during-competition.html, accessed 18 June 2021).

Nistelberger, H. M., A. H. Pálsdóttir, B. Star, R. Leifsson, A. T. Gondek, L. Orlando, J. H. Barrett, et al. (2019), 'Sexing Viking Age Horses from Burial and Non-Burial Sites in Iceland Using Ancient DNA', *Journal of Archaeological Science*, 101: 115–22.

Noble, D. (1969), 'The Mesopotamian Onager as a Draught Animal', in P. J. Ucko and G. W. Dimbleby (eds), *The Domestication and Exploitation of Plants and Animals*, 485–8, London: Gerald Duckworth & Co.

Oates, D. and J. Oates (2001), 'The Excavations', in D. Oates, J. Oates and H. MacDonald, *Excavations at Tell Brak 2: Nagar in the Third Millennium BC*, 15–98, London: British School of Archaeology in Iraq.

Oates, D., J. Oates and H. McDonald (2001), *Excavations at Tell Brak 2: Nagar in the Third Millennium BC*, London: British School of Archaeology in Iraq.

Oates, J. (2001), 'Equid Figurines and "Chariot" Models' in D. Oates, J. Oates and H. MacDonald, *Excavations at Tell Brak 2: Nagar in the Third Millennium BC*, 279–93, London: British School of Archaeology in Iraq.

Oates, J. (2003), 'A Note on the Early Evidence for Horse and the Riding of Equids in Western Asia', in M. Levine, C. Renfrew and K. Boyle (eds), *Prehistoric Steppe Adaptation and the Horse*, 115–25, Cambridge: McDonald Institute for Archaeological Research.

Oates, J., D. Oates and H. McDonald (1997), *Excavations at Tell Brak 1: The Mitanni and Old Babylonian Periods*, Cambridge: McDonald Institute for Archaeological Research.

O'Connor, T. (2000), *The Archaeology of Animal Bones*, Stroud: Sutton.

Ogden, L. A., B. Hall and K. Tanita (2013), 'Animals, Plants, People, and Things: A Review of Multispecies Ethnography', *Environment and Society*, 4 (1): 5–24.

Olsen, S. L. (2006), 'Early Horse Domestication on the Eurasian Steppe', in M. A. Zeder, D. G. Bradley, E. Emshwiller and B. D. Smith (eds), *Documenting Domestication: New Genetic and Archaeological Paradigms*, 245–69, Berkeley: University of California Press.

Orlando, L. (2015), 'Equids', *Current Biology*, 25: R973–8.

Orlando, L., J. L. Metcalf, M. T. Alberdi, M. Telles-Antunes, D. Bonjean, M. Otte, F. Martin et al. (2009), 'Revising the Recent Evolutionary History of Equids Using Ancient DNA', *Proceedings of the National Academy of Sciences*, 106 (51): 21754–9.

Osthaus, B., L. Proops, I. Hocking and F. Burden (2013), 'Spatial Cognition and Perseveration by Horses, Donkeys and Mules in a Simple A-Not-B Detour Task', *Animal Cognition*, 16 (2): 301–5.

Otten, H. (1952), 'Pirva: Der Gott auf dem Pferde', *Jahrbuch für kleinasiatische Forschung*, 2: 62–73.

Outram, A. K., N. A. Stear, R. Bendrey, S. Olsen, A. Kasparov, V. Zaibert, N. Thorpe and R. P. Evershed (2009), 'The Earliest Horse Harnessing and Milking', *Science*, 323 (5919): 1332–5.

Ovadia, E. (1992), 'The Domestication of the Ass and Pack Transport by Animals: A Case of Technological Change', in O. Bar-Yosef and A. Khazanov (eds), *Pastoralism in the Levant: Archaeological Materials in Anthropological Perspectives*, 19–28, Madison: Prehistory Press.

Overton, N. J. and Y. Hamilakis (2013), 'A Manifesto for a Social Zooarchaeology: Swans and Other Beings in the Mesolithic', *Archaeological Dialogues*, 20 (2): 111–36.

Owen, D. I. (1979), 'A Thirteen Month Summary Account from Ur', in M. A. Powell and R. H. Sack (eds), *Studies in Honor of Tom B. Jones*, 57–70, Kevelaer: Butzon & Bercker.

Owen, D. I. (1991), 'The "First" Equestrian: An Ur III Glyptic Scene', *Acta Sumerologica*, 13: 259–74.

Özgüç, N. (1965), *Kültepe Mühür Baskilarinda Anadolu Grubu: The Anatolian Group of Cylinder Seals from Kültepe*, Ankara: Türk Tarih Kurumu Basimevi.

Panter, K. E. (2018), 'Cyanogenic Glycoside-Containing Plants', in R. C. Gupta (ed.), *Veterinary Toxicology: Basic and Clinical Principles*, 935–40, 3rd edn, London: Academic Press.

Pardee, D. (1985), *Les textes hippiatriques*, Paris: ERC.

Pardee, D. (2000), 'Les équidés à Ougarit au bronze récent: La perspective des textes', *Topoi. Orient-Occident*, 2 (1): 223–34.

Pardee, D. (2002), *Ritual and Cult at Ugarit*, Atlanta: Society of Biblical Literature.

Parrot, A. (1956), *Mission archéologique de Mari 1: Le temple d'Ishtar*, Paris: Geuthner.

Parrot, A. (1967), *Mission archéologique de Mari 3: Les temples d'Ishtarat et de Ninni-zaza*, Paris: Geuthner.

Pendlebury, J. D. S. (1951), *The City of Akhenaten: Part III. The Central City and the Official Quarters. The Excavations at Tell El-Amarna during the Seasons 1926–1927 and 1931–1936*, London: Egypt Exploration Society.

Peters, J. (1998), *Römische Tierhaltung und Tierzucht: Eine Synthese aus archäozoologischer Untersuchung und schriftlich-bildlicher Überlieferung*, Rahden/Westf.: Leidorf.

Peters, J., N. Pöllath and A. von den Driesch (2002), 'Early and Late Bronze Age Transitional Subsistence at Tall al 'Umayri', in L. G. Herr, D. R. Clark, L. T. Geraty,

R. W. Younker and O. S. LaBianca (eds), *Madaba Plains Project 5: The 1994 Season at Tall al-'Umayri and Subsequent Studies*, 305–47, Berrien Springs: Andrews University Press.

Petrie, F. (1931), *Ancient Gaza I: Tell El Ajjul*, London: British School of Archaeology in Egypt.

Petrie, F. (1932), *Ancient Gaza II: Tell El Ajjul*, London: British School of Archaeology in Egypt.

Petrie, F. (1933), *Ancient Gaza III: Tell El Ajjul*, London: British School of Archaeology in Egypt.

Petrie, F. (1934), *Ancient Gaza IV: Tell El Ajjul*, London: British School of Archaeology in Egypt.

Petrie, F., E. J. H. Mackay and M. A. Murray (1952), *The City of Shepherd Kings and Ancient Gaza V*, London: British School of Egyptian Archaeology and Bernard Quaritch.

Piggott, S. (1979), '"The First Wagons and Carts": Twenty-Five Years Later', *University of London Institute of Archaeology Bulletin*, 16: 3–17.

Piggott, S. (1983), *The Earliest Wheeled Transport: From the Atlantic Coast to the Caspian Sea*, London: Thames & Hudson.

Pilaar Birch, S. E. (2018), *Multispecies Archaeology*, Abingdon: Routledge.

Porada, E. (1947), *Seal Impressions from Nuzi*, New Haven: ASOR.

Porada, E. (1948), *Corpus of Ancient Near Eastern Seals in North American Collections*, New York: Pantheon.

Porter, A. (2002a), 'The Dynamics of Death: Ancestors, Pastoralism, and the Origins of a Third-Millennium City in Syria', *Bulletin of the American Schools of Oriental Research*, 325: 1–36.

Porter, A. (2002b), 'Communities in Conflict: Death and the Contest for Social Order in the Euphrates River Valley', *Near Eastern Archaeology*, 65 (3): 156–73.

Porter, A. (2012), 'Mortal Mirrors: Creating Kin through Human Sacrifice in Third Millennium Syro-Mesopotamia', in A. Porter and G. M. Schwartz (eds), *Sacred Killing*, 191–215, Winona Lake, IN: Eisenbrauns.

Porter, A., T. McClellan, S. Wilhelm, J. Weber, A. Baldwin, J. Colley, B. Enriquez, et al. (2021), '"Their Corpses Will Reach the Base of Heaven": A Third-Millennium BC War Memorial in Northern Mesopotamia?', *Antiquity*, 95 (382): 900–18.

Postgate, J. N. (1982), 'Abu Salabikh', in J. Curtis (ed.), *Fifty Years of Mesopotamian Discovery*, 48–61, London: British School of Archaeology in Iraq.

Postgate, J. N. (1984), 'Excavations at Abu Salabikh, 1983', *Iraq*, 46 (2): 95–113.

Postgate, J. N. (1986), 'The Equids of Sumer, Again', in R. H. Meadow and H.-P. Uerpmann (eds), *Equids in the Ancient World 1*, 194–204, Wiesbaden: Ludwig Reichert.

Postgate, J. N. (forthcoming), *Abu Salabikh Excavations 5*.

Postgate, J. N. and J. A. Moon (1982), 'Excavations at Abu Salabikh, 1981', *Iraq*, 44 (2): 103–36.

Postgate, N., T. Wang and T. Wilkinson (1995), 'The Evidence for Early Writing: Utilitarian or Ceremonial?', *Antiquity*, 69 (264): 459–80.

Potratz, J. A. H. (1938), *Das Pferd in der Frühzeit*, Rostock: Hinstorff.

Potratz, J. A. H. (1966), *Die Pferdetrensen des alten Orient*, Rome: Pontificium Institutum Biblicum.

Potts, D. T. (1999), *The Archaeology of Elam: Formation and Transformation of an Ancient Iranian State*, Cambridge: Cambridge University Press.

Potts, D. T. (2014), 'On Some Early Equids at Susa', in B. Cerasetti (ed.), *My Life Is Like the Summer Rose': Maurizio Tosi e l'archeologia come modo di vivere*, 643–7, Oxford: Archaeopress.

Pritchard, J. B. (1969), *Ancient Near Eastern Texts Relating to the Old Testament*, 3rd edn, Princeton: Princeton University Press.

Proops, L., F. Burden and B. Osthaus (2009), 'Mule Cognition: A Case of Hybrid Vigour?', *Animal Cognition*, 12 (1): 75–84.

Proops, L., K. Grounds, A. V. Smith and K. McComb (2018), 'Animals Remember Previous Facial Expressions That Specific Humans Have Exhibited', *Current Biology*, 28 (9): 1428–32.

Pulak, C. (1998), 'The Uluburun Shipwreck: An Overview', *International Journal of Nautical Archaeology*, 27 (3): 188–224.

Raccidi, M. (2012), 'Chariot Terracotta Models from Tell Arbid', *Polish Archaeology in the Mediterranean*, 21: 605–23.

Rainey, A. F. (1972), 'A Front-Line Report from Amurru', *Ugarit-Forschungen*, 3: 131–49.

Rainey, A. F. (2014), *The El-Amarna Correspondence: A New Edition of the Cuneiform Letters from the Site of El-Amarna Based on Collations of All Extant Tablets*, Leiden: Brill.

Raulwing, P. (2000), *Horses, Chariots and Indo-Europeans: Foundations and Methods of Chariotry Research from the Viewpoint of Comparative Indo-European Linguistics*, Budapest: Archaeolingua.

Raulwing, P. (2004), 'Indogermanen, Indoarier und *Maryannu* in der Streitwagenforschung: Eine rezeptions- und wissenschaftsgeschichtliche Spurenlese', in M. Fansa and S. Burmeister (eds), *Rad und Wagen: der Ursprung einer Innovation: Wagen im Vorderen Orient und Europa*, 515–31, Mainz: Zabern.

Raulwing, P. (2005), 'The Kikkuli Text (CTH 284): Some Interdisciplinary Remarks on Hittite Training Texts for Chariot Horses in the Second Half of the 2nd Millennium B.C.', in A. Gardeisen (ed.), *Les équidés dans le monde Méditerranéen antique*, 61–75, Lattes: Edition de l'Association pour le développement de l'archéologie en Languedoc-Roussillon.

Raulwing, P. (2009), 'The Kikkuli Text: Hittite Training Instructions for Chariot Horses in the Second Half of the 2nd Millennium B.C. and Their Interdisciplinary Context', 1–21 (https://www.academia.edu/3039204/The_Kikkuli_Text_Hittite_Training_Instructions_for_Chariot_Horses_in_the_Second_Half_of_the_2nd_Millennium_B_C_and_Their_Interdisciplinary_Context, accessed 18 June 2021).

Raulwing, P. and J. Clutton-Brock (2009), 'The Buhen Horse: Fifty Years after Its Discovery', *Journal of Egyptian History*, 2 (1–2): 1–106.

Raulwing, P., K. M. Linduff and J. H. Crouwel, eds (2019), *Equids and Wheeled Vehicles in the Ancient World: Essays in Memory of Mary A. Littauer*, Oxford: BAR.

Reade, J. (1973), 'Tell Taya (1972–73): Summary Report', *Iraq*, 35 (2): 155–87.

Recht, L. (2011), 'Sacrifice in the Bronze Age Aegean and Near East: A Poststructuralist Approach', PhD dissertation, Dublin: Trinity College Dublin.

Recht, L. (2014), 'Perfume, Women and the Underworld in Urkesh: Exploring Female Roles through Aromatic Substances in the Bronze Age Near East', *Journal of Intercultural and Interdisciplinary Archaeology* 2014, (1): 11–24.

Recht, L. (2018), '"Asses Were Buried with Him": Equids as Markers of Sacred Space in the Third and Second Millennia BC in the Eastern Mediterranean', in L. D. Nebelsick, J. Wawrzeniuk and K. Zeman-Wiśniewska (eds), *Sacred Space: Contributions to the Archaeology of Belief*, 65–94, Warsaw: Institute of Archaeology, Cardinal Stefan Wyszynski University in Warsaw.

Recht, L. (2019), 'Animals as Social Actors: Cases of Equid Resistance in the Ancient Near East', *Cambridge Archaeological Journal*, 29 (4): 593–606.

Recht, L. (forthcoming a), 'Equids at the End of the Bronze Age on Cyprus', in P. M. Fischer and T. Bürge (eds), *Decline of Bronze Age Civilisations in the Mediterranean*.

Recht, L. (forthcoming b), 'Animals, Violence and Inequality in Ancient Mesopotamia', in S. Murray and T. Leppard (eds), *Coercion, Violence, and Inequality in Archaeological Perspective*.

Recht, L. and C. E. Morris (2021), 'Chariot Kraters and Horse-Human Relations in Late Bronze Age Greece and Cyprus', *Annual of the British School at Athens*, 116: 95–132.

Recht, L. and C. Tsouparopoulou, eds (2021), *Fierce Lions, Angry Mice and Fat-Tailed Sheep: Animal Encounters in the Ancient Near East*, Cambridge: McDonald Institute for Archaeological Research.

Reviv, H. (1972), 'Some Comments on the *Maryannu*', *Israel Exploration Journal*, 22 (4): 218–28.

Richter, T. (2004), 'Der Streitwagen im alten Orient im 2. Jahrtausend v. Chr. – Eine Betrachtung anhand der keilschriftlichen Quellen', in M. Fansa and S. Burmeister (eds), *Rad und Wagen: Der Ursprung einer Innovation: Wagen im Vorderen Orient und Europa*, 507–14, Mainz: Zabern.

Ritvo, H. (2004), 'Animal Planet', *Environmental History*, 9: 204–20.

Roaf, M. (1982), 'The Hamrin Sites', in J. Curtis (ed.), *Fifty Years of Mesopotamian Discovery*, 40–7, London: British School of Archaeology in Iraq.

Robb, J. (2010), 'Beyond Agency', *World Archaeology*, 42 (4): 493–520.

Robertson-Mackay, M. E. (1980), 'A "Head and Hooves" Burial beneath a Round Barrow, with Other Neolithic and Bronze Age Sites, on Hemp Knoll, near Avebury, Wiltshire', *Proceedings of the Prehistoric Society*, 46 (December): 123–76.

Rogers, R. A. and L. A. Rogers (1988), 'Notching and Anterior Bevelling on Fossil Horse Incisors: Indicators of Domestication?', *Quaternary Research*, 29: 72–4.

Romano, L. (2019), 'Abu Tbeirah and Area 1 in the Second Half of the 3rd Mill. BC', in L. Romano and F. D'Agostino (eds), *Abu Tbeirah Excavations I: Area 1. Last Phase and Building A – Phase 1*, 59–91, Rome: Sapienza University Press.

Rossel, S., F. Marshall, J. Peters, T. Pilgram, M. D. Adams and D. O'Connor (2008), 'Domestication of the Donkey: Timing, Processes, and Indicators', *Proceedings of the National Academy of Sciences*, 105 (10): 3715–20.

Rothschild, B. M., D. R. Prothero and C. Rothschild (2001), 'Origins of Spondyloarthropathy in Perissodactyla', *Clinical and Experimental Rheumatology*, 19: 628–32.

Rova, E. (2012), '"Themes" of Seal Images and Their Variants: Two New Examples from Tell Beydar', in G. B. Lanfranchi, D. M. Bonacossi, C. Pappi and S. Ponchia (eds), *Leggo! Studies Presented to Frederick Mario Fales on the Occasion of His 65th Birthday*, 745–61, Wiesbaden: Harrassowitz.

Russell, N. (2011), *Social Zooarchaeology: Humans and Animals in Prehistory*, Cambridge: Cambridge University Press.

Sallaberger, W. (1996a), 'Nagar in den frühdynastischen Texten aus Beydar', in K. van Lerberghe and G. Voet (eds), *Languages and Cultures in Contact: At the Crossroads of Civilizations in the Syro-Mesopotamian Realm. Proceedings of the 42th RAI*, 393–407, Leuven: Peeters.

Sallaberger, W. (1996b), 'Grain Accounts: Personnel Lists and Expenditure Documents', in F. Ismail, W. Sallaberger, P. Talon and K. van Lerberghe (eds), *Administrative Documents from Tell Beydar (Seasons 1993–1995)*, 89–106, Turnhout: Brepols.

Sallaberger, W. (1998), 'The Economic Background of a Seal Motif: A Philological Note on Tell Beydar's Wagons', in M. LeBeau (ed.), *About Subartu: Studies Devoted to Upper Mesopotamia*, 173–5, Turnhout: Brepols.

Sallaberger, W. (2004), 'Schlachtvieh aus Puzriš-Dagān: Zur Bedeutung dieses königlichen Archivs', *Jaarbericht 'Ex Oriente Lux'*, 38: 45–62.

Salonen, A. (1950), *Notes on Wagons and Chariots in Ancient Mesopotamia*, Helsinki: Societas Orientalis Fennica.

Salonen, A. (1956), *Hippologica Accadica*, Helsinki: Suomalainen Tiedeakatemia.

Sapir-Hen, L., Y. Gadot and O. Lipschits (2017), 'Ceremonial Donkey Burial, Social Status, and Settlement Hierarchy in the Early Bronze III: The Case of Tel Azekah', in J. S. E. Lev-Tov, P. Wapnish and A. S. Gilbert (eds), *The Wide Lens in Archaeology: Honoring Brian Hesse's Contributions to Anthropological Archaeology*, 259–70, Atlanta: Lockwood Press.

Schaeffer, C. F.-A. (1938), 'Les fouilles de Ras Shamra-Ugarit', *Syria*, 19 (4): 313–34.

Schaeffer, C. F.-A. (1949), *Ugaritica II*, Paris: Geuthner.

Schaeffer, C. F.-A. (1954), 'Fouilles de Ras Shamra-Ugarit', *Syria*, 31 (1): 14–67.

Schmitt, R. (2013), 'Astarte, Mistress of Horses, Lady of the Chariot: The Warrior Aspect of Astarte', *Die Welt des Orients*, 43 (2): 213–25.

Schubert, M., M. Mashkour, C. Gaunitz, A. Fages, A. Seguin-Orlando, S. Sheikhi, A. H. Alfarhan, et al. (2017), 'Zonkey: A Simple, Accurate and Sensitive Pipeline to

Genetically Identify Equine F1-Hybrids in Archaeological Assemblages', *Journal of Archaeological Science*, 78: 147–57.

Schwartz, G. M. (2012), 'Archaeology and Sacrifice', in A. Porter and G. M. Schwartz (eds), *Sacred Killing*, 1–32, Winona Lake, IN: Eisenbrauns.

Schwartz, G. M. (2013), 'Memory and Its Demolition: Ancestors, Animals and Sacrifice at Umm El-Marra, Syria', *Cambridge Archaeological Journal*, 23 (3): 495–522.

Schwartz, G. M. (2016), 'After Interment/Outside the Tombs: Some Mortuary Particulars at Umm El-Marra', in C. Felli (ed.), *How to Cope with Death: Mourning and Funerary Practices in the Ancient Near East*, 189–215, Pisa: Edizioni ETS.

Schwartz, G. M., H. H. Curvers, S. Dunham and B. Stuart (2003), 'A Third-Millennium B.C. Elite Tomb and Other New Evidence from Tell Umm El-Marra, Syria', *American Journal of Archaeology*, 107 (3): 325–61.

Schwartz, G. M., H. H. Curvers, S. Dunham, B. Stuart and J. A. Weber (2006), 'A Third-Millennium B.C. Elite Mortuary Complex at Umm El-Marra, Syria: 2002 and 2004 Excavations', *American Journal of Archaeology*, 110 (4): 603–41.

Schwartz, G. M., H. H. Curvers, S. Dunham and J. A. Weber (2012), 'From Urban Origins to Imperial Integration in Western Syria: Umm El-Marra 2006, 2008', *American Journal of Archaeology*, 116 (1): 157–93.

Shai, I., H. J. Greenfield, A. Brown, S. Albaz and A. M. Maeir (2016), 'The Importance of the Donkey as a Pack Animal in the Early Bronze Age Southern Levant: A View from Tell eṣ-Ṣāfi/Gath', *Zeitschrift des Deutschen Palästina-Vereins*, 132 (1): 1–25.

Sherratt, A. (1981), 'Plough and Pastoralism: Aspects of the Secondary Products Revolution', in I. Hodder, G. Isaac and N. Hammond (eds), *Pattern of the Past: Studies in Honour of David Clarke*, 261–305, Cambridge: Cambridge University Press.

Sherratt, A. (1983), 'The Secondary Exploitation of Animals in the Old World', *World Archaeology*, 15 (1): 90–104.

Shev, E. T. (2016), 'The Introduction of the Domesticated Horse in Southwest Asia', *Archaeology, Ethnology & Anthropology of Eurasia*, 44 (1): 123–36.

Shir-Vertesh, D. (2012), '"Flexible Personhood": Loving Animals as Family Members in Israel', *American Anthropologist*, 114 (3): 420–32.

Smith, A. V., L. Proops, K. Grounds, J. Wathan and K. McComb (2016), 'Functionally Relevant Responses to Human Facial Expressions of Emotion in the Domestic Horse (*Equus Caballus*)', *Biology Letters*, 12 (2): 20150907.

Smith, D. G. and F. A. Burden (2013), 'Practical Donkey and Mule Nutrition', in R. J. Geor, P. A. Harris and M. Coenen (eds), *Equine Applied and Clinical Nutrition*, 304–16, Edinburgh: Saunders Elsevier.

Smith, J. Z. (1987), 'The Domestication of Sacrifice', in R. Hamerton-Kelly (ed.), *Violent Origins*, 191–235, Stanford: Stanford University Press.

Speiser, E. A. (1935), *Excavations at Tepe Gawra I: Levels I-VIII*, Philadelphia: University of Pennsylvania Press.

Spruytte, J. (1983), *Early Harness Systems: Experimental Studies*, trans. M. A. Littauer, London: J.A. Allen.

Stager, L. E. (2006), 'Chariot Fittings from Philistine Ashkelon', in S. Gitin, J. E. Wright and J. P. Dessel (eds), *Confronting the Past: Archaeological and Historical Essays on Ancient Israel in Honor of William G. Dever*, 169–76, Winona Lake, IN: Eisenbrauns.

Starke, F. (1995), *Ausbildung und Training von Streitwagenpferde: Eine hippologisch orientierte Interpretation des Kikkuli-Textes*, Wiesbaden: Harrassowitz.

Starr, R. F. S. (1937), *Nuzi: Report on the Excavations at Gorgan Tepa near Kirkuk, Iraq*, Cambridge, MA: Harvard University Press.

Starr, R. F. S. (1939), *Nuzi: Report on the Excavations at Gorgan Tepa near Kirkuk, Iraq*, Cambridge, MA: Harvard University Press.

Steinkeller, P. (2005), 'The Priestess *Égi-zi* and Related Matters', in Y. Sefati, P. Artzi, C. Cohen, B. L. Eichler and V. A. Hurowitz (eds), *'An Experienced Scribe Who Neglects Nothing': Ancient Near Eastern Studies in Honor of Jacob Klein*, 301–10, Bethesda: CDL Press.

Stépanoff, C. and J.-D. Vigne, eds (2019), *Hybrid Communities: Biosocial Approaches to Domestication and Other Trans-Species Relationships*, London: Routledge.

Stol, M. (2011), 'Pferde, Pferdekrankheiten und Pferdemedezin in altbabylonischer Zeit', in L. Oswald (ed.), *Hippologia Ugaritica: Das Pferd in Kultur, Wirtschaft, Kriegführung und Hippiatrie Ugarits: Pferd, Esel und Kamel in biblischen Texten*, Münster: Ugarit-Verlag.

Stol, M. (2016), *Women in the Ancient Near East*, Berlin: De Gruyter.

Strommenger, E. (2017), *Die Kleinfunde von Habuba Kabira-Tall*, Wiesbaden: Harrassowitz.

Svendsen, E. D. (2009), *The Complete Book of the Donkey*, Shrewsbury: Kenilworth Press.

Tatin, L., B. F. Darreh-Shoori, C. Tourenq, D. Tatin and B. Azmayesh (2007), 'Up-Date on the Behaviour and Status of the Critically Endangered Onager, *Equus Hemionus Onager*, from Iran', *Exploration into the Biological Resources of Mongolia*, 10: 253–9.

Taylor, W., T. Treal, J. Bayarsaikhan and T. Tuvshinjargal (2015), 'Equine Cranial Morphology and the Identification of Riding and Chariotry in Late Bronze Age Mongolia', *Antiquity*, 89 (346): 854–71.

Tegetmeier, W. B. and C. L. Sutherland (1895), *Horses, Asses, Zebras, Mules and Mule Breeding*, London: Horace Cox.

Tenney, J. S. (2011), *Life at the Bottom of Babylonian Society: Servile Laborers at Nippur in the 14th and 13th Centuries, B.C.*, Leiden: Boston.

The Donkey Sanctuary (2016), *Donkey Care Book: Everything You Need to Know for the Lifelong Welfare of Your Donkeys and Mules*, 5th edn, Sidmouth: The Donkey Sanctuary.

The Donkey Sanctuary (2018), 'Factsheet: Colic in Donkeys' (www.thedonkeysanctuary.org.uk/sites/uk/files/2018-12/colic-in-donkeys-20181213.pdf, accessed 18 June 2021).

The Donkey Sanctuary (2019), 'The Mules and Men of World War I – Remembrance Day 2019' (www.thedonkeysanctuary.org.uk/news/the-mules-and-men-of-world-war-i-remembrance-day-2019, accessed 18 June 2021).

Thureau-Dangin, F. and M. Dunand (1936), *Til Barsib*, Paris: Geuthner.

Travis, L. (2004), *The Mule*, London: J. A. Allen.

Tsouparopoulou, C. (2012), 'The "K-9 Corps" of the Third Dynasty of Ur: The Dog Handlers at Drehem and the Army', *Zeitschrift für Assyriologie und Vorderasiatische Archäologie*, 102 (1): 1–16.

Tsouparopoulou, C. (2013), 'Killing and Skinning Animals in the Ur III Period: The Puzriš-Dagan (Drehem) Office Managing Dead Animals and Slaughter By-Products', *Altorientalische Forschungen*, 40 (1): 150–82.

Tsouparopoulou, C. (2015), *The Ur III Seals Impressed on Documents from Puzriš-Dagān (Drehem)*, Heidelberg: Heidelberger Orientverlag.

Tsouparopoulou, C. and L. Recht (2021), 'Dogs and Equids in War in Third Millennium BC Mesopotamia', in L. Recht and C. Tsouparopoulou (eds), *Fierce Lions, Angry Mice and Fat-Tailed Sheep: Animal Encounters in the Ancient Near East*, 279–89, Cambridge: McDonald Institute for Archaeological Research.

Tsukimoto, A. (1997), 'From Lullû to Ebla: An Old Babylonian Document Concerning a Shipment of Horses', in B. Pongratz-Leisten, H. Kühne and P. Xella (eds), *Ana šadî labnāni lū allik: Beiträge zu altorientalischen und mittelmeerischen Kulturen: Festschrift für Wolfgang Röllig*, 407–12, Neukirchen-Vluyn: Neukirchener Verlag.

Turner, S. (2021), *The Horse in New Kingdom Egypt: Its Introduction, Nature, Role and Impact*, Abercromby Press.

Twiss, K. C., J. Wolfhagen, R. Madgwick, H. Foster, G. A. Demirergi, N. Russell, J. L. Everhart et al. (2017), 'Horses, Hemiones, Hydruntines? Assessing the Reliability of Dental Criteria for Assigning Species to Southwest Asian Equid Remains', *International Journal of Osteoarchaeology*, 27: 298–304.

Uerpmann, H.-P. (1986), 'Halafian Equid Remains from Shams Ed-Din Tannira in Northern Syria', in R. H. Meadow and H.-P. Uerpmann (eds), *Equids in the Ancient World 1*, 246–65, Wiesbaden: Ludwig Reichert.

Uerpmann, H.-P. (1995), 'Domestication of the Horse: When, Where, and Why?', in L. Bodson (ed.), *Le cheval et les autres équidés: Aspects de l'histoire de leur insertion dans les activités humaines*, 15–29, Liège: Université de Liège.

Uerpmann, H.-P. (2003), 'Gedanken und Beobachtungen zur Equiden-Hybridisierung im alten Orient', in R. Dittmann and B. Jacobs (eds), *Altertumswissenschaften im Dialog*, 549–66, Münster: Ugarit-Verlag.

van Buren, E. D. (1939), *The Fauna of Ancient Mesopotamia as Represented in Art*, Rome: Pontificum Institutum Biblicum.

Van De Mieroop, M. (2016), *A History of the Ancient Near East, ca. 3000–323 BC*, 3rd edn, Chichester: Wiley-Blackwell.

van Koppen, F. (2001), 'The Organisation of Institutional Agriculture in Mari', *Journal of the Economic and Social History of the Orient*, 44 (4): 451–504.

van Koppen, F. (2002), 'Equids in Mari and Chagar Bazar', *Altorientalische Forschungen*, 29 (1): 19–30.

van Loon, M. (1975), 'First Results of the 1972 Excavations at Tell Selenkahiye', in Rencontre assyriologique internationale (ed.), *Le temple et le culte: Compte rendu de la vingtieme Rencontre Assyriologique Internationale*, 21–5, Leiden: Nederlands Historisch-Archaeologisch Instituut te Istambul.

Veenhof, K. R. (1972), *Aspects of Old Assyrian Trade and Its Terminology*, Leiden: Brill.

Veenhof, K. R. (1989), 'Status and Offices of an Anatolian Gentleman: Two Unpublished Letters of Huharimataku from Kārum Kanish', in K. Emre, B. Hrouda, M. J. Mellink and Nimet Özgüç (eds), *Anatolia and the Ancient Near East: Studies in Honor of Tahsin Özgüç*, 515–25, Ankara: Türk Tarih Kurumu Basımevi.

Veenhof, K. R. (1997), '"Modern" Features in Old Assyrian Trade', *Journal of the Economic and Social History of the Orient*, 40 (4): 336–66.

Veenhof, K. R. (2013), 'The Archives of Old Assyrian Traders: Their Nature, Functions and Use', in M. Faraguna (ed.), *Archives and Archival Documents in Ancient Societies: Legal Documents in Ancient Societies IV*, 27–71, Trieste: EUT Edizioni Università di Trieste.

Veenhof, K. R. and J. Eidem (2008), *Mesopotamia: The Old Assyrian Period*, 5th edn, Fribourg and Göttingen: Academic Press Vandenhoeck & Ruprecht.

Veldmeijer, A. J. and S. Ikram, eds (2013), *Chasing Chariots: Proceedings of the First International Chariot Conference (Cairo 2012)*, Leiden: Sidestone.

Veldmeijer, A. J. and S. Ikram, eds (2018), *Chariots in Ancient Egypt: The Tano Chariot, a Case Study*, Leiden: Sidestone.

Vila, E. (1998), 'Interpreting the Faunal Remains of El Kowm 2 - Caracol (IVth Millenium BC, Syria)', in H. Buitenhuis, L. Bartosiewicz and A. M. Choyke (eds), *Archaeozoology of the Near East III: Proceedings of the Third International Symposium on the Archaeozoology of Southwestern Asia and Adjacent Areas*, 120–9, Groningen: ARC.

Vila, E. (2005), 'Des inhumations d'équidés retrouvées à Tell Chuera (bronze ancien, Syrie du nord-est)', in A. Gardeisen (ed.), *Les équidés dans le monde Méditerranéen antique*, 197–205, Lattes: Edition de l'Association pour le développement de l'archéologie en Languedoc-Roussillon.

Vila, E. (2006), 'Data on Equids from Late Fourth and Third Millennium Sites in Northern Syria', in M. Mashkour (ed.), *Equids in Time and Space*, 101–23, Oxford: Oxbow.

Vila, E. (2010), 'Les vestiges de chevaux à Tell Chuera: Premières datations', in J. Becker, R. Hempelmann and E. Rehm (eds), *Kulturlandschaft Syrien: Zentrum und Peripherie, Festschrift für Jan-Waalke Meyer*, 607–21, Münster: Ugarit-Verlag.

Virolleaud, C. (1932), 'Un nouveau chant du poème d'Aleïn-Baal', *Syria*, 13 (2): 113–63.

Vita, J.-P. (2008), 'Le char de guerre en Syrie et Palestine au bronze récent', in P. Abrahami and L. Battini (eds), *Les armées du Proche Orient ancien, IIIe-Ier mill. av. J.-C., actes du colloque international organisé à Lyon les 1er et 2 décembre 2006*, 57–69, Oxford: John and Erica Hedges.

von Dassow, E. (2008), *State and Society in the Late Bronze Age Alalakh under the Mitannian Empire*, Maryland: Bethesda.

Wapnish, P. (1997), 'Middle Bronze Equid Burials at Tell Jemmeh and a Reexamination of a Purportedly "Hyksos" Practice', in E. D. Oren (ed.), *The Hyksos: New Historical and Archaeological Perspectives*, 335–68, Philadelphia: University Museum, University of Pennsylvania.

Waring, G. (2003), *Horse Behavior*, 2nd edn, Norwich, NY: Noyes Publishing.

Warmuth, V., A. Eriksson, M. A. Bower, G. Barker, E. Barrett, B. K. Hanks, S. Li, et al. (2012), 'Reconstructing the Origin and Spread of Horse Domestication in the Eurasian Steppe', *Proceedings of the National Academy of Sciences*, 109 (21): 8202–6.

Watanabe, C. (1998), 'Symbolism of the Royal Lion Hunt in Assyria', in J. Prosecký (ed.), *Intellectual Life of the Ancient Near East: Papers Presented at the 43rd Rencontre Assyriologique International, Prague, July 1–5, 1996*, 439–50, Prague: Academy of Sciences of the Czech Republic, Oriental Institute.

Watelin, L. and S. Langdon (1934), *Excavations at Kish IV: 1925–1930*, Paris: Geuthner.

Watson, W. G. E. (2011), 'Semitic and Non-Semitic Terms for Horse-Trappings in Ugaritic', *Aula Orientalis*, 29: 155–76.

Way, K. C. (2010), 'Assessing Sacred Asses: Bronze Age Donkey Burials in the Near East', *Levant*, 42 (2): 210–25.

Way, K. C. (2011), *Donkeys in the Biblical World: Ceremony and Symbol*, Winona Lake, IN: Eisenbrauns.

Weber, J. A. (2001), 'A Preliminary Assessment of Akkadian and Post-Akkadian Animal Exploitation at Tell Brak', in D. Oates, J. Oates and H. MacDonald (eds), *Excavations at Tell Brak 2: Nagar in the Third Millennium BC*, 345–50, London: British School of Archaeology in Iraq.

Weber, J. A. (2008), 'Elite Equids: Redefining Equid Burials of the Mid- to Late 3rd Millennium BC from Umm El-Marra, Syria', in E. Vila, L. Gourichon, A. M. Choyke and H. Buitenhuis (eds), *Archaeozoology of the Near East VIII: Actes des huitièmes rencontres internationales d'archéozoologie de l'Asie du sud-ouest et des régions adjacentes*, 499–519, Lyon: Maison de l'Orient et de la Méditerrannée.

Weber, J. A. (2012), 'Restoring Order: Death, Display, and Authority', in A. Porter and G. M. Schwartz (eds), *Sacred Killing*, 159–90, Winona Lake, IN: Eisenbrauns.

Weber, J. A. (2017), 'Elite Equids 2: Seeing the Dead', in M. Mashkour and M. J. Beech (eds), *Archaeozoology of the Near East 9: Proceedings of the 9th Conference of the Aswa (AA) Working Group: Archaeozoology of Southwest Asia and Adjacent Areas*, 340–52, Oxford: Oxbow.

Weber, J. A. (forthcoming), 'Equids' in final Tell Umm el-Marra publication.

Weidner, E. (1952), 'Weisse Pferde im alten Orient', *Bibliotheca Orientalis*, 9: 157–9.

Weil, K. (2010), 'A Report on the Animal Turn', *Differences*, 21 (2): 1–23.

Wickens, C. L. and C. R. Heleski (2010), 'Crib-Biting Behavior in Horses: A Review', *Applied Animal Behaviour Science*, 128 (1): 1–9.

Wilkens, B. (2003), *Archeozoologia: Manuale per lo studio dei resti faunistici dell'area Mediterranea* (www.archeozoologia.it/, accessed 18 June 2021).

Willerslev, R. (2007), *Soul Hunters: Hunting, Animism, and Personhood among the Siberian Yukaghirs*, Berkeley: University of California Press.

Winter, I. J. (1985), 'After the Battle Is Over: The "Stele of the Vultures" and the Beginning of Historical Narrative in the Art of the Ancient Near East', *Studies in the History of Art*, 16: 11–32.

Wiseman, D. J. (1953), *The Alalakh Tablets*, New York: AMS Press.

Wiseman, D. J. (1968), 'The Tell al Rimah Tablets, 1966', *Iraq*, 30 (2): 175–205.

Woolley, L. (1934), *Ur Excavations II: The Royal Cemetery*, Philadelphia: University of Pennsylvania Press.

Woolley, L. (1955), *Alalakh: An Account of the Excavations at Tell Atchana in the Hatay, 1937-1949*, London: Society of Antiquaries.

Wrede, N. (2003), *Uruk: Terrakotten I. Von der 'Ubaid- bis zur altbabylonischen Zeit*, Mainz am Rhein: Philipp von Zabern.

Wygnańska, Z. (2017), 'Equid and Dog Burials in the Ritual Landscape of Bronze Age Syria and Mesopotamia', *ARAM*, 1&2: 141–60.

Yannai, E. (2008), 'Tel Lod', in E. Stern (ed.), *The New Encyclopedia of Archaeological Excavations in the Holy Land*, 1913–15, Jerusalem: Israel Exploration Society.

Yon, M. (2006), *The City of Ugarit at Tell Ras Shamra*, Winona Lake, IN: Eisenbrauns.

Zarins, J. (1978), 'The Domesticated Equidae of Third Millennium B.C. Mesopotamia', *Journal of Cuneiform Studies*, 30: 3–17.

Zarins, J. (1986), 'Equids Associated with Human Burials in Third Millenium B.C. Mesopotamia: Two Complementary Facets', in R. H. Meadow and H.-P. Uerpmann (eds), *Equids in the Ancient World 1*, 164–93, Wiesbaden: Ludwig Reichert.

Zarins, J. (2014), *The Domestication of Equidae in Third-Millennium BCE Mesopotamia*, with R. Hauser, Bethesda: CDL Press.

Zeder, M. A. (1986), 'The Equid Remains from Tal-e Malyan, Southern Iran', in R. H. Meadow and H.-P. Uerpmann (eds), *Equids in the Ancient World 1*, 367–412, Wiesbaden: Ludwig Reichert.

Zeder, M. A. (1998), 'Pigs and Emergent Complexity in the Ancient Near East', in S. M. Nelson (ed.), *Ancestors for the Pigs in Prehistory*, 109–22, Pennsylvania: University of Pennsylvania Museum of Archaeology and Anthropology.

Index of Place Names

Place names from online appendices not included here.

Subject Index